The Unofficial Guide to
LEGO® MINDSTORMS™ Robots

The Unofficial Guide to LEGO® MINDSTORMS™ Robots

Jonathan B. Knudsen

O'REILLY®

Beijing · Cambridge · Farnham · Köln · Paris · Sebastopol · Taipei · Tokyo

The Unofficial Guide to LEGO® MINDSTORMS™ Robots
by Jonathan B. Knudsen

Copyright © 1999 O'Reilly & Associates, Inc. All rights reserved.
Printed in the United States of America.

Published by O'Reilly & Associates, Inc., 101 Morris Street, Sebastopol, CA 95472.

Editor: Mike Loukides

Production Editor: Nicole Arigo

Printing History:

> October 1999:   First Edition.

ISBN: 1-56592-692-7
[M]

[12/99]

For Kristen
who helps me reach my dreams

Table of Contents

Preface

This is a book for people who build and program LEGO® robots with the Robotics Invention System (RIS)™ set. This book is the answer to the question, "How can I push this thing as far as it will go?" Once you've built a few robots and written a few programs, you'll probably be itching for *more*: more complex robots, more powerful programming environments, more sensors, and more fun. This book will take you there.

About This Book

For many of us, plastic LEGO bricks are the best toy money can buy. When I was five and broke my leg, a little LEGO set was the high point of my six-week convalescence. I grew up building spaceships and planetary rovers, wearing grooves in the ends of my fingernails from endlessly putting together and taking apart my creations. In high school, I shifted into the TECHNIC™ product line—what could be better than cars with real shifting and pistons that worked?

In the Fall of 1998, The LEGO Group released the Robotics Invention System (RIS), a set that was part of a new product line called MINDSTORMS™. This set entered the world like a lightning bolt—finally, the chance to make LEGO models that moved, sensed, and thought! The LEGO Group made 80,000 of these sets in 1998 and sold every one. Although The LEGO Group was aiming for young adults, 11 and older, the RIS has also hypnotized many people in their 20s, 30s, and beyond.

A vibrant, inventive online community sprang up around MINDSTORMS robots. In some ways, this book is an introduction to the most important developments in that community—alternate programming environments and advanced building techniques. But this book goes farther than that, painting a backdrop of the theories and practices of mobile robotics.

Building and programming robots is exhilarating. It's fun to build something that moves and thinks, in a sense; at the same time, you're learning a lot about how things work, mechanically, and how to write programs that can deal with the real world. This book is designed to take you to the next level of building and programming, all in the spirit of fun and learning.

This book's chapters come in two basic flavors. Five chapters have robot projects, complete with building instructions and programs. Four chapters describe various programming environments for LEGO MINDSTORMS robots, including code examples and debugging tips. The first and last chapters don't fit in either category.

Here's a description of each chapter in this book:

Chapter 1, *Robotics and MINDSTORMS*, introduces the field of mobile robotics and describes how the LEGO MINDSTORMS Robotic Invention System fits in the larger picture of the field.

Chapter 2, *Hank, the Bumper Tank*, is the first building project—a tank-style robot that avoids obstacles in its path. This chapter discusses basic mechanical features like gears and bumpers.

Chapter 3, *Trusty, a Line Follower*, covers a slightly trickier robot—a line-follower. It uses a light sensor to follow a black line on the floor.

Chapter 4, *Not Quite C*, introduces the Not Quite C (NQC) language. NQC is an excellent environment for programming robots. The chapter includes descriptions of NQC's functions as well as many examples.

Chapter 5, *Minerva, a Robot with an Arm*, contains another building project—by far the most complex robot in the book. You'll learn about directional transmissions and other neat stuff.

Chapter 6, *pbFORTH*, discusses an innovative programming environment based on a language called Forth.

Chapter 7, *A Remote Control for Minerva*, is another project-based chapter. Using a second robot kit, you can build a remote control for the robot from Chapter 5.

Chapter 8, *Using Spirit.ocx with Visual Basic*, talks about how to control and program your robots using Microsoft's Visual Basic.

Chapter 9, *RoboTag, a Game for Two Robots*, shows how to create a pair of robots that play tag.

Chapter 10, *legOS*, discusses legOS, a programming environment that enables you to program your robots with C, C++, or assembly code.

Chapter 11, *Make Your Own Sensors*, describes how you can build sensors for your robots easily and inexpensively.

Appendix A, *Finding Parts and Programming Environments*, describes various parts you can get to expand your RIS set and where to find them. It also includes a summary of the programming environments that are available for RIS.

Appendix B, *A pbFORTH Downloader*, contains the source code for a program that downloads Forth code to your robots. It's a supplement to Chapter 6.

Appendix C, *Future Directions*, describes some interesting emerging technologies related to LEGO robots. These are ideas or projects that weren't fully baked as this book went to press.

About the Examples

Versions

This book covers a handful of rapidly evolving technologies. The versions used in this book are as follows:

RCX
>   Version 1.0

NQC
>   Version 2.0b1

pbFORTH
>   Version 1.0.7

legOS
>   The March 30, 1999 build, a patched version of 0.1.7

Downloading

All of the examples in this book can be downloaded from *http://www.oreilly.com/ catalog/lmstorms/*. This site also provides a listing of the "Online Resources" that appear at the end of each chapter.

Font Conventions

Constant width is used for:

- Function and subroutine names

- Source code

- Example command-line sessions—the input you type is shown in boldface

Italic is used for:

- Pathnames and filenames
- New terms where they are defined
- Internet addresses, such as domain names and URLs

Boldface is used for the names of buttons.

 This is a note with information that supplements the text.

 This is a warning with a cautionary message for the reader.

Request for Comments

If you find typos, inaccuracies, or bugs, please let us know. You can reach O'Reilly by mail, telephone, fax, or email:

> O'Reilly & Associates, Inc.
> 101 Morris Street
> Sebastopol, CA 95472
> (800) 998-9938 (in the U.S. or Canada)
> (707) 829-0515 (international or local)
> (707) 829-0104 (fax)
> *bookquestions@oreilly.com*

Please let us know what we can do to make the book more helpful to you. We take your comments seriously, and will do whatever we can to make this book as useful as it can be.

Acknowledgments

This book is the result of a crazy idea I had in mid-1998, when I first heard that the Robotics Invention System was coming. LEGO robots sounded like something O'Reilly readers would like to play with—why not write a book about them? I'd like to thank Mike Loukides and Tim O'Reilly for having the vision to believe in this book. Thanks to Mike, again, for excellent help and feedback.

I'd like to thank my parents for buying me LEGO sets when I was a kid. Did you ever expect something like this?

Many thanks go to my wife, Kristen, for helping to create this book. She first suggested its project-oriented organization; she gave me excellent feedback on many of its chapters; she got me RolyKits to help organize my pieces; she is able to keep a straight face when we tell people I'm writing a book about LEGO robots; she stayed up late nights helping me finish the book.

I'm grateful to my daughter, Daphne, who finally believes that building LEGO robots is part of my job. "Want to see Daddy," she said one day. Kristen explained, "No, no, sweetheart, Daddy's working right now." With tears in her eyes, Daphne said, "Daddy's not working. Daddy play LEGOs." Someday, I promise, I'll let Daphne play with the whole set, not just the bendy purple things. And thanks to my sons, Luke and Andrew, just for being great guys. You can build robots someday too, if you wish.

The building instructions in this book were a special challenge. I first sketched out the building instructions with photos from a digital camera. Once these were finished, Kristen took over 475 photographs with a regular camera. We selected the best and sent them off to the O'Reilly illustration department. These photographs were scanned in and meticulously touched up, cropped, edited, and manipulated to produce the instructions that you see in the book. I owe many thanks to Rob Romano for his hard work on these instructions.

This book has had an excellent set of technical reviewers. Ralph Hempel, Todd Lehman, Russel Nelson, Suzanne Rich, John Tamplin, ActivMedia Robotics (*http://www.activrobots.com/*), and Ben Williamson provided insightful and authoritative feedback on a draft of this book. Thanks also to Stephan Somogyi for encouraging me to include more information about using a Macintosh with MINDSTORMS.

1

Robotics and MINDSTORMS

This is a book about creating robots with the LEGO® MINDSTORMS™ Robotic Invention System (RIS)™. If you've always dreamed of building and programming your own robots, this is your big chance—the RIS set makes it easy to get started. There are a lot of enthusiastic RIS owners out there already: other people have built robots that pick up empty soda cans; robots that seek light; robots that play tag; walking robots with two, four, six, or even eight legs; robots that can be controlled over the Internet; working computer peripherals like a plotter and an optical scanner; and robots that simulate a Tsunami and a tornado.* You can build anything you can imagine. RIS gives you a chance to breathe life into LEGO creations, making them move and respond to their surroundings. You can create a tank that scurries into the dark, or a monorail car that traverses your living room on a string. You can create robots that hop, walk, and drive around with a mind of their own.

Furthermore, by owning the RIS set, you become part of a worldwide community of enthusiasts. The RIS set is a common ground for building robots; if you build something cool, other people will be able to build it too. Similarly, you can build and modify other people's creations. LEGO bricks, therefore, are a kind of *lingua franca* for mechanical design.

You have many options when it comes to building and programming robots. LEGO bricks, of course, can be assembled in many different ways. Part of this book is about building robots; it includes five projects that you can build yourself. But you also have lots of options for programming your robot. Aside from the "official" software that comes with RIS, the inventive MINDSTORMS community

---

* Internet links to pictures of some of these robots are included in the "Online Resources" section at the end of this chapter.

has produced a bevy of other options. The most important ones are described in this book.

This chapter describes the basic concepts of robotics and creates a backdrop for the MINDSTORMS product line. I'll also cover different approaches to programming mobile robotics. Finally, I'll describe the RIS set itself. If you're in a hurry to start building something, skip ahead to Chapter 2, *Hank, the Bumper Tank.*

What Is a Robot?

A robot is a machine whose behavior can be programmed. This is a broad definition —it includes things like VCRs and microwave ovens, a far cry from the talking androids you might be thinking of. Robots have five fundamental components:

1. A *brain* controls the robot's actions and responds to sensory input. Usually the brain is a computer of some kind.

2. A robot's *body* is simply the physical chassis that holds the other pieces of the robot together.

3. *Actuators* allow the robot to move. These are usually motors, although there are many other possibilities, such as hydraulic pistons.

4. *Sensors* give a robot information about its environment. A touch sensor, for example, can tell a robot that it has come in contact with something else.

The last component is not always obvious:

5. A *power source* supplies the juice needed to run the brain, actuators, and sensors.

For example, think about a robot that spraypaints cars in a factory. Its brain is probably a garden-variety desktop computer. The body is a big arm with a paint sprayer at the end. The actuators are motors or pneumatic pistons that move the arm around. Position and rotation sensors are used so the robot knows where the sprayer is and what direction it's pointing. The whole thing is plugged into a wall socket for power.

Mobile Robots

Mobile robots present special challenges. These robots can move their bodies around from place to place. Why is this capability difficult? Many more things can go wrong if your robot is free to move around rather than being bolted to one place. Being mobile multiplies the number of situations your robot needs to be able to handle.

Mobile robots actually come in two varieties: *tethered* and *autonomous*. A tethered robot "cheats" by dumping its power supply and brain overboard, possibly relying on a desktop computer and a wall outlet. Control signals and power are run through a bundle of wires (the tether) to the robot, which is free to move around, at least as far as the tether will allow.

Autonomous mobile robots are even more challenging. These robots need to bring everything along with them, including a power supply and a brain. The power supply is typically an array of batteries, which adds a lot of weight to the robot. The brain is also constrained because it has to fit on the robot, not weigh a ton, and be frugal about sucking power out of the batteries.

This Is Tough Stuff

The field of autonomous mobile robotics is extremely challenging. Have you ever seen an autonomous mobile robot, besides in the movies? Probably not. If you have been lucky enough to see such a robot, was it doing something useful? Probably not. If the robot was supposed to do something useful, did it work? Probably not.

If it wasn't so hard to make autonomous mobile robots, the world would be full of them. Wouldn't it be nice to have a robot do your laundry or drive you to the airport? But the cold truth is that it's unbelievably difficult to make a robot that can do even the simplest of tasks. It all comes down to one fact: *it's very hard to deal with the real world.*

To understand this, think about how you might try to make a robot to vacuum your living room. This is a pretty simple task to describe: basically you just want to move the vacuum back and forth over the rug until the whole thing is clean. Suppose you modify your vacuum cleaner so that it can move around on its own, by adding more motors and a small computer brain. Just consider the staggering complexity:

- How does the robot keep from getting tangled up in its own power cord, assuming it's a tethered robot? If it's not tethered, you need to find a power supply that will run the robot for long enough to clean at least one room.

- How does the robot know where it's been already? How does the robot know where it is? How does it know where to go next?

- How does the robot navigate around obstacles like table legs and furniture?

- How does the robot recognize things it shouldn't vacuum, like money, or toys, or your cats?

You can answer these questions, but not well, not simply, and not cheaply. After years of sweat and expense, you might produce a robot that could vacuum a room, but only under very closely controlled conditions. Add a rocking chair, or drop a child's toy in the middle of the room, and you'd probably have to start all over again.

Another reason that robotics is so challenging is that it spans many different disciplines. Suppose that you want to go down in your basement and build a mobile robot. Without some sort of kit, you'd probably need to take along a team of highly educated, highly paid engineers, including:

- An electrical engineer chooses the brain, sensors, and maybe the actuators, and wires them all together. This person probably selects the power supply, as well.

- A mechanical engineer designs the body and possibly selects the actuators. The mechanical person needs to be familiar with the other components of the robot (brain, sensors, actuators, and power supply) so that everything fits together mechanically.

- A computer programmer writes the software for the robot. This task usually requires intimate knowledge of the brain, sensors, and actuators that the electronics and mechanical people have chosen.

- For specialized designs, you might even want to have a chemical engineer to select or design the power supply.

It is very rare for a single person to be knowledgeable in all of these fields. Designing a mobile robot, then, is often a collaborative effort, which makes it even more complex.

Autonomous mobile robots, for the most part, are still confined to the research programs of colleges, universities, and governments. This research is divided into two camps: the big robot people and the little robot people.

Big Is Beautiful

The big robot people believe that the robot should understand its environment and "think," more or less the same way that a human does. This is the traditional Artificial Intelligence (AI) approach to robotics. In this approach, the robot takes input from its sensors and tries to build a map of its surroundings. This process alone is very complicated: the robot might use a pair of video cameras or some more exotic sensors to examine its surroundings, while heavy-duty computers analyze all the sensor data and attempt to build a map. Finally, in a process called task planning, the robot tries to figure out how it will accomplish an objective—getting from one point to another, or picking up an object, or some other simple task. In this respect, again, the robot is expected to think like a human being. The heavy computing requirements of the AI approach consume a lot of power, which implies a bulky, heavy power supply. Hence, the robot can be pretty big—and expensive, too.

He Ain't Heavy, He's My Robot

A good example of the "big iron" approach to mobile robots is Ambler, developed by Carnegie Mellon University and the Jet Propulsion Laboratory. This behemoth stands about 5 m (16.4 ft) tall, is up to 7 m (23.0 ft) wide, and weighs 2500 kg (5512 lb). It moves at a blistering 35 cm (13.8 in) per minute. Just sitting still, it consumes 1400 W of power. Ask it to walk and it sucks up just about 4000 W. You can see a photograph of Ambler at *http://ranier.oact.hq.nasa.gov/telerobotics_page/Photos/Ambler.jpg*.

Small Is Beautiful

Little robot people like to tease the big robot people for building tremendously large, tremendously expensive machines that don't have the dexterity of a six-month-old baby. The little robot people make small mobile robots based around inexpensive, off-the-shelf parts. They like to see themselves as mavericks, achieving decent results at a fraction of the cost and complexity of big robotics.

One of the interesting ideas behind small robot research is the idea that quantity might get the job done rather than quality. Instead of building a single bulky, complex robot to explore the surface of Mars, why not send a thousand robots the size of mice to do the same job? So what if a few of them fail? Small robots offer a new and innovative way to approach big problems.

The small robotics approach reduces the number of engineers you need in your basement. It makes robotics accessible to sophisticated hobbyists—people with technical knowledge and some extra time and money. If you take the small robot approach, you'll probably use standard batteries for power, which eliminates the need for a chemical engineer to design a power supply. Small robots are usually based on an existing, cheap microprocessor, which makes the electrical engineer's job a little easier. But you still need quite a bit of expertise:

- The electrical engineer still has to select sensors and actuators and wire them to the microprocessor. These parts are inexpensive and can be bought from hobby stores or electronics parts stores.
- The computer programmer still needs a pretty low-level understanding of the microprocessor and the attached sensors and actuators.
- You still need a mechanical engineer to design the robot's body.

The sophisticated hobbyist can do all of these things alone. But you have to be determined and have a lot of free time and money. There are a couple of ways to make things easier:

- You could buy a prebuilt robot brain. Some companies sell kits that are designed specifically to be used as robot brains. This approach saves you the trouble of selecting a microprocessor and getting it running, but you still have to select sensors and actuators and attach them to the brain somehow.

- You could use a modular construction kit to build the robot's body. LEGO® bricks are one possiblity—in fact, researchers and students at the Massachusetts Institute of Technology (MIT) have been using LEGO bricks for mechanical prototyping for over a decade.

An even better simplication, of course, is the MINDSTORMS™ Robotics Invention System itself.

What Is MINDSTORMS?

MINDSTORMS is the name of a product line sold by The LEGO Group. The LEGO Group has a handful of product lines that cater to different age groups, some of which are shown in Table 1-1.

Table 1-1. Representative LEGO Product Lines

Product Line Name	Suggested Ages
LEGO® PRIMO™	3 months to 24 months
LEGO® DUPLO™	18 months to 6 years
LEGO® SYSTEM™	3 years to 12 years
LEGO® TECHNIC™	7 years to 16 years
LEGO® MINDSTORMS™	11 years and older

The centerpiece of MINDSTORMS is the Robotics Invention System (RIS), a set for building robots. It makes the challenges and excitement of mobile robotics accessible to anyone with $200US and a desktop computer (PC). It gives you a chance to solve problems in innovative ways. Best of all, it's a lot of fun.

The RIS set eliminates many of the difficulties of building mobile robots:

- The set comes with a robot brain called the RCX.* The RCX is a small computer that is neatly packaged in a palm-sized LEGO brick.

---

* Some people think RCX stands for Robotic Controller X. According to the MINDSTORMS web site, RCX stands for Robotic Command Explorer.

- Two touch sensors and one light sensor are included in the RIS set. Wiring the sensors to the RCX is as simple as snapping LEGO bricks together.

- The set also includes two motors. Like the sensors, they can be connected to the RCX by just snapping LEGO bricks together.

- The RCX uses six standard AA batteries for power. It also includes a power jack. You can supply power in either polarity, even AC, from 9V to 12V.

- The set includes more than 700 LEGO pieces that you can use to build the body of the robot.

- You can write programs for the brain using an intuitive, highly visual programming environment on your PC. Programs are sent to the RCX over an infrared (IR) data link. The set includes an IR tower that attaches to one of the serial ports on your PC. Just point the tower at the RCX, and you're ready to download programs.

You don't need an electrical engineer anymore because the brain, sensors, and actuators that come with the RIS set are easy to hook up. You don't need a computer programmer anymore because the programming environment is easy to use. And you don't need a mechanical engineer because building a body is as simple as building a LEGO model.

Figure 1-1 illustrates the basic setup. Building a robot using MINDSTORMS consists of four steps:

1. Build the robot's body.

2. Write a program for the robot using software tools on your PC.

3. Download the program to the robot.

4. Run the program.

This is only a sketch of the process, of course; it's likely you'll repeat the steps many times as you gradually improve the mechanical design and software of your robot.

You can create a program on your PC using the MINDSTORMS software. Then you need to download it to the RCX using the IR link. Once the program is downloaded, your robot is ready to go.

Is it a good deal? Yes. You could build a comparable setup by buying the pieces separately, but it would cost more and would not be nearly as easy to use.

Meet the RCX

The RCX is a robot brain in the form of a bulky LEGO brick. Figure 1-2 shows a photograph of the top of the RCX.

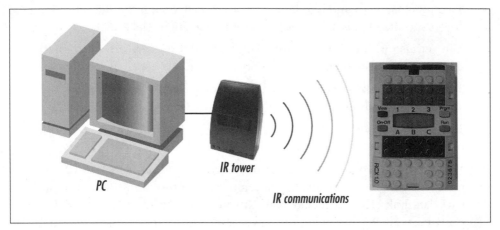

Figure 1-1. Basic MINDSTORMS setup

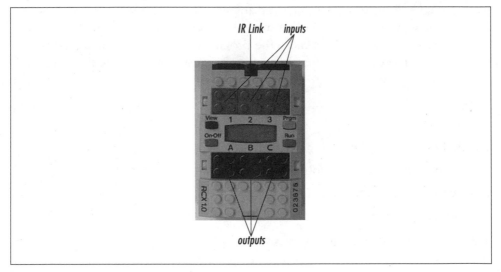

Figure 1-2. The RCX, a robot brain

The RCX is a small computer with the following features:

outputs

Three output ports, labeled A, B, and C, are located near the center of the brick. The robot's actuators (motors or lights) can be attached to these ports.

inputs

Three input ports, labeled 1, 2, and 3, are provided. Various types of sensors can be attached to these ports to allow the RCX to find out about its environment.

screen

> The RCX includes a small LCD screen. This screen displays helpful informa-
> tion such as sensor readings and output port settings.

sound

> The RCX is capable of producing beeps of different frequencies.

front panel buttons

> Four buttons are provided to control the RCX. You can select a program, start
> it, and stop it. You can also view the values of attached sensors or check the
> settings on output ports.

IR communications link

> The RCX communicates with your PC through the IR (infrared) link, similar to
> that on a television remote control. It can also communicate with other RCXs
> through this link.

About the Software

The CD-ROM that comes with RIS contains a lot of software. Basically it can all be
distilled down to three pieces:

documentation

> The RIS software includes extension tutorials about setting up and program-
> ming the RCX. These include animations, movies, and detailed, step-by-step
> instructions. When you first begin using the software, it is in *guided mode*,
> which means the software tells you what to do next. This is a good way to get
> used to the software and the RCX.

programming environment

> The RIS software includes an environment you can use to write programs
> that will run on the RCX. In the computer world, this technique is called
> *cross-compiling*, meaning you write a program on one computer that you
> intend to run on another. In this case, you use your PC to write a program
> that will be run on the RCX. As you'll see, there are many ways to write
> programs for your RCX; the official environment that comes with RIS is only
> one of them. This book will introduce you to four powerful alternate pro-
> gramming environments.

program downloader

> Once you've written a program for the RCX, you need to know how to run it.
> The RIS software includes a *program downloader* for this purpose. The pro-
> gram downloader is a special application that runs on your PC. It knows how
> to transmit your robot programs into the RCX using the IR link.

What About MacOS and Linux?

Currently, the software that comes with RIS runs only on Windows. If you have MacOS or Linux, however, you can still program your robots, just not with the official software. The best option, at least to get started, is NQC, which is described in Chapter 4. Appendix A, *Finding Parts and Programming Environments*, lists the different packages that are available. If you really want visual-style programming (like RCX Code), you can purchase ROBOLAB, which provides a similar (but more powerful) environment on MacOS.

There's one final wrinkle if you want to program from MacOS: you'll need a suitable cable. The following web page describes the issues of programming the RCX from MacOS, including cables: *http://www.enteract.com/~dbaum/lego/macmind/index.html.*

You can purchase a Macintosh IR tower cable from Pitsco LEGO DACTA for $15US. See Appendix A for details.

Expansion Sets

Aside from the basic RIS set, the MINDSTORMS product line also includes expansion sets. These sets provide additional parts and software to supplement the RIS set. Two such sets exist, each selling for about $50US:

Extreme Creatures
> This set comes with about 150 LEGO pieces and is designed so you can add decorative jaws and claws to your robots. It includes a light that can be attached to one of the output ports of the RCX.

Robosports
> This expansion set includes about 90 LEGO pieces, two balls, two pucks, and an additional motor. It's oriented towards robots that can play different sports.

A third expansion set, *Exploration Mars*, should be released sometime in 1999.

Among LEGO enthusiasts, the consensus is that the expansion sets are not as good a value as the RIS set itself. If you're looking for extra pieces, it might be better to buy a LEGO TECHNIC set instead. If you're looking for additional sensors and motors, by themselves, there are other ways to get these. See Appendix A, *Finding Parts and Programming Environments*, for details.

Other Sets

RIS isn't the only game in town. In 1999, two new MINDSTORMS sets were released: the Droid Developer Kit and the Robotics Discovery Set. Both sets are based on the same technology as RIS. They have more limited capabilities than RIS with the intent of making them easier to use.

What Now?

Now that you have some background in mobile robots and LEGO MINDSTORMS, what should you do? Play.

Read the manuals, follow the instructions on the MINDSTORMS CD, and have fun with your new toy. When you're thirsty for more, come back and read the rest of this book. It will tell you everything you need to know to push your MIND-STORMS set as far as it can go.

Online Resources

One of the most exciting things about MINDSTORMS is the online community that supports it. On the one hand, LEGO's official MINDSTORMS site provides some interesting information as well as a chance for RIS owners to exchange designs and ideas. But in the months since the release of MINDSTORMS, many unofficial sites have appeared. These cover a broad range of topics: clever mechanical designs, novel sensors, alternate programming environments, even a new operating system for the RCX. I'll list references to online resources at the end of each chapter in this book; my lists are also available online at *http://www.oreilly.com/catalog/lmstorms/*. There's a lot of information out there.

LEGO MINDSTORMS
http://www.legomindstorms.com/
> This is the official site of MINDSTORMS. It contains handy tips and mildly informative articles. If you own a MINDSTORMS RIS set, you can sign up for your own little corner of this web site, where you can post pictures of your creations and even the programs that run them.

LEGO Worlds
http://www.lego.com/
> This is the official site of The LEGO Group. It's a good place to go to browse through different product lines and to get a sense of the entire company's product offerings.

Robotics
http://www.lugnet.com/robotics/
> LUGNET (the international fan-created LEGO Users Group Network) forms the hub of the online LEGO universe. LUGNET hosts many useful discussion groups; a whole hierarchy of them is devoted to robotics. This URL will take you to the top level of the LEGO robotics discussion groups, which is further

subdivided into more specific interests. LUGNET is an outstanding, searchable resource.

Lego Mindstorms Internals
http://www.crynwr.com/lego-robotics/
This page, maintained by Russell Nelson, contains many fascinating nuggets of information about RIS and the things you can do with it.

RCX Internals
http://graphics.stanford.edu/~kekoa/rcx/
This page presents the results of Kekoa Proudfoot's reverse engineering efforts on the RCX, which enabled the development of interesting technologies like NQC, pbFORTH, and legOS. For hard-core geeks, this page is fascinating reading. Kekoa is, to quote Russell Nelson, a "minor deity" in the online MINDSTORMS world.

LEGO on my mind: Roboworld
http://homepages.svc.fcj.hvu.nl/brok/legomind/robo/
This comprehensive unofficial site contains a helpful section that introduces MINDSTORMS RIS and its TECHNIC doppelgänger, CyberMaster™.

LEGO MINDSTORMS WebRing
http://members.tripod.com/~ssncommunity/webrings/legoms_index.html
A web ring is a set of sites that are all linked to each other. You can traverse forward or backward through the entire ring if you wish, or visit sites in a random order. Browsing the MINDSTORMS web ring is a good way to acquaint yourself with the MINDSTORMS online community.

LEGO MindStorms Gallery
http://member.nifty.ne.jp/mindstorms/
This Japanese web site, maintained by someone named Joe, includes photographs and descriptions of many, many different robots, including several flavors of walkers. The text is mostly in Japanese, but the pictures are fascinating, even if you can't read the text.

Ben's Lego Creations
http://www.pobox.com/~benw/lego/
Ben Williamson is a very gifted mechanical designer. This visually clean web site details Ben's creations, including a working plotter, a treaded robot with a grabber arm, an intelligent truck, and other pearls.

Lego
http://www.mop.no/~simen/lego.htm
Simen Svale Skogsrud maintains this fascinating site. It contains, among other interesting things, a detailed description of a MINDSTORMS-based optical scanner.

Lego

http://www.fischer-mellbin.com/Marcus/Lego/lego.html

This web site belongs to Marcus Fischer-Mellbin, a ten-year-old with a penchant for natural disasters. Along with other models, you'll find photographs and descriptions of a MINDSTORMS-based Tsunami and tornado.

The Epistemology and Learning Group

http://el.www.media.mit.edu/groups/el/

The Epistemology and Learning Group (E&L group) at MIT's prestigious Media Lab basically developed the RCX that is the centerpiece of MINDSTORMS. This web site provides an overview of the E&L group and describes its aspirations and current projects.

The MIT Programmable Brick

http://el.www.media.mit.edu/groups/el/projects/programmable-brick/

The MIT Programmable Brick is the forerunner of the RCX. Looking through this site is like leafing through the RCX's family photograph album.

Crickets: Tiny Computers for Big Ideas

http://fredm.www.media.mit.edu/people/fredm/projects/cricket/

If MINDSTORMS robots aren't small enough for you, take a look at Crickets, another project from the fine people at MIT. Hardly larger than a nine-volt battery, Crickets are a very tiny mobile robot platform. Crickets are not publically available, but this site can give you the inspiration to build your own tiny robots.

What's New at Eureka

http://www.eureka.com/whatsnew/robotvac.htm

I'm not the only one who doesn't want to vacuum the floor. This page at Eureka describes the Eureka Robot Vac, a kind of concept car in the world of vacuum cleaners. Supposedly it will navigate through a room, around obstacles and over electrical cords, vacuuming as it goes. My favorite part: "Switch on the robot vac and you'll hear a robotic tone." What's a robotic tone?

2

Hank, the Bumper Tank

Hank is the first robot we'll be building. He is a friendly robot who explores the floor of a room. Whenever he bumps into an obstacle, like a chair leg or a shoe, he backs up, turns away from the obstacle, and goes forward again. This chapter includes complete building and programming instructions so that you can build Hank yourself. Hank is a fairly simple robot that will serve as a good jumping-off point to discuss:

- Various means of locomotion

- Bumper design

- The use of gears

- Motors

- Software multitasking

Figure 2-1 shows a picture of the completed robot. I suggest you begin by building and programming Hank. Let him run around your floor for a while. Then come back and read the rest of the chapter, where I'll talk about some of Hank's interesting features.

About the Building Instructions

The building instructions for the robots in this book are comprised of pictures, with a little bit of explanation here and there. Each step shows you the parts you need as well as how they fit together. There are, however, some names with which you should be familiar, so that I don't end up describing everything as a "doo-hickey" or a "little gray thingy." The parts you need to know are beams, plates, shafts, gears, bushings, and wire bricks.

Figure 2-1. Hank, a friendly robot

Beams, plates, and shafts are characterized by their length. For beams, at least, this corresponds to how many studs (bumps) are on the beam. Figure 2-2 shows a photograph of some beams, plates, and shafts with their corresponding lengths. The "u" stands for "units."

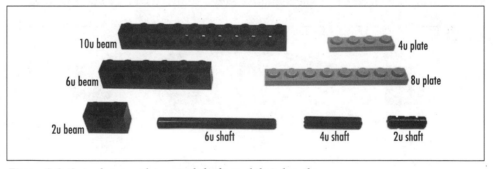

Figure 2-2. Some beams, plates, and shafts and their lengths

Gears, for the most part, are described by the number of teeth they have. A 24t gear, for example, has 24 teeth. (The "t" stands for "teeth.") Figure 2-3 shows a photograph of the various types of gears that come with the RIS kit.

There are two types of bushings in the RIS kit: regular and half-size. Both fit on shafts and are used for securing a shaft in place or for spacing. Figure 2-4 shows the bushings.

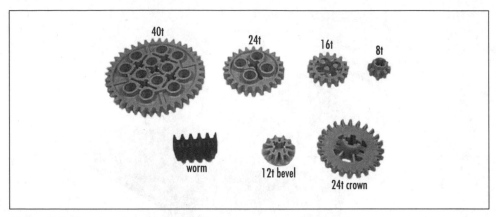

Figure 2-3. Gears

Figure 2-4. Full and half-size bushings

Finally, the term *wire brick* refers to the part shown in Figure 2-5. This piece is used to make an electrical connection between a sensor or motor and the RCX.

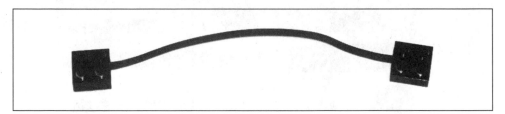

Figure 2-5. A wire brick

Building Instructions*

Create Hank's main chassis as shown in the next two steps; this will hold the RCX, the motors, and the bumpers.

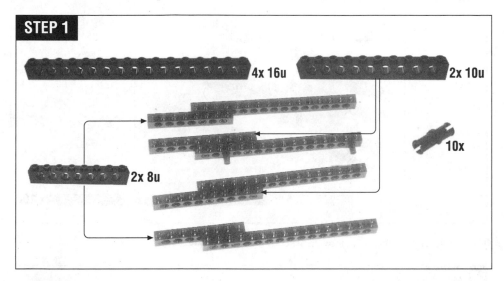

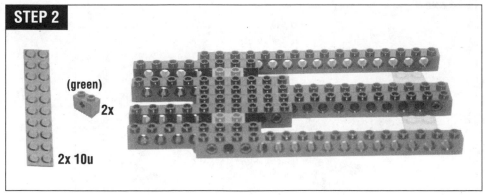

Attach the shafts as shown. Hank's treads will be mounted on these shafts. The front pair do not rotate, while the rear pair should. Don't push the front pair all the way in; you'll need to fit the tread wheel and another bushing on the end.

---

* The parts included with RIS 1.5 are slightly different than those in RIS 1.0. If you're building Hank using RIS 1.5, you should use two bushings instead of the green pieces in Step 2.

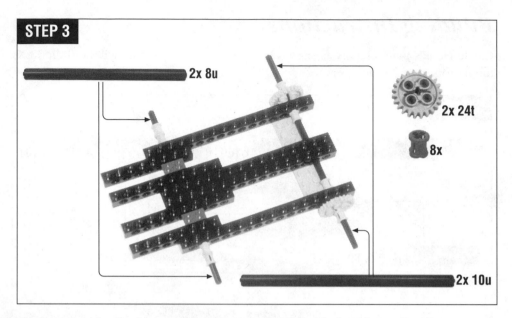

The back tread wheels are anchored to the shafts with the 16t gears.

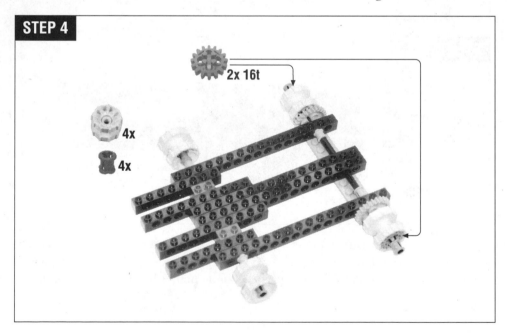

STEP 5

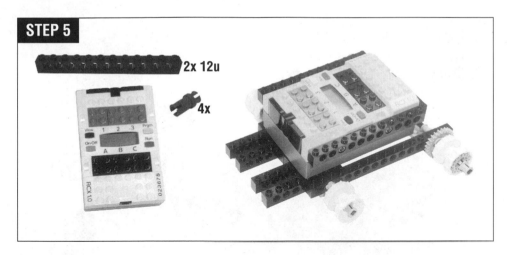

2x 12u

4x

STEP 6

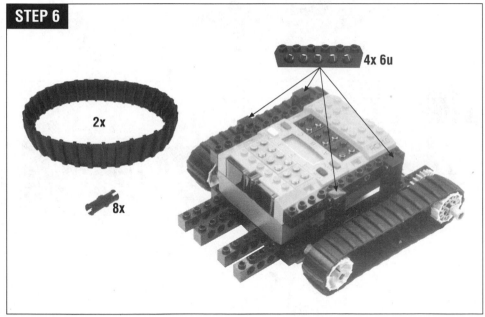

4x 6u

2x

8x

Next, start building support for the drive motors.

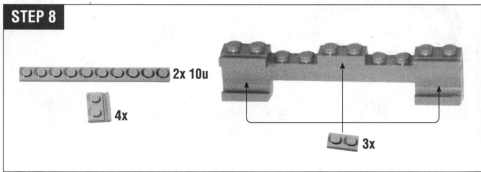

STEP 9

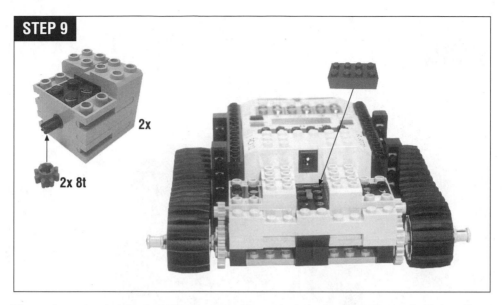

Place the wire bricks on the motors, then anchor them down with the yellow plates. The wires themselves will fit into the grooves on the top of the motors.

STEP 10

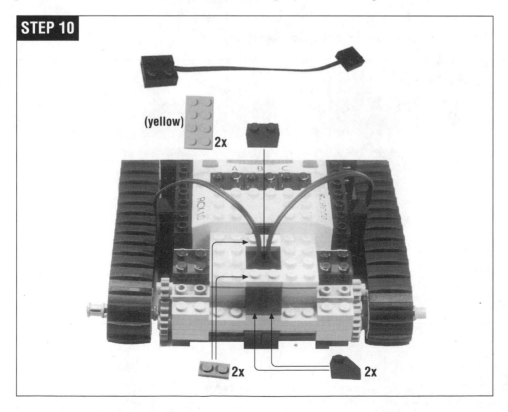

Attach the motor wires to output A and output C.

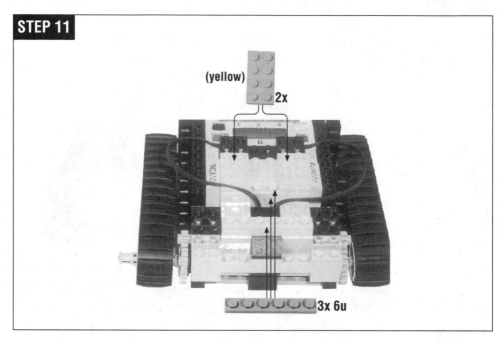

Next, build the platform for the front bumpers.

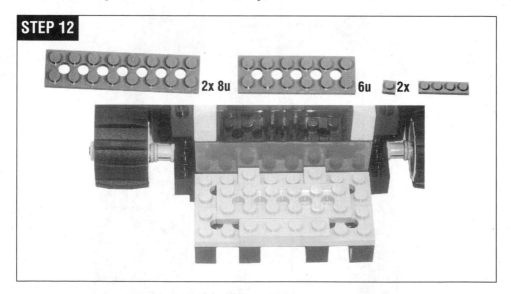

STEP 13

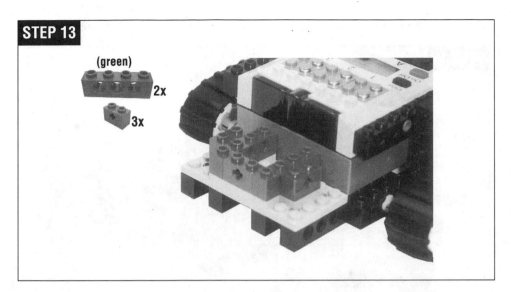

(green)

2x

3x

The touch sensors are attached only by the shaft that runs through them.

STEP 14

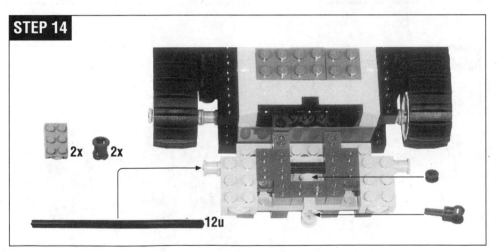

2x 2x

12u

Hank's left bumper is next. A light touch on the bumper pushes the touch sensor.

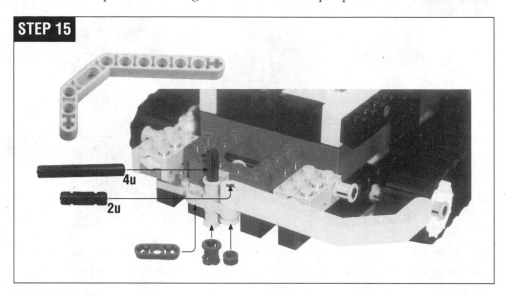

Hank's right bumper works exactly the same way.

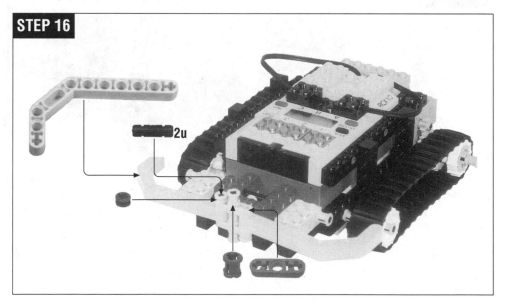

The bushings are pushed onto the plate in the next step. Note that the bushings are not symmetrical; one side will push into the plate, and the other side won't.

STEP 17

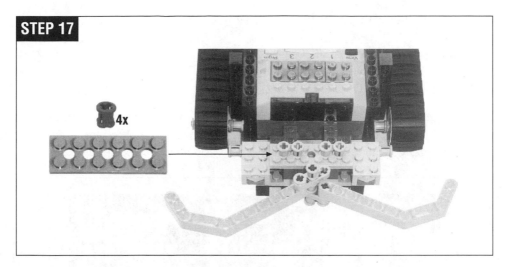

Finish Hank by attaching the bumper touch sensors to input 1 and input 3. Slide the blue rubber bands onto the bumpers and anchor them to the bushings from the last step. The rubber bands keep the bumpers from swinging forward.

STEP 18

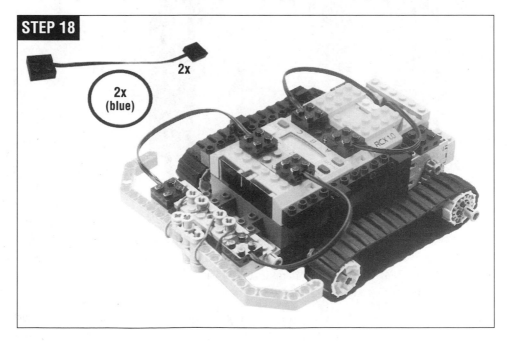

A Simple Program

Now that you've built a robot, you need a program to make it work. Hank's mission in life is to explore the world.

His basic program works something like this:

```
go forward
if I've bumped into something
   back up
   turn away from the obstacle
   start over
```

This program translates pretty simply into the RIS programming environment, as shown in Figure 2-6. The program assumes that the two motors are attached to outputs A and C, while the touch sensors should be attached to inputs 1 and 3.

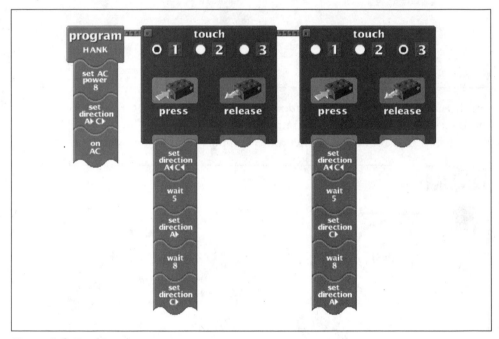

Figure 2-6. Hank's program

To create this program, enter the RIS software. Choose **Program RCX** from the main menu, then **RCX Code**. Use the menus on the left side of the screen to click and drag out different program "blocks." If you're not familiar with this process, you should probably go back and take a look at LEGO's official documentation, either the printed material or the computer-based tutorial.

Once you have created the program, download it and run it. (You can download or save a program by right-clicking on the main program block.) If everything goes right, Hank should amble around on your floor, trying to avoid things he bumps into. If you have pets, this would be a good time to introduce them to your new toy.

Hank is a pretty simple robot, but you still may run into trouble:

- If your robot spins in place or goes backward instead of forward, you may need to adjust the wires that connect the motors to the outputs. Remove one of the wires and turn it 180° around. This will reverse the direction of the attached motor. If the robot is moving backward instead of forward, turn both wires around.

- Hank may not run well on very thick carpet, because there's not much space between the bottom of the body and the floor.

Once you've got things running smoothly, read on. I'll describe Hank's most interesting features in the rest of this chapter.

Locomotion

Hank gets around in the world on a pair of treads, like a tank or a bulldozer. This is just one approach to the general problem of locomotion. Different designs have different merits—you should choose a locomotion method based on what kind of terrain you're expecting your robot to encounter.

Treads

Hank's treads have some interesting properties. Foremost among these is *zero turning radius*, which is a fancy way of saying that a treaded robot can turn around in one place. (I'll explain why it's a *radius* a little later.) Each tread is driven by one of the motors, so all you need to do to turn is move the treads in opposite directions at the same speed. This turning, however, is accomplished with a good deal of friction. Both treads slip on the driving surface. Tanks in Veteran's Day parades can really chew up roads this way.

The large surface of the treads is one of their other assets. Treads are good for driving on jagged or slippery terrain. Hank should do pretty well driving over uneven obstacles, like a small pile of LEGO bricks.

Differential Drive

Treads are a special kind of *differential drive*, in which two wheels are each driven by a motor. The wheels are mounted on either side of the robot, like the treads. Figure 2-7 shows a top view of such a robot.

Independent drive wheels behave a lot like treads. If you run them both forward at the same speed, the robot moves forward. Run the drive wheels in opposite directions, and the robot will spin in place. This design also exhibits zero turning radius, but without the slipping of the treads.

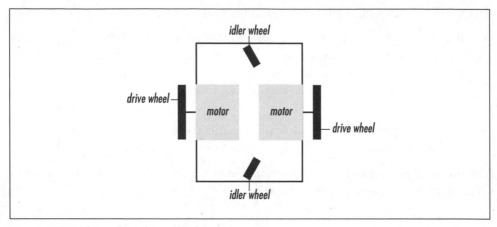

Figure 2-7. Independent drive wheels

Zero turning radius is nice in robots that measure how far each wheel travels. (You could do this using rotation sensors.) Once you know how far each wheel on a differential drive robot has traveled, you can calculate with a fair degree of accuracy the location of the robot relative to its starting point.

The *idler wheels* don't drive or steer the robot. They exist to keep the robot from tipping over. They can turn freely to point in whatever direction the rest of the robot is moving. Figure 2-8 shows a typical idler wheel.

Figure 2-8. An idler wheel

Cars

Modern automobiles demonstrate another popular approach to locomotion. Cars have four wheels, two in front and two in back. The back wheels drive the robot (or car) forward and reverse, while the front wheels are used for steering. Figure 2-9 shows how this looks.

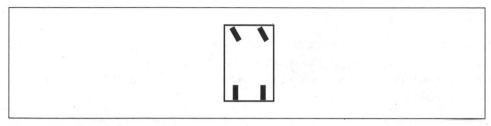

Figure 2-9. Car-style locomotion

Rear-wheel drive is simpler because it decouples the drive mechanism from the steering mechanism. But you could obviously build front-wheel drive robots, with enough parts. Whichever system you choose, this design does not have a zero turning radius. (You can't spin in place in your car.) The term *turning radius* comes from what happens when a car-style robot drives in circles, as shown in Figure 2-10.

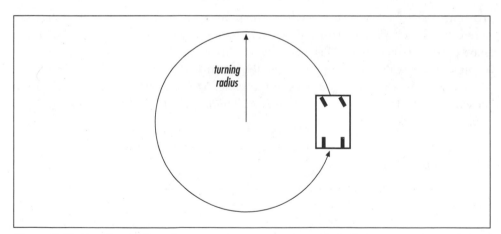

Figure 2-10. Turning radius of a car

This type of design can be difficult to maneuver, as you'll know if you've ever tried to parallel park a car. The other subtlety of this design involves the back drive wheels. When the car turns, the back wheels must turn at different speeds. Consider Figure 2-10 again—the inside back wheel has a smaller distance to go than the outside wheel.

This means that you can't simply connect the two drive wheels with a shaft and hook it up to a motor. You need something trickier, called a *differential* (not the same as differential drive).

A simple variation on the car design is the tricycle design. In this design, a single wheel, instead of a pair, is used for steering.

Exotic Drives

There are three other interesting drives that should be mentioned. The first of these is *synchro drive*. In this scheme, the robot has three or more identical wheels. Each of the wheels pivots on its vertical center. All of the wheels point in the same direction, as shown in Figure 2-11.

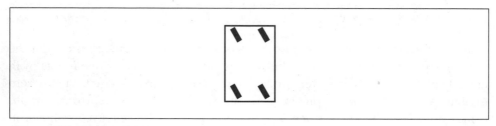

Figure 2-11. Synchro drive

To turn, the robot swivels the wheels to point in a new direction. This has the interesting side effect that the robot can change direction even though its body stays oriented the same. This property could be useful for robots that need to communicate with the computer over the IR link. The key to building synchro drive robots is a piece called a large turntable. You can order these pieces from Pitsco® LEGO DACTA®; see Appendix A, *Finding Parts and Programming Environments*, for details.

The *tri-star* wheel is another interesting idea. Figure 2-12 shows a side view of a tri-star robot and a close-up of the wheel assembly.

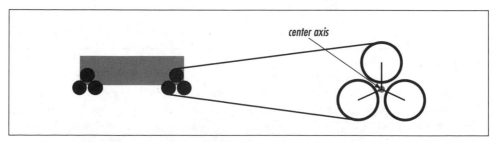

Figure 2-12. Side view of the tri-star design

Each wheel assembly is actually composed of three wheels arranged in a triangular fashion. The robot drives these wheels to move. When a large obstacle (like a step) is encountered, the entire wheel assembly rolls on its center axis. In essence, the entire wheel assembly acts like a large triangular wheel. This large wheel size enables the tri-star design to drive over large obstacles.

Killough's platform is an interesting variation on the wheels-within-a-wheel concept. It's really too exotic to describe here; the "Online Resources" lists two web pages that contain photographs and diagrams of this platform.

Bumpers and Feelers

Hank uses the touch sensors to figure out when he bumps into something. But it's not really enough to put a touch sensor just on the front of your robot, because then it could be activated only in one specific spot. Instead, Hank uses a pair of bumpers to detect touches across the entire front of the robot.

The idea of a bumper is to make a large area sensitive to touch so that the robot can detect collisions with a wide variety of objects—chair legs, walls, pets, rocks, trees, and so forth.

Hank uses bumpers that rest lightly against the touch sensors. When the bumper is pressed anywhere along its length, the touch sensor is then also pressed. A slightly different approach is to make a bumper that is held tightly against the sensor. When the bumper collides with something, the sensor actually turns *off* instead of *on*.

The trick with bumpers is to make them sensitive but not too sensitive. The bumper needs to trigger the touch sensor when the robot bumps into something. On the other hand, it should not trigger the touch sensor when the robot starts or stops moving abruptly or when it's driving over a bumpy surface.

Gears

Gears are clever mechanical devices that can be used to trade speed for power or to translate motion from one axis to another. A gear, in essence, is a disk with teeth on its edge. It has a space in its center where you can put a shaft. Gears have three primary purposes:

1. You can trade speed for power by using a small gear to drive a larger gear. The shaft on the larger gear will turn more slowly but more powerfully than the shaft on the smaller gear.

2. The opposite effect—trading power for speed—occurs if you use a large gear to drive a smaller gear. The shaft on the smaller gear will turn faster than the one on the larger gear, but with less power.

3. You can use gears to transfer motion from one axis to another. The gears in Hank's body transfer motion from the motors to the drive axles of the treads, as shown in Figure 2-13.

Figure 2-13. Using gears to transfer motion

The Palette of LEGO Gears

LEGO offers an impressive array of gears. The LEGO community has adopted names for these gears, which I will use throughout this book. Refer back to Figure 2-3; it shows the gears that come with RIS and their names. For the most part, gears are named based on the number of teeth they have. The 40t gear, for example, has 40 teeth. The number of teeth is directly proportional to the gear's radius, so the 24t gear has a radius exactly three times as large as the 8t gear.

Specialty Gears

You're probably comfortable with the 8t, 16t, 24t, and 40t gears. They can be put together to transfer rotational motion from one axis to another. In particular, these gears are used to transfer motion between *parallel* axes.

The gears in the bottom row of Figure 2-3 can be used to transfer motion between *perpendicular* axes. Two of these are *bevel* and *crown* gears.

The *worm* gear is a real character, for two reasons:

1. While the other gears attach firmly to the shaft, the worm gear can slide freely along the shaft. If you want it to stay in one place, you'll need to anchor it down somehow.

2. The worm gear really works only one way: you drive the worm gear, and it drives another gear. There's no way to turn the other gear and have it translate to motion in the worm gear.

Do the Math

The mathematics of gears can be described in a high school physics class. The two important equations have to do with *torque* and *angular velocity*.

Here's the equation for torque, which is a measure of the power in a turning shaft:

$$\tau = Fr$$

In this case, τ is torque, F is force, and r is the distance from the center of the rotation to the point where the force is applied. For a gear, this is the distance from the center (where the shaft runs through) to the teeth. This is the same as the radius of the gear. Suppose, then, that you have an 8t gear driving a 24t gear.

The equation for the torque of the 8t gear's shaft is this:

$$\tau_8 = Fr$$

The radius of the 24t gear is exactly three times the radius of the 8t gear. The force is the same where the teeth of the two gears meet. Therefore, the torque on the shaft on the 24t gear is exactly three times the torque on the 8t gear's shaft:

$$\tau_{24} = 3Fr = 3\tau_8$$

Angular velocity is the measure of how fast a shaft rotates. The angular velocity of a shaft can be expressed in terms of the velocity of a point on the gear as follows:

$$\omega = \frac{v}{r}$$

Here, ω is the angular velocity, v is the velocity of the point on the gear, and r is the distance between the point and the center of the gear. For the example I just described (an 8t gear driving a 24t gear), the angular velocity of the 24t gear is exactly one third of the angular velocity of the 8t gear. You can figure this out because the velocities of the gear teeth must be the same:

$$\omega_8 = \frac{v}{r}$$

$$\omega_{24} = \frac{v}{3r} = \frac{\omega_8}{3}$$

In general, then, it's easy to figure out the ratios of torque and angular velocity for two mating gears, just by figuring out the ratios of gear teeth. If you use an 8t gear to drive a 40t gear, you'll end up with fives times the torque and one fifth the angular velocity.

Of Geared and Ungeared Motors

There's one more topic related to gears that's important. Most electric motors turn too fast and with too little power to be useful. Gears are usually used to swap speed for power until a good balance is achieved. This process is called *gearing down* or *gear reduction*.

The motors that come with RIS are *internally geared*, which means that the motor case actually contains an electric motor and some number of gears. The output shaft is already adjusted to turn at a reasonable speed with a reasonable amount of power. This means you can attach wheels directly to these motors to drive your robot around.

The LEGO group makes four different kinds of motors that can be driven from the outputs of the RCX:

standard motor

> This has been the standard motor of the LEGO TECHNIC line for many years. It is an *ungeared* motor, which means its output shaft rotates very rapidly, with little power, when electricity is applied. To do any useful work with it, you'll probably have to use gears to reduce its output speed.

micro motor

> This is a tiny motor with low speed and low power. You probably can't use this motor to move your robot, but it could be useful for lighter tasks. It's harder to find than the other motors.

geared motor

> Two of these motors come with the MINDSTORMS RIS kit. They are internally geared so that the output shaft has enough power to drive your robot around. They are more efficient than the standard motor. The geared motor is shown in Figure 2-14.

Figure 2-14. The geared motor

train motor

LEGO sells an entire line of train sets. The train motor can be controlled by your RCX; as a matter of fact, you can make an "intelligent" train by mounting the RCX in one of the cars.

For a Rainy Day

To see exactly how efficient the geared motors are, try this experiment. Use one of the "wire bricks" to attach two motors to each other. When you turn the shaft of one motor, the other motor's shaft will turn simultaneously. What's going on here? Just as you can supply power to make the motor turn, turning the motor with your hand generates power. This power is transferred to the other motor, where it's converted back to the movement of the shaft.

Of course, you haven't actually built anything useful. But it's a good demonstration of the efficiency of these motors. The shaft on the second motor turns at nearly the same speed as the first motor, which means very little energy is lost in converting mechanical energy to electrical energy and vice versa.

If you have a choice of motors, you'll probably always use a geared motor. It is more efficient, more convenient, and less bulky than the standard motor. The micro motor is hard to find and not strong enough for most tasks.

How can you get more motors? RIS comes with two motors, but there are three outputs on the RCX. You can get another motor in the RoboSports expansion set, but it'll cost you $50.

You can order extra motors from the LEGO Shop-at-Home service, one of The LEGO Group's best-kept secrets. This service is available in the United States at (800) 835-4386. They have a variety of sets and spare parts—the item numbers for the motors are as follows:

- Standard motor, item 5114

- Micro motor, item 5119

- Geared motor, item 5225

- Train motor, item 5300

You can also order the first three motors from Pitsco LEGO DACTA: (800) 362-4308.

For more information on extra parts and ordering, see Appendix A.

Multitasking

Don't be fooled by the simplicity of the RIS programming environment—it hides some pretty messy details. Hank's simple program demonstrates a powerful feature of the RCX software: *multitasking*. This is a term from the computer world—it just means that the RCX can do more than one thing at a time. Each of the two instruction sequences hanging off the touch sensor watchers is a separate task, and they can actually execute at the same time. To see this in action, touch one of Hank's bumpers to trigger the first task, then touch the other bumper shortly afterward. (To really see this effect, you could try putting in longer delay times in Hank's program.)

The sensor watchers in RCX Code exhibit another interesting property. If you trigger a sensor watcher, the code for that watcher begins executing. If you trigger the same sensor watcher again, while the watcher code is still executing, the watcher code starts over again from the beginning.

The relationship between the programs you create in RCX Code and the tasks that run on the RCX is not always clear. Tasks and subroutines are declared explicitly in NQC, one of the alternate programming environments for the RCX. See Chapter 4, *Not Quite C*, for details.

Figure 2-15 shows how the multitasking nature of the RCX can get you into trouble. The figure shows an alternate program for Hank. At first glance, it makes sense. The main program starts Hank moving forward. When one of the bumpers is touched, the robot backs up, waits, turns, waits, and starts going forward.

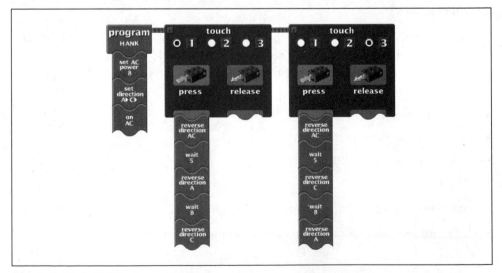

Figure 2-15. A slightly dangerous program

A serious problem occurs if the same bumper is quickly hit twice. Suppose the bumper on input 1 is hit once. It begins executing its sensor watcher code by reversing the direction of the motors. The robot travels backwards for half a second, then output A reverses direction and the robot spins in place. Suppose, now, that the bumper on input 1 is triggered again, before output C's direction is reversed again. The sensor watcher routine will begin again, reversing the direction of both the motors. Hank, therefore, will begin spinning the other direction instead of moving backwards. Then output A's direction reverses, and the robot moves forward. Finally, output C's direction reverses, and the robot spins in place again, instead of moving forward.

There are two solutions to this problem. First, you can be more explicit about controlling outputs. Instead of just reversing the output directions in the sensor watcher routines, you could specifically set the directions and turn on the motors. This technique is shown in Hank's first program, in Figure 2-6. It doesn't matter if the sensor watchers are interrupted before they finish, because the directions of the motors are always set explicitly. The other solution is to structure your program differently. If your sensor watchers don't have any delays built into them, for example, they will be much less likely to be interrupted.

Online Resources

The Art of LEGO Design
ftp://cherupakha.media.mit.edu/pub/people/fredm/artoflego.pdf
> This is an outstanding paper about building with LEGO parts. It includes helpful tips on making strong structures and using gears. The paper is written by Fred Martin, one of the people at the MIT Media Lab whose programmable brick work formed the basis of the RCX. I highly recommend this paper, especially if you are having trouble getting things to fit together.

Fred's 6.270 Home Page
http://lcs.www.media.mit.edu/people/fredm/projects/6270/
> For a deeper treatment of many aspects of small mobile robotics, read the course guide for MIT's famous 6.270 class. In this class, students build robots from the ground up. *The 6.270 Robot Builder's Guide* was written by Fred Martin; it is a real bonanza of information and advice.

Doug's LEGO Technic Tri-Star Wheel ATV and Robotics page
http://www.net-info.com/~dcarlson/
> Doug Carlson's fascinating page is full of pictures of his implementations of the tri-star design, synchro drive, and the Killough platform. For sheer mechanical finesse, this page is hard to beat.

Killough's mobile robot platform
http://carol.wins.uva.nl/~leo/lego/killough.html

This part of Leo Dorst's acclaimed site gives some background and explanation of the Killough platform.

Synchronicity
http://members.xoom.com/jknudsen/Synchronicity/Synchronicity.html

This page has photographs of my own synchro drive robot, which has three wheels and a compact design.

Pitsco LEGO DACTA
http://www.pitsco-legodacta.com/

This is the official home page of Pitsco LEGO DACTA. Many of the interesting things that Pitsco LEGO DACTA sells are not listed online, but you can call and order a catalog. Make sure you get the LEGO DACTA catalog, as Pitsco has an entirely different catalog that doesn't have anything to do with LEGO. This is the place to order the Robolab software that allows you to program your RCX from a Macintosh.

Dacta Spares from Pitsco
http://www.ee.nmt.edu/~jmathis/dacta.html

This unofficial site contains images of some of the interesting pages in the Pitsco LEGO DACTA catalog, including the pages with the motors and sensors.

LEGO Motors
http://www.enteract.com/~dbaum/lego/motors.html

This page contains a concise description of the three kinds of motors.

3

Trusty, a Line Follower

In this chapter, you'll build Trusty, a simple robot that exhibits a behavior called *line following*. This means that Trusty, shown in Figure 3-1, can drive along a sort of "track" defined by a thick black line on the floor. Your RIS kit includes a "Test Pad," which is simply a large piece of white paper with some black lines and other marks on it. Trusty will follow the large black oval on this paper faithfully until he runs out of battery power.

Figure 3-1. Trusty, a line follower

As you can see in Figure 3-1, Trusty's main feature is a downward pointing light sensor. This sensor is the key to line following. The light sensor can distinguish between the white background of the Test Pad and the black line drawn on it. As you'll discover, this feature doesn't make line following easy to program; but it does make it possible.

Building Instructions

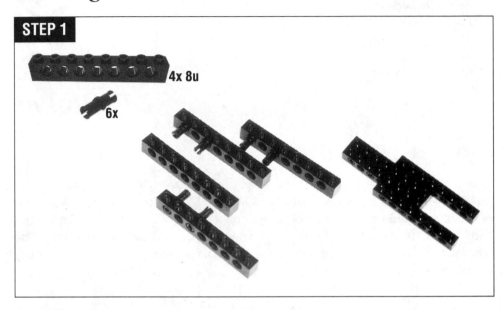

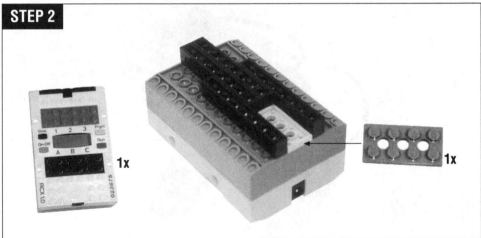

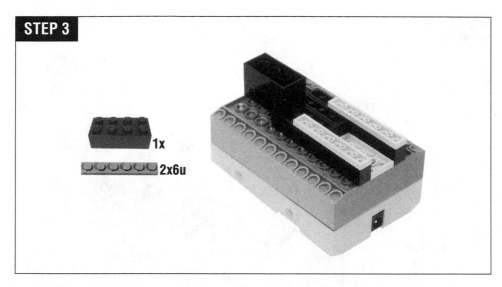

STEP 3

1x

2x6u

In Step 4, make sure the top bushing allows the idler wheel to rotate freely by putting the round side next to the plate. If you put it on the other way, the idler wheel will be locked in place.

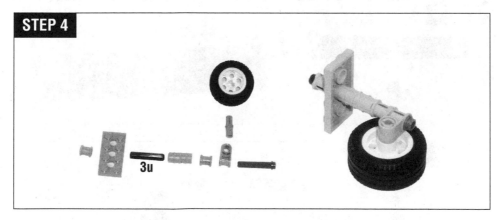

STEP 4

3u

Be sure to attach the wire bricks to the motors before putting them on Trusty.

STEP 5

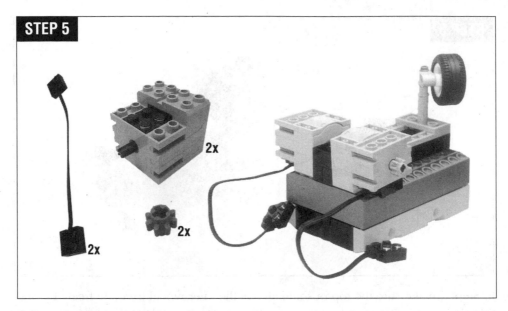

Next, build the support for the light sensor.

STEP 6

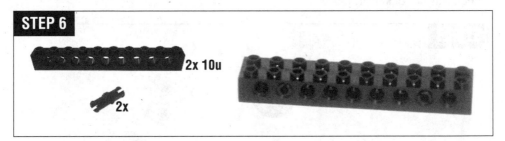

STEP 7

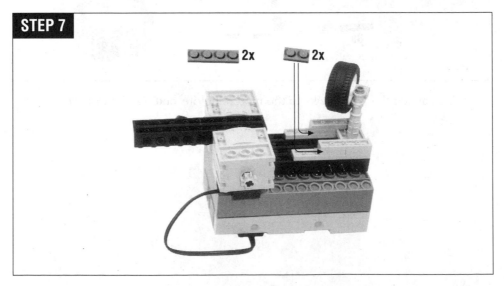

The 2u beams between the motors will hold the ends of the drive shafts. Make sure that you can see the holes.

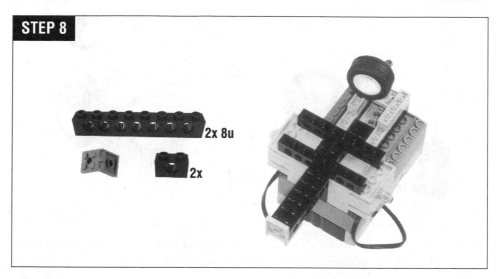

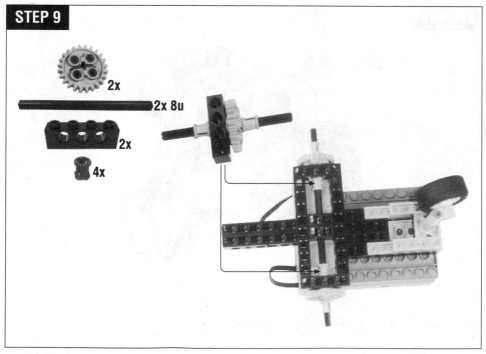

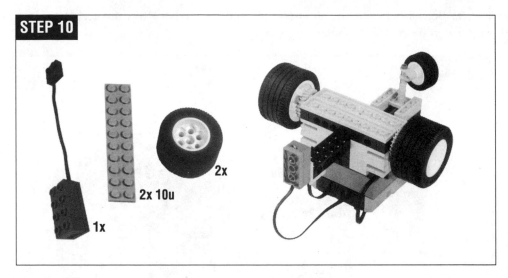

Flip the robot over and attach the wires as shown. The motors are attached to output A and output C, while the light sensor is attached to input 2.

Some Tricky Programming

It's surprisingly hard to convince our robot to follow a black line on the floor. (A lot of things in mobile robotics are surprisingly hard, as we discussed in Chapter 1, *Robotics and MINDSTORMS*.) The simplest way to describe the program is this:

```
if I'm on the line, go straight forward
if I'm off the line, find the line and start over
```

It's the "find the line" part that's difficult. When Trusty's light sensor goes off the black line, Trusty has no way of knowing if he's on the right or the left side of the line. Ideally, Trusty would turn back to the line and start going straight again. He would proceed in a zigzag fashion along the line.

State

Even if Trusty doesn't know which side of the line he's on, he can make a pretty good guess. If he knows he drove off the left side of the line last time, it's a pretty good bet he'll drive off the right side the next time. Figure 3-2 shows a likely path as Trusty tries to stay on the line.

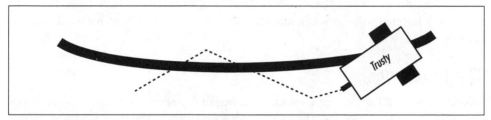

Figure 3-2. Trusty zigzags along the black line

With this in mind, Trusty's algorithm can be more specific:

```
if I'm on the line, go straight forward
if I'm off the line {
    turn back the opposite direction from the way I turned last time
    if I still don't find the line, turn farther back the other direction
}
```

Another way of looking at this is to say that Trusty now has two possible *states*:

1. Just turned left (turn right next)

2. Just turned right (turn left next)

By keeping track of this state, Trusty can figure out the best way to turn the next time he drives off the black line.

Could I Please Have a Variable?

Some kind of variable is needed if Trusty is to keep track of his state. Said another way, Trusty needs some kind of memory to remember which way he last turned. This highlights one of the weak points of RCX Code (the RIS programming environment), its lack of variables.

The environment does provide a counter, which we'll use in lieu of a variable to hold the turning direction. Although you can't assign values directly to the counter, you can do two things: reset it to zero and add one to it. Trusty will use just two values, 0 and 1, to mean turn left and turn right, respectively.

Coping with Failure

Our basic assumption about Trusty is that he will drive off the black line on alternating sides. But this probably won't really happen all the time, particularly if the black line has curves in it. What Trusty needs is some way to figure out if he's turning the wrong way, away from the line instead of toward it. For this purpose, we'll use a timer. If Trusty doesn't find the line within a certain time interval, we'll have him switch state and turn back the other way.

The real world is a very challenging place. You should always assume that bad things will happen to your robot and try to create a program that responds appropriately.

The Program

Figure 3-3 shows Trusty's basic program. It begins by setting the two motors to the forward direction at speed 4. The central decision point is the light sensor watcher. If the sensor sees the black line, Trusty moves straight ahead. If the sensor sees the white background, then the program resets the timer and calls a subroutine called `toggle`. This subroutine turns the robot left or right, alternating each time it is called.

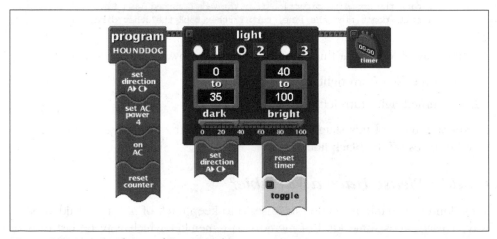

Figure 3-3. A top-level view of Trusty's software

Use your own values for the thresholds of the light sensor watcher. The values shown in Figure 3-3 are calibrated to my particular light sensor and may not work with yours.

The timer is used in case Trusty happens to turn the wrong way. Suppose, for example, that he runs off the right side of the black line twice in a row. The first time, he would turn left to find the line again. The second time, however, he would turn right, away from the line. The timer is used to limit this behavior. If Trusty is turning and the timer goes off, then Trusty automatically turns back the other way. Figure 3-4 shows the timer watcher, which calls the same `toggle` subroutine if the robot is still off the line.

You might be wondering why the timer counts for one half second. Why not three quarters of a second, or a full second? Remember that the timer keeps Trusty from turning around completely. The timer value is based on observation—if Trusty is turning toward the line, he will find it within a half second. If he is turning away from the line, he can be pretty sure he's missed it after a half second. A line-follower with a different mechanical design might need a different timer value.

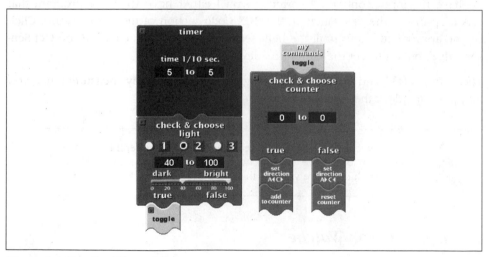

Figure 3-4. Details of Trusty's software

Figure 3-4 also shows the `toggle` subroutine itself. All it does is examine the value of the counter. If it's 0, then the robot is set to turn left and the counter value is changed to 1. The next time `toggle` is called, the robot turns right and the counter value is reset to 0. It's useful to have `toggle` as a subroutine because it is called from two places in Trusty's program.

The Light Sensor

Working with the light sensor can be a little tricky. As measured by the RCX, the light sensor outputs a value from 0 (dark) to 100 (bright). However, the signal generated by the sensor has some *noise* in it, which means the value jumps around unpredictably. To use a light sensor effectively, then, you need to figure out what the interesting values are and how to respond to them.

Testing Light Sensor Values

The easiest way to figure out what values your light sensor is generating is to use the RCX's **View** button. Press **View** repeatedly until a little arrow appears under the input with the sensor. The RCX's screen should show the value of the sensor. You can place Trusty so the light sensor is over the line, and then observe the value. Now see what values you get when Trusty is off the line. You should also try the green area of the Test Pad, and try all the measurements with the room both dark and light. This should give you a good feel for the values that are important.

The **View** button only works if the input is configured to measure a light sensor. To have the input configured correctly, you'll either have to run a program that sets it up or use the **Test Panel**, in the **RCX Code** section of the RIS software. Click on the appropriate input until the light sensor appears. Then click on the **Get Sensor Values** button to get the current readings.

The choice of 35 and 40 in Trusty's program is based on my measurements; you may want to adjust these values for your specific conditions.

 Don't expect to get the same readings from two different light sensors, even under the same conditions with the same RCX. Always test the values before you use them in a program.

The Light Sensor Watcher

What's going on with that sensor watcher in Figure 3-3? It's actually two sensor watchers rolled into one. The following pseudocode shows how it works:

```
if the sensor value is in the range from 0 to 35 (but wasn't previously),
   execute the "dark" commands
if the sensor value is in the range from 40 to 100 (but wasn't previously),
   execute the "bright" commands
```

Figure 3-5 shows a hypothetical graph of the light sensor value, along with the times when the dark and bright commands will be executed. Nothing happens until the sensor value enters either the dark or bright value ranges.

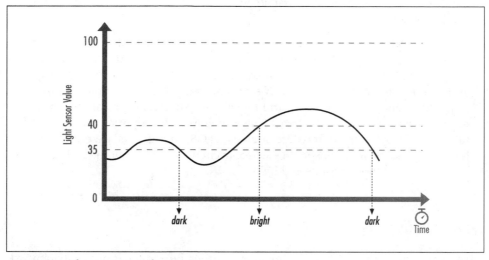

Figure 3-5. The sensor watcher

Remember that the RCX runs some tasks at the same time. If the dark commands and bright commands both take a while to execute, it's possible they may overlap. If the light sensor reading gets into the bright range and abruptly drops back into the dark range, the dark commands will start running while the bright commands are still in progress. You should be aware of this possibility and structure your code to deal with it. In Trusty's program, the dark and bright commands both execute quickly so they won't overlap.

Ambient Light

You have to be careful with the light sensor; its value depends on all the light it receives. This includes the reflected light from the red light that's part of the sensor as well as room light and sunlight.* In a line-following robot like Trusty, you really want to measure only the reflected light. In this case, it's in your interests to block out the room lighting, sunlight, light from your kid brother's flashlight, and anything else distracting. The light level that's present in a certain place is called the *ambient* light. In a robot like Trusty, you might try surround the light sensor with dark bricks to block out the ambient light. This can improve the accuracy of your sensor measurements. In this particular case, I didn't think it was necessary, but you might like to give it a whirl.

---

* The light sensor is even sensitive to the infrared light that is produced from the IR port.

Where's That Red Light Coming From, Anyhow?

Isn't it odd that the light sensor, an input device, has a red light on it? How did that happen? And how is that possible with only two wires connecting the sensor to the RCX?

The basic role of the RCX's inputs is to measure the value of the sensor. For certain types of sensors, like the light sensor, the RCX also provides power to the sensor. It does this by very quickly alternating between providing power and taking a measurement. The RCX sends power to the light sensor for about 3 ms (thousandths of a second) and takes a measurement for about .1 ms. It repeats this cycle over and over. (These timings only apply to the standard firmware. In an alternate firmware such as legOS, the timings are entirely different.) Inside the light sensor, an electronic circuit smooths out the pulses and provides steady power to the red light.

Idler Wheels

Trusty's two main drive wheels determine whether he moves forward, backward, or turns. But without at least one more wheel, Trusty can't balance and will tip forward or backward. Trusty's third wheel is a good example of an *idler wheel*. An idler wheel provides support for the robot but doesn't constrain its motion. It does this by rotating freely on a vertical axis. The front wheels on shopping carts are idler wheels, as are the casters under furniture. Ideally, an idler wheel can easily swivel in response to changes in the robot's direction. You've already seen Trusty's idler wheel in Figure 2-8.

Make your idler wheels sturdy! One of Trusty's early designs could follow a line just fine. But after about a minute of back-and-forth turning, the idler wheel broke off the bottom, and Trusty was left lying on his back, twitching.

Using Two Light Sensors

You can buy more light sensors for about $20US each (see the "Online Resources" section at the end of this chapter). By adding one more light sensor to Trusty, we can simplify his program and make his movement along the black line smoother.

Adding the Sensor

To add the second light sensor to Trusty, just move over the one that's already there. You can leave the original one attached to input 2 and just add the second one to input 3. Figure 3-6 shows how to do this.

Figure 3-6. Adding a second light sensor to Trusty

Programming

With two side-by-side light sensors, Trusty's algorithm is pretty simple. If both sensors are on the line, we just drive forward. If only one of the sensors is on the line, we simply turn back to the line. If both sensors go off the line, we don't do anything; the robot must already be turning and should return to the line soon. This logic can be represented by a simple map from the sensor values to the motor settings, as shown in Table 3-1.

Table 3-1. Mapping from Sensor Inputs to Motor Outputs

Left Light Sensor (2)	Right Light Sensor (3)	Left Motor (A)	Right Motor (C)	Result
dark	dark	forward	forward	Go forward
dark	bright	stop	forward	Turn left
bright	dark	forward	stop	Turn right
bright	bright	-	-	No change

It's cumbersome to implement this algorithm in RCX Code. Figure 3-7 shows the program, which is based around two sensor watchers. But go ahead and try it out; it works well even if it looks kind of strange. In Chapter 4, I'll show you how this algorithm (as well as the single-light-sensor Trusty) can be reprogrammed in NQC.

The program centers around two sensor watchers, one for each light sensor. Whenever either sensor sees light or dark, the value of the other is examined. Based on the values of the two sensors, the motors are set according to Table 3-1.

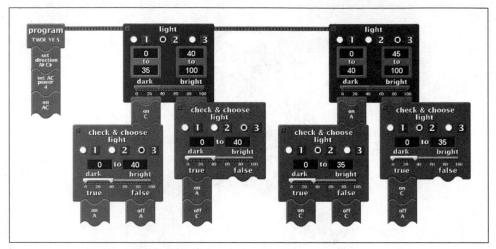

Figure 3-7. Programming Trusty with two light sensors

Online Resources

LEGO World Shop
http://www.legoworldshop.com/

> The RIS kit itself is available at this online store, although you can probably get it cheaper at a local retailer. However, the online store also carries items you won't find locally, like extra motors, touch sensors, light sensors, and even a remote control that sends messages to the RCX's IR port. You can even buy an extra RCX, although it's a much better value to spring for a whole RIS kit.

LEGO MINDSTORMS Sensor Input
http://www.plazaearth.com/usr/gasperi/lego.htm

> This is the authoritative resource for RCX sensor information. It describes how the sensors work, how you can modify sensors, and how you can build your own sensors. It includes schematic diagrams, handy graphs, and photographs.

LEGO Light Sensor
http://www.plazaearth.com/usr/gasperi/light.htm

> For the real skinny on LEGO's light sensor, check out this page. It includes a photograph of the circuit board inside the sensor, a schematic diagram, and graphs of the sensor's response with and without the LED.

4

Not Quite C

Once you've written a few programs in RCX Code, it feels a little constrictive. For one thing, there aren't any variables. It would be nice if your robot could remember things, like how many obstacles it's encountered or what the temperature was three minutes ago. In RCX Code, the only thing remotely resembling a variable is the counter. Back in Chapter 3, *Trusty, a Line Follower*, I used the counter to remember which way to turn. The counter was always a 0 or a 1, indicating whether the robot should turn left or right. But it's tough going, and if you try anything more complicated, the counter is not going to get the job done.

The lack of variables is only one of the limitations of RCX Code. Two other important limitations are:

- Although you can define subroutines (called "My Commands"), you can't call one subroutine from another. Likewise, a subroutine can't call itself.

- You can't control the RCX's display very well. It would be really nice, for debugging purposes, to be able to show values on the display.

The LEGO Group aimed the Robotics Invention System at people who had never programmed before. For this group, RCX Code is a gentle way to get started with programming mobile robots. But RIS is exceedingly popular with programmers and other technically savvy people, who are frustrated by the limitations of RCX Code. If you're reading this chapter, this probably includes you.

Since RIS was released in the Fall of 1998, the MINDSTORMS community has produced an amazing stream of clever, innovative software designed to overcome the limitations of RCX Code. Most of this software is available, free of charge, on the Internet. In this chapter, I'll describe one of the most popular packages: Not Quite C (NQC). NQC allows you to write programs for your RCX with a text-based language. I'll describe the syntax and commands of this language, with copious examples. If you've programmed in C, NQC will look familiar. If you have never programmed in C, don't worry; NQC is easy to learn.

This chapter presents NQC in four steps:

1. To get you started with NQC, this chapter begins with a simple example.

2. To understand how NQC works, you need to understand the software that's running on the RCX. This chapter describes the important pieces of the RCX's software architecture.

3. This chapter provides a detailed listing of NQC's commands, with examples.

4. Finally, this chapter contains software for Trusty written in NQC.

A Quick Start

Let's get right to the good stuff with a working example. First, you'll need to download and install NQC. It's available for MacOS, Linux, and Windows. Navigate to the NQC web site (*http://www.enteract.com/~dbaum/lego/nqc/*), and follow the instructions to download and install the latest version. The examples in this book were written with the NQC version 2.0b1.

Once it's installed, enter the following program using a text editor. This program operates Hank, the robot from Chapter 2, *Hank, the Bumper Tank*. Save the program in a file called *Hank.nqc*.

```
#define BACK_TIME 50
#define TURN_TIME 80

task main() {
  SetSensor(SENSOR_1, SENSOR_TOUCH);
  SetSensor(SENSOR_3, SENSOR_TOUCH);
  OnFwd(OUT_A + OUT_C);
  while (true) {
    if (SENSOR_1 == 1) {
      PlayTone(440, 50);
      OnRev(OUT_A + OUT_C);
      Wait(BACK_TIME);
      OnFwd(OUT_A);
      Wait(TURN_TIME);
      OnFwd(OUT_C);
    }
    if (SENSOR_3 == 1) {
      PlayTone(880, 50);
      OnRev(OUT_A + OUT_C);
      Wait(BACK_TIME);
      OnFwd(OUT_C);
      Wait(TURN_TIME);
      OnFwd(OUT_A);
    }
  }
}
```

Now compile the source code using the nqc command:

```
C:\>nqc Hank.nqc

C:\>
```

If you made a mistake typing in the program, nqc gives you a list of errors. Otherwise, you're ready to download the program with the –d option:

```
C:\>nqc -d Hank.nqc
Downloading Program:.....complete

C:\>
```

(If you need to specify a serial port different from the default, use the –S option.)

Go ahead and run the program. When you're done playing, come back and get some background on the software that runs the RCX.

RCX Software Architecture

Writing a program for the RCX involves a handful of software layers, both on the development PC and on the RCX itself. Figure 4-1 shows an overview of the important pieces.

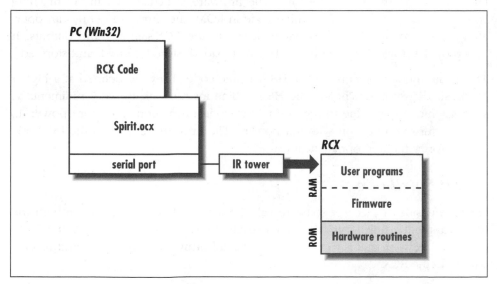

Figure 4-1. RCX software architecture

ROM

The RCX is a small computer that is based on a Hitachi H8/3292 microcontroller. The RCX contains two kinds of memory: Read Only Memory (ROM) and Random

Access Memory (RAM). As its name implies, ROM cannot be written. It is programmed at the factory and cannot be changed. RAM, on the other hand, can be written and read as many times as you want, with one catch: it needs power. If you take the batteries out of your RCX, the contents of the RAM are erased. Under normal circumstances, however, the batteries preserve the contents of the RAM.

When you first get your RCX, it has some stuff in ROM and an empty RAM. The RCX's ROM routines know a little bit about the RCX's hardware. These routines can run the motors or access the sensors. Most importantly, the ROM routines know how to receive code from the IR port and place it in RAM.

Firmware

One of the first things you have to do with your RCX is download the *firmware*. The firmware is, essentially, an operating system for your RCX. The routines in ROM know how to download a set of firmware from the IR port and store it in RAM. The firmware is capable of more than just processing the ROM routines. It shows a clock on the display of the RCX. It can recognize and respond to the **View** button. Most importantly, it can receive robot programs over the IR port and run them.

Although at first it sounds like the firmware and the robot programs are the same kind of animal, this is not the case. The firmware is actual Hitachi H8 machine code. Together with the H8 machine code in ROM, the firmware defines an operating system for the RCX. It provides access to the RCX's inputs and outputs. It also provides a way for programs to be downloaded, stored, started, and stopped.

The actual robot programs are not H8 machine code. They are defined at a higher level called *bytecode*. Whereas the H8 machine instructions are very rudimentary, such as "move this value to register 1," bytecode instructions are more powerful, such as "turn output 2 on with full power." The firmware interprets the bytecode and performs the appropriate action.

About Spirit.ocx

On the PC side, a piece of software called *Spirit.ocx* handles interaction with the RCX via the IR link. *Spirit.ocx* can execute bytecode commands on the RCX, download new programs to the RCX, download firmware to the RCX, and receive data from the RCX.

The RCX Code programming environment sits on top of *Spirit.ocx*. It provides the click-and-drag programming environment that you're already familiar with. RCX Code converts these graphic programs into bytecode and uses *Spirit.ocx* to download the programs to the RCX.

Spirit.ocx is a regular ActiveX control, which means its functions are accessible from programming languages like Visual Basic and Visual C++.

Spruce Up That Resume

Writing programs for the RCX is an example of *cross-compiling* for an *embedded system*, a phrase that is bound to sound good on your resume. Cross-compiling means that you are writing programs on one computer (your PC) that will run on another computer (the RCX). An embedded system is a computer that is part of some other device. For example, microwave ovens and mobile phones both contain embedded systems. Modern cars contain dozens of embedded systems, as well.

The usual way to develop software for a chip like the Hitachi H8 would be to use a cross compiler running on a PC. You would write source code (probably in C or assembly language) on your PC and use the cross-compiler to create H8 machine code from the source. Then you would probably use a special PC peripheral, called a *burner*, to place the machine code on some sort of programmable memory chip.

The final step would be to physically place the memory chip in the embedded system. When the embedded system boots up, the software you just wrote will run.

The RIS software simplifies this process in two important ways. First, it provides a graphic programming environment that's very accessible, particularly for people who haven't programmed before. Second, programs are downloaded to the RCX over the IR link and stored in RAM. This feature eliminates the complexity of dealing with memory chips and burners yourself.

The cross-compilation step is a little different, too, because RCX programs are bytecode rather than machine code. But it's still cross-compilation: the end result is bytecode rather than H8 machine code.

A Day in the Life of a Program

Let's examine the typical life of a robot program:

1. The program's life begins when you create something in RCX Code. RCX Code compiles your program to bytecode.

2. RCX Code uses *Spirit.ocx* to download the program to one of the RCX's five program slots. The compiled bytecode is transferred to the RCX via the IR link.

3. The program is now available in RAM. When you run it, the firmware interprets the bytecode in your program and performs the appropriate tasks.

NQC Overview

Where does NQC fit in? NQC is a replacement for the software on the PC, both RCX Code and *Spirit.ocx*. NQC source code is stored in simple text files, just like C, C++, or Java source code. NQC compiles these source files to bytecode and can download them to the RCX using the IR tower. NQC is a good way to overcome the limitations of RCX Code. But because it produces bytecode programs, it's still subject to the limitations of the firmware's bytecode interpreter.

Because NQC talks to the IR tower directly, without depending on *Spirit.ocx*, it is very portable. NQC runs on MacOS (using MPW), Linux, and of course Windows 95, 98, and NT. RCX Code, by contrast, only runs on Windows.*

NQC was developed by Dave Baum, who maintains the official web site at *http:// www.enteract.com/~dbaum/lego/nqc/*. His web site also includes pithy documentation for the language.

If you're using NQC on Windows, you might want to also use RCX Command Center (RcxCC). RcxCC is a Windows application that wraps around NQC. It provides a syntax-colored program editor, push-button compilation and downloading, real-time control of the RCX, and a host of other useful features. Although NQC is fairly easy to use all by itself, RcxCC gives you an even smoother ride. See the "Online Resources" at the end of this chapter for a URL and more information.

This chapter covers the important commands of NQC. If you have a background in C programming, the syntax and control structures will look familiar. If you don't have a background in C, don't worry: NQC is easy to learn. I've included lots of example programs to demonstrate how things work. I won't cover NQC exhaustively; several excellent web pages detail the entire language. See the "Online Resources" section at the end of this chapter for details.

main

NQC programs are organized into one or more *tasks*. A task is simply some set of instructions that execute in order. A task is analogous to a *thread* in other programming environments. A single program may consist of several tasks that execute at the same time.

Tasks have names. Every program should have a special task called **main**. When the **Run** button is pressed, the RCX begins the program by running **main**. If you define other tasks, you have to explicitly start and stop them. The **main** task is the only one that is automatically run by the RCX. I'll explain more about starting and stopping tasks later.

---

* As this book goes to press, a standalone MacOS version of NQC is being released in beta test form. Now you can run NQC on MacOS without MPW.

Output Commands

NQC includes several commands for controlling the outputs of the RCX. You've already seen one of these, OnFwd, in our first simple example.

On(const outputs)

> This command turns on the specified outputs. The outputs should be some combination of the constant values OUT_A, OUT_B, and OUT_C. Multiple outputs can be specified by adding them together, as shown in the first example. When an output is turned on, its current power and direction are consulted to determine what actually happens.

Off(const outputs)

> This command turns off the specified outputs, putting them in brake mode. For motors, this means that the motor shaft will be hard to turn.

Float(const outputs)

> Float() is really a variation of Off(). No power is sent to the output, but the shaft of an attached motor will turn freely. This is a useful option if you want your robot to coast to a stop.

You can set the direction of outputs with the following three commands:

Fwd(const outputs)

> Use this command to set the direction of the specified outputs to forward.

Rev(const outputs)

> This command sets the direction of the specified outputs to reverse.

Toggle(const outputs)

> To switch the direction of one or more outputs, use this command.

To determine the output power, use the following command:

SetPower(const outputs, expression speed)

> This command sets the power of the given outputs. Any expression that evaluates to a value from one to seven can be used as the speed. You may use the constant values OUT_LOW (1), OUT_HALF (4), and OUT_FULL (7) if you desire.

To fully determine an output's actions, you should set its mode, direction, and power explicitly. By default, all three outputs are set to full power and the forward direction. Therefore, calling On() is enough to get the motors running.

NQC provides two handy "combination" commands:

OnFwd(const outputs)

> This command turns on the specified outputs in the forward direction.

OnRev(const outputs)

> This command turns on the specified outputs in the reverse direction.

These commands set the mode and direction of the outputs in one fell swoop, but you should still set the power level explicitly with a call to `SetPower()`.

For timed actions, the following command will come in handy:

OnFor(const outputs, expression time)
>   This command turns on the specified outputs for the given time, measured in hundredths of a second. Then the given outputs are turned off (in brake mode, not in float mode).

The following example runs outputs A and C forward, waits one second, then reverses outputs A and C. After another second, the outputs are turned off.

```
task main() {
  SetPower(OUT_A + OUT_C, OUT_HALF);

  Fwd(OUT_A + OUT_C);
  OnFor(OUT_A + OUT_C, 100);

  Rev(OUT_A + OUT_C);
  OnFor(OUT_A + OUT_C, 100);
}
```

The `On()`, `Off()`, `Float()`, `Fwd()`, `Rev()`, and `Toggle()` commands are really shorthand for these lower-level output commands:

SetOutput(const outputs, const mode)
>   This command sets the mode for the given outputs. The outputs are specified in the same way as in the `Fwd()` and `Rev()` commands. The value of `mode` should be one of the constants `OUT_ON`, `OUT_OFF`, and `OUT_FLOAT`.

SetDirection(const outputs, const direction)
>   This command determines the direction of the supplied outputs. The `direction` parameter should be `OUT_FWD`, `OUT_REV`, or `OUT_TOGGLE`. `OUT_TOGGLE` is a special value that sets the direction of the output to the opposite of its current value.

In general, I recommend you don't call `SetDirection()` with the `OUT_TOGGLE` value. If you explicitly set the directions of your outputs, your program will be clearer. Furthermore, in programs with more than one task, your program is more likely to behave as you expect.

Input Commands

Before you can read a value from one of the RCX's inputs, you need to tell the RCX what type of sensor is attached to the input. NQC provides a command that does just this:

SetSensor(expression sensor, const configuration)

This command tells the RCX how to configure the given input. Valid values for **sensor** are SENSOR_1, SENSOR_2, and SENSOR_3, which represent the three inputs of the RCX. The sensor configurations are detailed in Table 4-1. See Appendix A, *Finding Parts and Programming Environments*, which lists the sensors that are available for the RCX.

Table 4-1. NQC Sensor Modes

Configuration	Sensor Type	Input Value	ClearSensor()
SENSOR_TOUCH	Touch	1 (pressed) or 0 (not pressed)	-
SENSOR_LIGHT	Light	0 (dark) to 100 (bright)	-
SENSOR_ROTATION	Rotation	16 units per full rotation	yes
SENSOR_CELSIUS	Temperature	Celsius degrees times 10	-
SENSOR_FAHRENHEIT	Temperature	Fahrenheit degrees times 10	-
SENSOR_PULSE	Touch	Count of presses	yes
SENSOR_EDGE	Touch	Count of state transitions	yes

The actual sensor value can be read using SENSOR_1, SENSOR_2, and SENSOR_3. These are shorthand for the following command:

SensorValue(const input)

This command returns the current value of the given input, which should be 0, 1, or 2, for input 1, input 2, and input 3 respectively. The values returned from an input depend on the input's configuration and are described in Table 4-1.

SENSOR_1, SENSOR_2, and SENSOR_3 actually have a dual purpose in life. Their first purpose is to identify the inputs on the RCX to commands like SetSensor(). Their second purpose is to retrieve values from the inputs. Thus, there are two distinct uses for SENSOR_1, SENSOR_2, and SENSOR_3.

The SENSOR_PULSE and SENSOR_EDGE configurations are variations on SENSOR_TOUCH. The SENSOR_PULSE configuration counts the times the touch sensor has been pressed, while SENSOR_EDGE counts the transitions from on to off and from off to on. When you read the value of an input in one of these configurations, the input value is the accumulated count.

The configurations that keep a count can be reset with a call to ClearSensor() (as shown in Table 4-1):

ClearSensor(expression sensor)

This command resets the current count for the given input to 0.

Edges and Pulses

If you examine the output of a touch sensor, over time, it looks something like this:

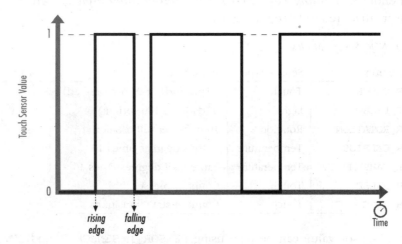

The transitions from 0 to 1 and from 1 to 0 are called *edges*. A transition from 0 to 1 is a rising edge, while a transition from 1 to 0 is a falling edge.

The SENSOR_EDGE configuration counts all edges, rising or falling. SENSOR_PULSE is a little more selective—it counts rising edges only.

The following example plays a sound after every fourth press on the touch sensor. It begins by configuring input 1 to count touch presses with the SENSOR_PULSE configuration. Then it enters an endless loop, repeatedly testing the value of input 1. If it is 4, a sound is played, and the count for input 1 is reset.

```
task main() {
  SetSensor(SENSOR_1, SENSOR_PULSE);
  while(true) {
    if (SENSOR_1 == 4) {
      PlaySound(SOUND_DOWN);
      ClearSensor(SENSOR_1);
    }
  }
}
```

The SetSensor() command actually configures an input's *type* and *mode* at the same time. The input type describes the electrical characteristics of the attached sensor, while the mode determines how the sensor values are interpreted. If you need finer control over the inputs than you can get from SetSensor(), use the SetSensorType() and SetSensorMode() commands:

SetSensorType(expression sensor, const type)

> This command specifies the type of sensor attached to the given input. Input types are listed in Table 4-2. This command specifies how the RCX should treat an input, electrically speaking. The SENSOR_TYPE_LIGHT type, for example, supplies power to the sensor. (I described this back in Chapter 3.)

Table 4-2. Input Type Constants

Type Constant	Sensor Type
SENSOR_TYPE_TOUCH	Touch sensor
SENSOR_TYPE_TEMPERATURE	Temperature sensor
SENSOR_TYPE_LIGHT	Light sensor (powered)
SENSOR_TYPE_ROTATION	Rotation sensor (powered)

SetSensorMode(expression sensor, const mode)

> Use this command to set the mode of the given input. While the SetSensor-Type() command is used to specify the electrical characteristics of the input, the SetSensorMode() command specifies how the input value should be processed. The modes are listed in Table 4-3.

Table 4-3. Input Mode Constants

Mode Constant	Description
SENSOR_MODE_RAW	Raw sensor value from 0 to 1023
SENSOR_MODE_BOOL	Either 1 or 0
SENSOR_MODE_EDGE	Counts transitions from 1 to 0 and vice versa
SENSOR_MODE_PULSE	Counts transitions from 1 to 0
SENSOR_MODE_PERCENT	Percent from 0 to 100
SENSOR_MODE_CELSIUS	Celsius temperature
SENSOR_MODE_FAHRENHEIT	Fahrenheit temperature
SENSOR_MODE_ROTATION	Shaft angle, 16 counts per full revolution

Internally, input values initially have a raw value from 0 to 1023. Raw values are converted to the input values that your program sees by a process that depends on the input mode. Three of the modes count events: SENSOR_MODE_EDGE, SENSOR_MODE_PULSE, and SENSOR_MODE_ROTATION. The other modes perform a mathematical scaling operation on the raw input value.

For example, if the input mode is SENSOR_MODE_PERCENT, the RCX converts the raw value into a percent according to the equation:

$$inputValue = 100 \cdot \frac{rawValue}{1023}$$

If you wanted to attach a temperature sensor to input 2 and measure Celsius values, you would do the following:

```
SetSensorType(SENSOR_2, SENSOR_TYPE_TEMPERATURE);
SetSensorMode(SENSOR_2, SENSOR_MODE_CELSIUS);
```

The `SetSensor()` command, which I described first in this section, is a convenient way of specifying both an input type and an input mode. Table 4-4 shows what types and modes correspond to the configurations that `SetSensor()` recognizes.

Table 4-4. Input Configurations, Types, and Modes

Input Configuration	Input Type	Input Mode
SENSOR_TOUCH	SENSOR_TYPE_TOUCH	SENSOR_MODE_BOOL
SENSOR_PULSE	SENSOR_TYPE_TOUCH	SENSOR_MODE_PULSE
SENSOR_EDGE	SENSOR_TYPE_TOUCH	SENSOR_MODE_EDGE
SENSOR_LIGHT	SENSOR_TYPE_LIGHT	SENSOR_MODE_PERCENT
SENSOR_CELSIUS	SENSOR_TYPE_TEMPERATURE	SENSOR_MODE_CELSIUS
SENSOR_FAHRENHEIT	SENSOR_TYPE_TEMPERATURE	SENSOR_MODE_FAHRENHEIT
SENSOR_ROTATION	SENSOR_TYPE_ROTATION	SENSOR_MODE_ROTATION

Timers

The RCX has four internal timers, numbered 0, 1, 2, and 3. They count in increments of 100 ms, or once every 1/10 seconds. NQC includes two commands for interacting with the timers:

Timer(const n)

   This returns the value of the specified timer, which should be 0, 1, 2, or 3. The number returned is the number of 1/10 seconds since the timer was cleared.

ClearTimer(const n)

   This command resets the value of the given timer to 0. The timer begins counting up again immediately.

Random Numbers

NQC has a simple command for creating random numbers. Random numbers are often useful in robot programming. For example, a robot that tries to drive around obstacles can easily get stuck in a corner if it always backs up and turns exactly the same way to get away from an obstacle. A robot that backs up for a random amount of time and turns for a random amount of time is less likely to get stuck in this way. The command for generating random numbers is:

Random(const n)

   This command returns a random number between 0 and n.

Program Flow

You've seen how to control the RCX's outputs and inputs. But robot programs aren't very interesting unless they can make decisions and repeat actions. In this section, I'll sketch out NQC's program control commands. NQC supports a standard set of conditional branches and loops; if you've ever programmed in other languages (particularly C), this will look familiar.

Waiting

Although it might not seem important, NQC includes a command that tells the robot to do nothing for a certain amount of time. This is often useful if you need to allow some time for something to happen—maybe the robot needs to move forward or turn for a little while, or you want to give a sound time to play. The command is:

Wait(expression ticks)

> This command causes the current task to pause for the supplied hundredths of a second; a call to `Wait(100)` will pause the task for a full second. Note that this only applies to the current task—other tasks will continue to execute. I'll talk more about tasks a little later.

A variation on this theme is the concept of waiting for an event, like a press on a touch sensor, or a certain time of day. The following command waits for a condition to become true:

until (boolean condition) [statements]

> Use this command to wait for the given condition to become true. You could, for example, wait for the value of input 1 to become 4 like this:[*]
>
> ```
> until (SENSOR_1 == 4);
> ```

This particular **until** has an empty body, which means it won't do anything each time the condition is tested—it simply waits until the condition is true. The following program beeps every half second until you press a touch sensor on input 1 four times:

```
task main() {
  SetSensor(SENSOR_1, SENSOR_PULSE);
  until (SENSOR_1 == 4) {
    PlaySound(SOUND_CLICK);
    Wait(50);
  }
}
```

---

[*] As in C, conditional expressions are very different from evaluations. Use == to compare values and = to assign values.

Loops

A loop is a series of commands that you want to be executed repeatedly. NQC offers three flavors of loop:

repeat (expression value) [statements]

> This command simply repeats the given statements `value` times.

while (boolean condition) [statements]

> This loop repeats the supplied statements until `condition` is no longer true.

do [statements] while (boolean condition)

> This loop is similar to `while` but the statements are executed before the `condition` is tested. The statements will always be executed at least once, which is not true for a `while` loop.

Let's look at an example. The following code plays a sound every half second while a light sensor attached to input 3 sees dark:

```
while (SENSOR_3 < 35) {
  PlaySound(0);
  Wait(50);
}
```

Notice how curly braces are used to bracket the statements that belong to the `while` loop. If you have only one command in the body of the `while`, you can omit the braces like this:

```
while (SENSOR_3 < 35)
  Wait(50);
```

Conditionals

To test a condition, use the `if` command.

if (boolean condition) [statements]

> This command executes the given statements only if `condition` is true.

if (boolean condition) [statements] else [statements]

> This is a simple variation on the basic `if` command. If the condition is false, the statements after the `else` are executed.

The following example turns different directions depending on the value of input 2:

```
SetPower(OUT_A + OUT_C, OUT_FULL);
if (SENSOR_2 < 50) {
  Fwd(OUT_A);
  Rev(OUT_C);
}
else {
  Rev(OUT_A);
  Fwd(OUT_C);
}
On(OUT_A + OUT_C);
```

Variables

To use a variable, you simply need to declare its name. Only integer variables are supported. Once a variable is declared, you can assign the variable values and test it in the body of the program. Here's a simple example:

```
int i;

task main() {
  i = 0;
  while (i < 10) {
    PlaySound(0);
    Wait(5 * i);
    i += 1;
  }
}
```

This example beeps at successively longer intervals. The variable, i, is declared in the very first line:

```
int i;
```

Values are assigned to the variable using the = operator:

```
i = 0;
```

You can also assign input values to variables, like this (not part of the example):

```
i = SENSOR_2;
```

In the following line, one is added to the value in variable i:

```
i++;
```

This is really shorthand for the following:

```
i += 1;
```

The += operator, in turn, is shorthand for this:

```
i = i + 1;
```

Using #define for Constants and Macros

Constant values can be assigned meaningful names using #define. This is a idiom that will be familiar to C programmers. Here is an example:

```
#define POWER 5

task main() {
  SetPower(OUT_A + OUT_C, POWER);
  On(OUT_A + OUT_C);
}
```

NQC replaces every occurrence of POWER with 5 in your source code before compiling it. Although this may not seem like a big deal, it is; #define lets you create readable names for things that might otherwise be cryptic. It also lets you define things that might need to be adjusted throughout your program in one place. Your program, for example, might have multiple places where it set the outputs to power level 5. Instead of explicitly putting 5 all the way through your program, you can use the constant value POWER. If you later decide you want the power level to be 7, you just have to change the definition of POWER, instead of finding all the places in your program where the output power is set.

You can also create *macros* with #define. A macro is a kind of miniature program. Usually you'll define a macro for something you want to do frequently. The following program uses three macros:

```
#define forward(power) \
    SetPower(OUT_A + OUT_C, power); \
    OnFwd(OUT_A + OUT_C);
#define left(power) \
    SetPower(OUT_A + OUT_C, power); \
    OnRev(OUT_A); OnFwd(OUT_C);
#define right(power) \
    SetPower(OUT_A + OUT_C, power); \
    OnFwd(OUT_A); OnRev(OUT_C);

task main() {
  forward(OUT_FULL);
  Wait(100);
  left(OUT_HALF);
  Wait(100);
  right(OUT_HALF);
  Wait(100);
  Off(OUT_A + OUT_C);
}
```

The preceding example shows off two features of macros. First, each macro has a parameter, power, that is used in the body of the macro. Second, the macros are split out to multiple lines by using a backslash.

Sounds and Music

Your RCX can play various prepackaged sounds, using the following command:

PlaySound(const n)

This command plays the sound represented by n. NQC includes constant names for each available sounds, as detailed in Table 4-5.

Table 4-5. RCX System Sounds

Sound Name	Description
SOUND_CLICK	Short beep
SOUND_DOUBLE_BEEP	Two medium beeps

Table 4-5. RCX System Sounds (continued)

Sound Name	Description
SOUND_DOWN	Descending arpeggio
SOUND_UP	Ascending arpeggio
SOUND_LOW_BEEP	Long low note
SOUND_FAST_UP	Quick ascending arpeggio (same as SOUND_UP but faster)

If you'd prefer to make your own music, you can play individual notes with the PlayTone() command:

PlayTone(const frequency, const duration)

This command plays a note with the given frequency for the specified duration. The frequency is in Hz, so 440 is the pitch of the A above middle C on a piano. The duration is in hundreths of a second. You can only specify integer values for the frequency, so don't expect the pitches to be exactly in tune. No one expects your little robot to sound like Pavorotti.

If you want to play a sequence of notes, you have to be a little tricky about it. Each time you call PlayTone(), the command returns almost immediately, without waiting for the sound you've requested to finish playing. The tone you've requested is put in a queue; the system plays it while the rest of your program executes. If you call PlayTone() repeatedly, the queue will fill up. Subsequent calls to PlayTone() will not fit on the queue and the tones you've requested will not be played. The queue is long enough to hold eight tones. If you want to play a sequence longer than this, you should insert calls to Wait() in your program so that the queue has time to empty out as notes are played.

The following example demonstrates this technique; it plays part of *Quando men vo*, from Giacomo Puccini's *La Bohème*.

```
#define SIXTH 12
#define HALF 3*SIXTH
#define BEAT 2*HALF
#define GRACE 6

task main() {
  PlayTone(330, 2*BEAT);
  Wait(2*BEAT + 2*SIXTH);
  PlayTone(115, SIXTH);
  PlayTone(208, SIXTH);
  PlayTone(247, SIXTH);
  PlayTone(330, SIXTH);
  PlayTone(311, 2*BEAT);
  Wait(4*SIXTH + 2*BEAT + 2*SIXTH);
  PlayTone(115, SIXTH);
  PlayTone(208, SIXTH);
  PlayTone(247, SIXTH);
```

```
        PlayTone(311, SIXTH);
        PlayTone(277, 3*BEAT);
        Wait(4*SIXTH + 3*BEAT + HALF);
        PlayTone(277, HALF);
        PlayTone(311, HALF);
        PlayTone(370, GRACE);
        PlayTone(330, HALF);
        PlayTone(311, HALF); Wait (2*HALF);
        PlayTone(277, HALF);
        PlayTone(330, HALF);
        PlayTone(220, HALF);
        PlayTone(220, 2*BEAT);
        Wait(GRACE + 5*HALF + 2*BEAT + HALF);
        PlayTone(247, HALF);
        PlayTone(277, HALF);
        PlayTone(330, GRACE);
        PlayTone(311, HALF);
        PlayTone(277, HALF); Wait (2*HALF);
        PlayTone(247, HALF);
        PlayTone(311, HALF);
        PlayTone(208, HALF);
        PlayTone(208, 2*BEAT);
        Wait(GRACE + 5*HALF + 2*BEAT + HALF);
    }
```

IR Communication

Your robot can send and receive data over its IR port. In NQC, three commands handle sending and receiving data:

SendMessage(expression m)

This command sends the given byte of data out the IR port.

Message()

Use this command to return the last byte of data received on the IR port.

ClearMessage()

This command clears the incoming message. You may want to do this after responding to an incoming message, to avoid responding more than once.

The Display

Although you can't control the display directly in NQC, you can configure it to some degree:

SelectDisplay(expression v)

This command tells the RCX to show the data source represented by v on its display. The legal values for v are shown in Table 4-6. You can achieve the same results by pressing the **View** button on the front of the RCX to show the state of the inputs or outputs, but the SelectDisplay() command allow you to do this as part of a program.

Table 4-6. Display Values

Value	Description
0	System clock
1	View Input 1
2	View Input 2
3	View Input 3
4	View Output A
5	View Output B
6	View Output C

You can set the clock in the RCX using the following macro:

SetWatch(const hours, const minutes)

> Use this macro to set the current time of the RCX's clock. Unfortunately, only constant values can be used.

The Datalog

With the default firmware, your RCX supports an interesting option called a *datalog*. The datalog is simply a list of numbers. You can create a new datalog and put numbers into it. Datalogs can be uploaded to your PC for analysis or display. The datalog commands are:

CreateDatalog(const size)

> This command tells the RCX to make space for the given number of elements. There is only one datalog, so this command will erase any previous datalog.

AddToDatalog(expression v)

> This command adds a value to the datalog. It's up to you to keep track of how many values are in the datalog. If you try to add values after the datalog is full, nothing happens.

The following example waits for a touch sensor on input 1 to be pressed. For each press, the value of timer 0 is stored in the datalog, which holds 20 values in this example:

```
int count;

task main() {
  CreateDatalog(20);
  ClearTimer(0);
  SetSensor(SENSOR_1, SENSOR_TOUCH);

  count = 0;
  until (count == 20) {
    until(SENSOR_1 == 1);
    AddToDatalog(Timer(0));
```

```
        count++;
        until(SENSOR_1 == 0);
    }
}
```

When you run this program, you'll notice the RCX shows the status of the datalog on the right side of the display. It looks kind of like a pie; as you add values to the datalog the pie fills up.

To upload a datalog to the PC, you can use nqc's **-datalog** option, which simply dumps the values to the screen:

```
C:\>nqc -datalog
8
12
16
19
23
25
27
29
31
33
39
47
52
56
59
62
65
68
71
75

C:\>
```

The datalog actually stores the source of every value. If you use a tool like RCX Command Center, it can show you the source of each value in the datalog. In Chapter 8, *Using Spirit.ocx with Visual Basic*, I'll show you how to write your own program in Visual Basic to retrieve the contents of the datalog.

Tasks

NQC gives you powerful control over *tasks* and *subroutines*. Each of the RCX's five programs is made up of one or more tasks. These tasks can execute at the same time, which is another way of saying that the RCX is multitasking.

Tasks are defined using the `task` command. Every program must have a `main` task which is executed when the program is first started. Other tasks must be started and stopped explicitly:

start taskname

This command starts the named task.

stop taskname

Use this command to stop the named task.

The following program controls its outputs from **main** and uses another task, **sing**, to play some music. The **sing** task has to be started from **main**; otherwise, its commands will never be executed.

```
task main() {
  start sing;
  while (true) {
    OnFwd(OUT_A);
    OnRev(OUT_C);
    Wait(100);
    OnFwd(OUT_C);
    OnRev(OUT_A);
    Wait(100);
  }
}

#define SIXTH 12
#define HALF 3*SIXTH
#define BEAT 2*HALF
#define GRACE 6

task sing() {
  PlayTone(330, 2*BEAT);
  Wait(2*BEAT + 2*SIXTH);
  PlayTone(115, SIXTH);
  PlayTone(208, SIXTH);
  PlayTone(247, SIXTH);
  PlayTone(330, SIXTH);
  PlayTone(311, 2*BEAT);
  Wait(4*SIXTH + 2*BEAT + 2*SIXTH);
  PlayTone(115, SIXTH);
  PlayTone(208, SIXTH);
  PlayTone(247, SIXTH);
  PlayTone(311, SIXTH);
  PlayTone(277, 3*BEAT);
  Wait(4*SIXTH + 3*BEAT + HALF);
  PlayTone(277, HALF);
  PlayTone(311, HALF);
  PlayTone(370, GRACE);
  PlayTone(330, HALF);
  PlayTone(311, HALF); Wait (2*HALF);
  PlayTone(277, HALF);
  PlayTone(330, HALF);
  PlayTone(220, HALF);
  PlayTone(220, 2*BEAT);
  Wait(GRACE + 5*HALF + 2*BEAT + HALF);
  PlayTone(247, HALF);
```

```
    PlayTone(277, HALF);
    PlayTone(330, GRACE);
    PlayTone(311, HALF);
    PlayTone(277, HALF); Wait (2*HALF);
    PlayTone(247, HALF);
    PlayTone(311, HALF);
    PlayTone(208, HALF);
    PlayTone(208, 2*BEAT);
    Wait(GRACE + 5*HALF + 2*BEAT + HALF);
    stop main;
    Float(OUT_A + OUT_C);
}
```

When the **sing** task is done playing music, it stops the **main** task with the **stop** command. Then it turns the motors off. The order is critical. If we turned off the motors and then stopped the **main** task, it's possible that **main** would turn on the motors again before it was stopped. Multithreaded programming is powerful but tricky.

Each RCX program can have up to ten tasks.

Subroutines

A *subroutine* is a group of commands that you will execute frequently. Subroutines offer a way to clean up your source code and reduce the size of compiled programs. Subroutines in NQC are defined in much the same way as tasks. The following program has one subroutine, called **wiggle()**. The **main** task shows how this subroutine is called:

```
task main() {
  wiggle();
  Wait(200);
  wiggle();
}

sub wiggle() {
  OnFwd(OUT_A);
  OnRev(OUT_C);
  Wait(20);
  OnFwd(OUT_C);
  OnRev(OUT_A);
  Wait(20);
  Off(OUT_A + OUT_C);
}
```

Subroutines execute as part of the task from which they are called. It works just as if the call to **wiggle()** was replaced with the commands it contains. The nice thing about subroutines is that their code is defined once, but you can call it as many times as you like from other places in your program. You could accomplish the same sorts of things with subroutines and macros, but subroutines are more efficient because the code is just compiled once. With a macro, the entire macro body would be placed at each point where it was called.

The RCX imposes three crippling restrictions on subroutines. First, you can't call another subroutine from within a subroutine. As a consequence, a subroutine also cannot call itself. Second, you can't pass parameters to a subroutine or get a return value. Third, no more than eight subroutines can be defined for a single program. These limitations are imposed by the RCX's bytecode interpreter, which is defined in the firmware. To get around restrictions like these, you'll need to use a different firmware, like legOS or pbForth.

Inlines

NQC does offer another interesting option, the *inline* subroutine. In source code, it looks a lot like a subroutine except with a C-style return type (always **void**):

```
void wiggle() {
  OnFwd(OUT_A);
  OnRev(OUT_C);
  Wait(20);
  OnFwd(OUT_C);
  OnRev(OUT_A);
  Wait(20);
  Off(OUT_A + OUT_C);
}
```

Inlines are called the same way as subroutines. The compiler actually places the code of the inline wherever it is called, almost like a macro or constant definition. This actually makes inlines appear a little more capable than subroutines: they can call other inlines or even subroutines. In NQC version 2.0, for example, you can define inlines with a parameter, like this:

```
void wiggleTime(int waitTime) {
  OnFwd(OUT_A);
  OnRev(OUT_C);
  Wait(waitTime);
  OnFwd(OUT_C);
  OnRev(OUT_A);
  Wait(waitTime);
  Off(OUT_A + OUT_C);
}
```

You can have more than one argument, if you wish. Just remember that inlines are really an example of *syntactic sugar*, something that makes your source code look pretty but doesn't necessarily result in better efficiency.

Arguments to inlines can be passed in four different ways. Table 4-7 summarizes the options.

Table 4-7. Argument Passing for Inlines

Type	By Value or By Reference?	Temporary Variable Used?
int	by value	yes
const int	by value	no
int&	by reference	no
const int&	by reference	no

If you pass `int` by value, the parameter's value is copied into a temporary variable (from the pool of 31) and used in the inline. `const int` passes by value, but the value must be a constant at compile time.

If you pass by reference, the variable that is passed in can actually be modified in the inline. In this code, for example, a `count` variable is incremented in the body of an inline:

```
task main() {
  int count = 0;
  while (count <= 5) {
    PlaySound(SOUND_CLICK);
    Wait(count * 20);
    increment(count);
  }
}

void increment(int& n) {
  n++;
}
```

The last option, `const int &`, is used when you want to pass a value that should not be changed. This is great for things like `Sensor()` and `Timer()`. For example, you might have an inline like this:

```
void forward(const int& power) {
  SetPower(OUT_A + OUT_C, power);
  OnFwd(OUT_A + OUT_C);
}
```

With this inline, you can do normal things, like passing a variable or constant:

```
int power = 6;
forward(power);

forward(OUT_HALF);
```

But you can also do trickier stuff, like this:

```
forward(Message());
```

You can basically accomplish the same stuff with `int` parameters and `const int&` parameters. The advantage of `const int&` is that no temporary variables are used.

Trusty Revisited

You've seen some small examples of NQC code. Now I'll show you how Trusty can be programmed using NQC. You'll be able to compare the NQC programs to the RCX Code programs from Chapter 3.

New Brains For Trusty

As you may recall, we used a counter to keep track of Trusty's state. The counter value was used to decide if Trusty would turn left or right the next time the light sensor left the black line. In NQC, we can store Trusty's state in a real variable. Plus, we'll use symbolic constants to represent state values.

```
int state;

#define LEFT 0
#define RIGHT 1
```

Trusty's program has two tasks. The first task (**main**) tests the value of the light sensor. If it is over the black line, the robot is set to move forward:

```
while (true) {
  if (SENSOR_2 < DARK2)
    OnFwd(OUT_A + OUT_C);
}
```

The **DARK2** and **POWER** constants are determined using **#define**s; this means it's easy to fiddle with their values, and our program is easy to read.

The second task takes care of things when the light sensor leaves the black line. Whenever the robot leaves the line, the **toggle()** subroutine is called. **toggle()** starts the robot turning. Then we wait a little while; if the robot is still not on the black line, we call **toggle()** again to turn back the other way:

```
task lightWatcher() {
  while (true) {
    if (SENSOR_2 > LIGHT2) {
      toggle();
      Wait(TIMEOUT);
      if (SENSOR_2 > LIGHT2) {
        toggle();
        Wait(TIMEOUT * 2);
      }
    }
  }
}
```

The **toggle()** subroutine performs two important functions. First, it makes Trusty turn, based on the value of the **state** variable. Second, it updates the value of **state**; if it was **RIGHT**, it will be **LEFT**, and vice versa.

Here is the whole program:

```
int state;

#define LEFT 0
#define RIGHT 1

#define DARK2 35
#define LIGHT2 40

#define POWER 7

#define TIMEOUT 50

task main() {
  state = LEFT;
  SetSensor(SENSOR_2, SENSOR_LIGHT);
  SetPower(OUT_A + OUT_C, POWER);
  start lightWatcher;

  while (true) {
    if (SENSOR_2 < DARK2)
      OnFwd(OUT_A + OUT_C);
  }
}

task lightWatcher() {
  while (true) {
    if (SENSOR_2 > LIGHT2) {
      toggle();
      Wait(TIMEOUT);
      if (SENSOR_2 > LIGHT2) {
        toggle();
        Wait(TIMEOUT * 2);
      }
    }
  }
}

sub toggle() {
  if (state == LEFT) {
    OnRev(OUT_A);
    OnFwd(OUT_C);
    state = RIGHT;
  }
  else {
    OnFwd(OUT_A);
    OnRev(OUT_C);
    state = LEFT;
  }
}
```

The **main** task performs three important initializations which I haven't mentioned yet. First, **main** initializes the value of the **state** variable. It just uses LEFT arbitrarily. Next, `main` configures input 2 for a light sensor. Finally, it starts the `lightWatcher` task.

Using Two Light Sensors

In this section, I'll present an NQC program that works with the two light sensor version of Trusty. As you may recall, programming this robot in RCX Code was cumbersome.

The programming is a lot cleaner in NQC. It's pretty straightforward to translate Table 3-1 into source code. The basic strategy is to use a state variable to represent the four states of the robot, represented by the four lines of Table 3-1. Then one task examines the sensors and updates the state variable. Another task examines the state variable and sets the motors appropriately.

The four possible states are represented by constant values. A fifth value, **INDETERMINATE**, is used when one or both of the light sensor values is not in the dark or light range:

```
#define BOTH_ON 3
#define LEFT_ON 1
#define RIGHT_ON 2
#define BOTH_OFF 0
#define INDETERMINATE 255
```

The **main** task simply tests the value of the **state** variable and sets the motors accordingly. No action is taken for **BOTH_OFF** and **INDETERMINATE**:

```
while (true) {
  if (state == BOTH_ON)
    OnFwd(OUT_A + OUT_C);
  else if (state == LEFT_ON) {
    Off(OUT_A);
    OnFwd(OUT_C);
  }
  else if (state == RIGHT_ON) {
    Off(OUT_C);
    OnFwd(OUT_A);
  }
}
```

A separate task, `watcher`, examines the light sensor values and sets the **state** variable. Here is the entire source code for the two sensor version of Trusty:

```
int state;

// "ON" refers to whether the light
//    sensor is on the line. If it is,
//    the light sensor is seeing black.
#define BOTH_ON 3
#define LEFT_ON 1
```

```
#define RIGHT_ON 2
#define BOTH_OFF 0
#define INDETERMINATE 255

// Thresholds for light and dark.
#define DARK2 35
#define LIGHT2 40
#define DARK3 40
#define LIGHT3 45

#define POWER 4

task main() {
  initialize();
  while (true) {
    if (state == BOTH_ON)
      OnFwd(OUT_A + OUT_C);
    else if (state == LEFT_ON) {
      Off(OUT_A);
      OnFwd(OUT_C);
    }
    else if (state == RIGHT_ON) {
      Off(OUT_C);
      OnFwd(OUT_A);
    }
  }
}

sub initialize() {
  SetSensor(SENSOR_2, SENSOR_LIGHT);
  SetSensor(SENSOR_3, SENSOR_LIGHT);
  SetPower(OUT_A + OUT_C, POWER);
  OnFwd(OUT_A + OUT_C);
  start watcher;
}

task watcher() {
  while (true) {
    if (SENSOR_2 < DARK2) {
      if (SENSOR_3 < DARK3) state = BOTH_ON;
      else if (SENSOR_3 > LIGHT3) state = LEFT_ON;
      else state = INDETERMINATE;
    }
    else if (SENSOR_2 > LIGHT2) {
      if (SENSOR_3 < DARK3) state = RIGHT_ON;
      else if (SENSOR_3 > LIGHT3) state = BOTH_OFF;
      else state = INDETERMINATE;
    }
    else state = INDETERMINATE;
  }
}
```

Online Resources

NQC—Not Quite C
http://www.enteract.com/~dbaum/lego/nqc/

> This is the official site for NQC. You can download the current release, read the documentation, or browse a FAQ. Dave Baum has packed a lot of useful information into this site, including such gems as how to create a cable to connect your Macintosh to the IR tower. This site also includes the definitive NQC documentation.

Lego Robots: RCX Command Center
http://www.cs.uu.nl/people/markov/lego/rcxcc/

> RCX Command Center (RcxCC), developed by Mark Overmars, is built on top of NQC. It's a Windows application that provides a friendly graphic interface to the features of NQC. It includes a syntax-colored program editor, real-time control of the RCX, utilities for making your RCX play music, and useful help files. I highly recommend this application.

Lego Robot Pages [NQC Tutorial]
http://www.cs.uu.nl/people/markov/lego/

> Mark Overmars, creator of RcxCC (the previous entry), has written a detailed introduction to NQC. It's available off his main web page as PDF, Word97, PostScript, or RTF. This document is a gentle and thorough introduction to NQC.

Kevin Saddi's NQC Reference Page
http://home1.gte.net/ksaddi/mindstorms/nqc-reference.html

> This page provides a distilled view of NQC. It's very handy when you can't remember the input type constants, or you'd like to see NQC's commands organized by function. Single-line code samples are also included.

Hitachi Single-Chip Microcomputer H8/3297 Series...
http://semiconductor.hitachi.com/products/pdf/h33th014d2.pdf

> This PDF document has all the crufty details on the Hitachi H8 that forms the heart of the RCX. The specific model is the H8/3292, which is covered in the manual. This information is not for casual browsing—you probably won't need to look here unless you start writing your own firmware. (Hitachi's web site is a little flakey. If you're having trouble with this URL, try starting at the URL *http://semiconductor.hitachi.com/h8/* and searching for the H8/3292.)

5

Minerva, a Robot with an Arm

Minerva is a mechanical marvel. Although she has the same wheel layout as Trusty, Minerva's drivetrain is radically different. In addition, she has a simple arm with a grabber, which allows her to pick up and drop small objects. Best of all, Minerva can be built with the pieces from the RIS alone. The grabber arm is operated by a single motor. The other motor powers the drivetrain, which moves the robot forward or spins it in place. Figure 5-1 shows a picture of this remarkable robot.

Figure 5-1. Minerva, a mechanical masterpiece

When you run Minerva's program, she drives straight forward. When the light sensor (mounted on the end of the grabber arm) sees something dark, Minerva stops driving. She uses the arm to try to pick up whatever the light sensor saw. Then she turns around and drives back to her starting point. She puts down whatever she's carrying, turns around, and is ready to start again.

Building Instructions

If there's one lesson to be learned from Minerva, it is that mechanical design is hard. I had to build this robot five times to get it right. And I don't mean I moved a few pieces around—I actually disassembled and rebuilt the robot that many times. The drivetrain alone took four tries before I got it right.*

Directional Transmission and Drivetrain

The long gray piece in Step 1 swivels freely on the shaft.

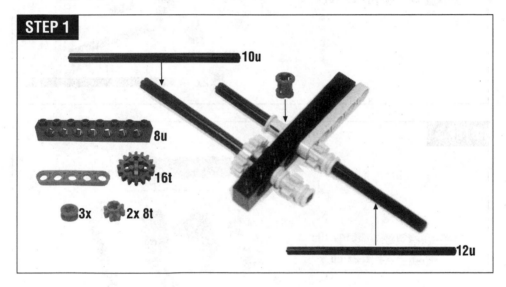

---

* Minerva uses almost all of the gears that come with RIS 1.0. Unfortunately, RIS 1.5 comes with fewer gears (five 12t gears instead of eight). To get the extra gears you'll need for Minerva, you can order the #5229 Gears & Differentials parts pack from the LEGO Shop At Home Service, (800) 453-4652. Cost is $4.50 including shipping.

The 8u shaft in Step 2 is loose and may fall out. It will be anchored in the next step. The 6u beam, like the long gray piece from Step 1, swivels freely on its shaft.

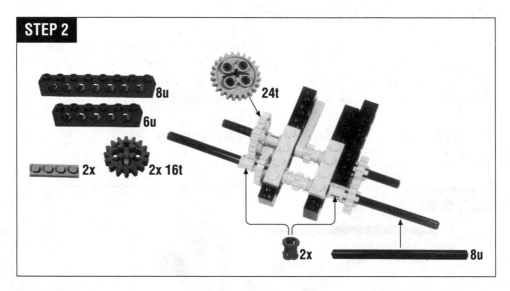

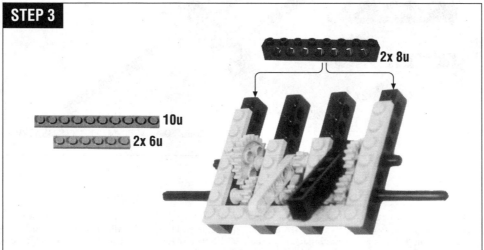

STEP 4

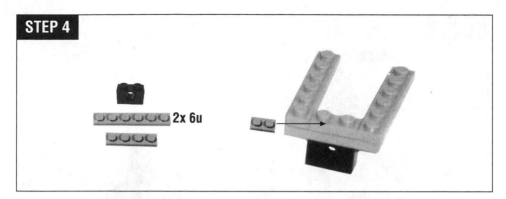

Make sure the bump on the long pin is up against the 4u beam.

STEP 5

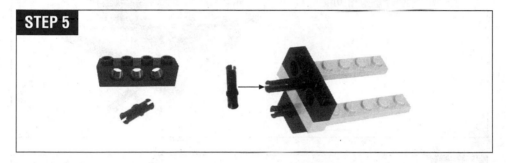

STEP 6

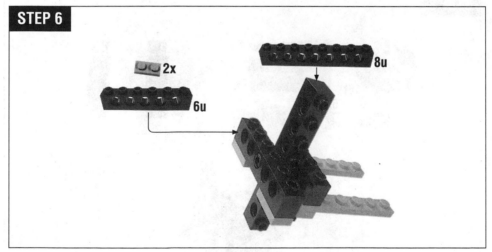

Before you put all of Step 7 together, make sure the swiveling parts from Steps 1 and 2 are pointing up, as shown.

STEP 7

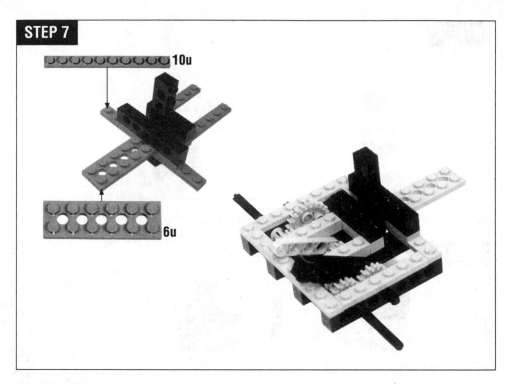

10u

6u

STEP 8

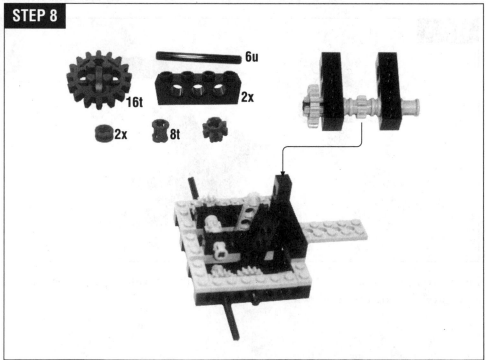

16t

6u

2x

2x

8t

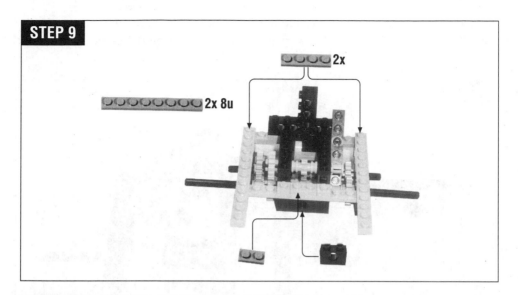

STEP 9

2x

2x 8u

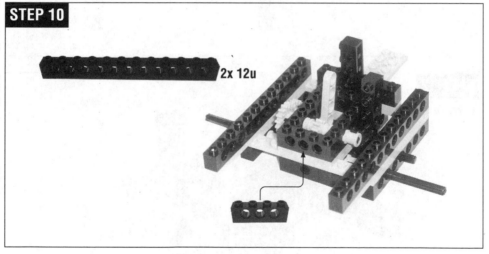

STEP 10

2x 12u

Step 11 is tricky. You'll need to slide the 8u shaft into the structure, adding bushings and gears as you go. The swiveling pieces from Steps 1 and 2 are now anchored.

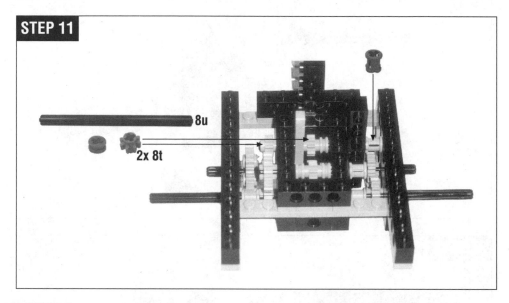

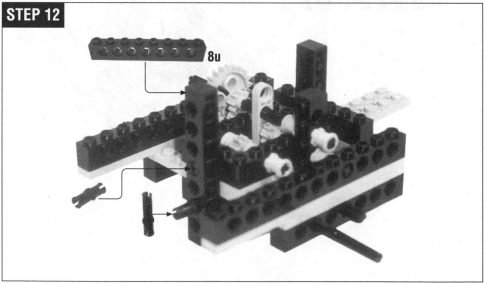

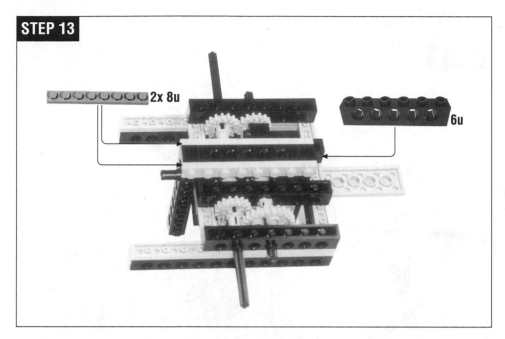

Step 14 is similar to Step 11; take a deep breath and go slowly.

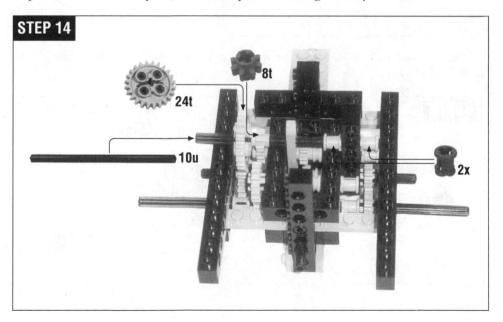

Grabber Arm

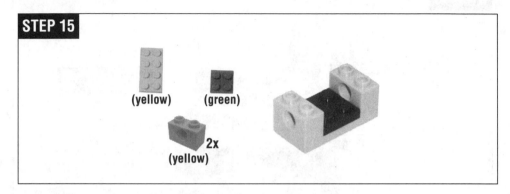

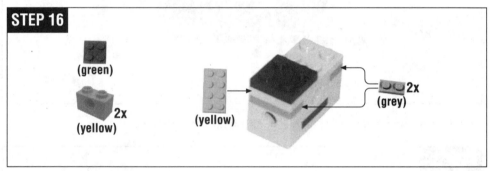

In Step 17, the half-bushings go between the center block and the cams (pear-shaped pieces).

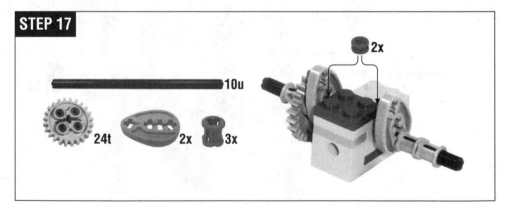

STEP 18

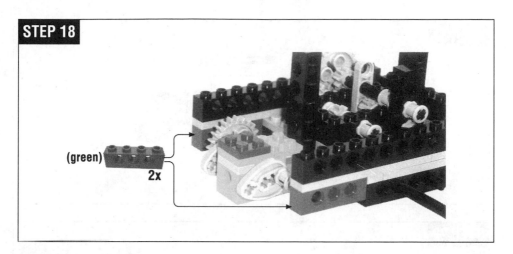

(green) 2x

STEP 19

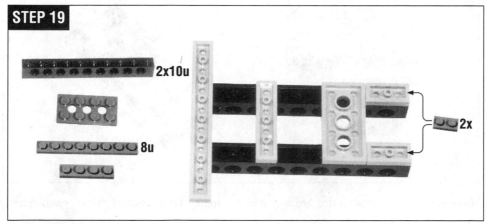

2x10u

8u

2x

STEP 20

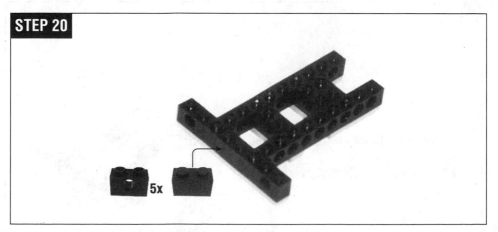

5x

STEP 21

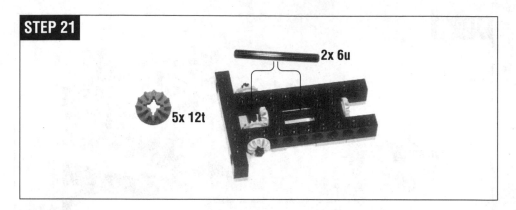

STEP 22

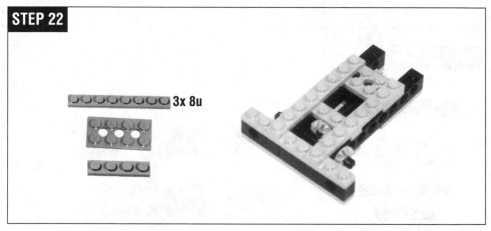

Make sure that the two sides are at the same angle. They should mirror each other.

STEP 23

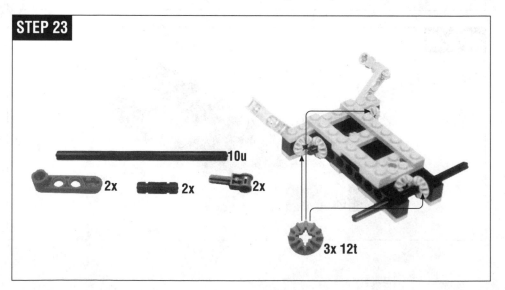

STEP 24

2x

(yellow)

2x

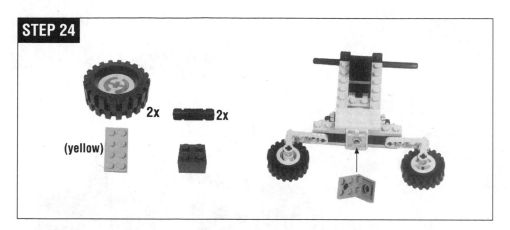

STEP 25

40t

24t

2x

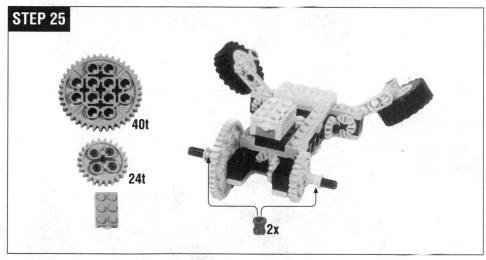

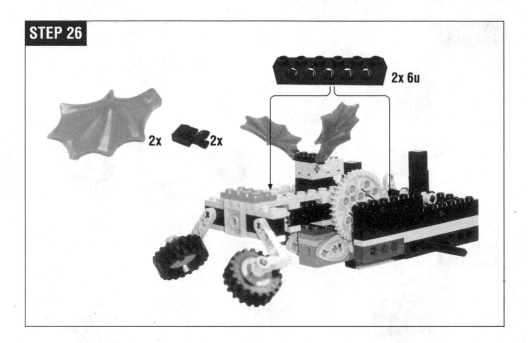

Structural Support

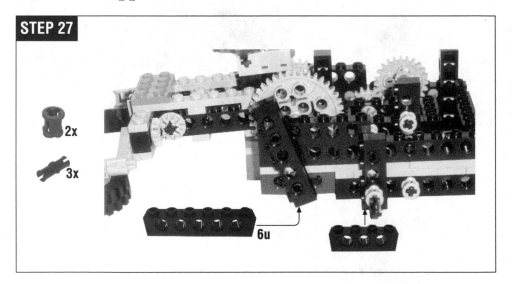

STEP 28

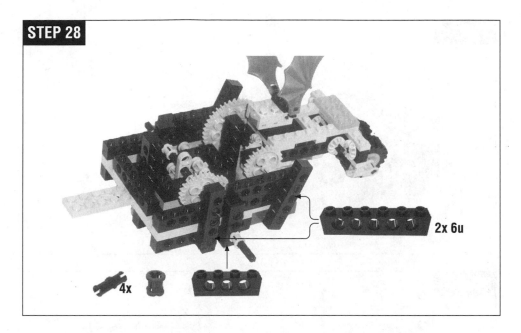

2x 6u

4x

Idler Wheel

STEP 29

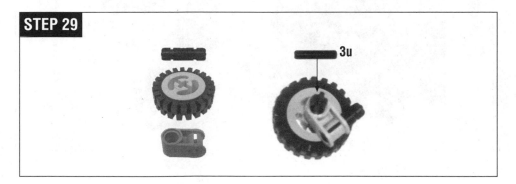

3u

STEP 30

STEP 31

Drive Motor

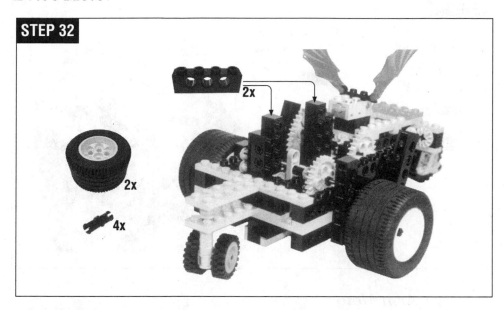

While you're putting the motor in, hold on to the worm gear so it doesn't slip off.

STEP 34

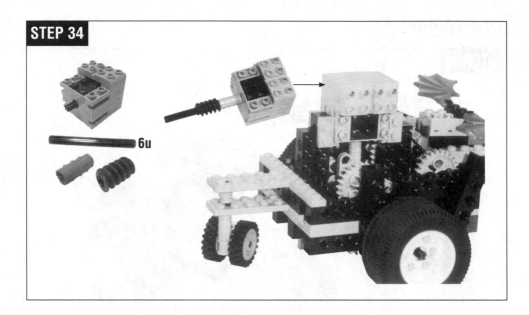

Grabber Arm Motor

STEP 35

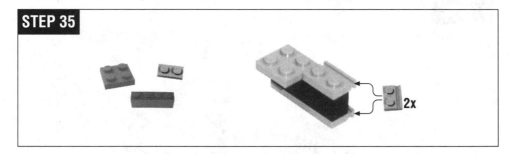

STEP 36

STEP 37

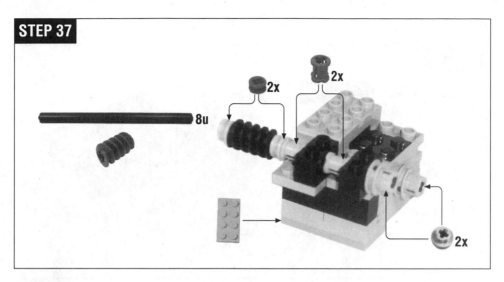

STEP 38

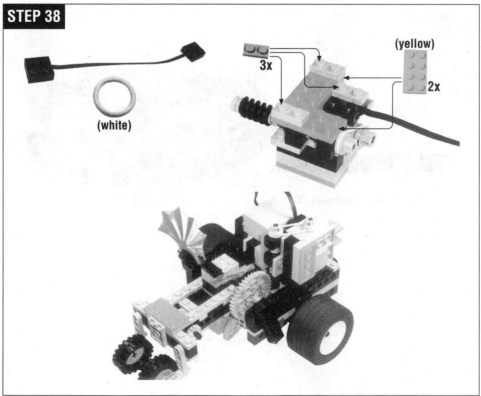

RCX

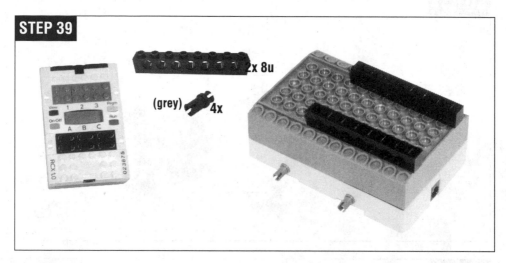

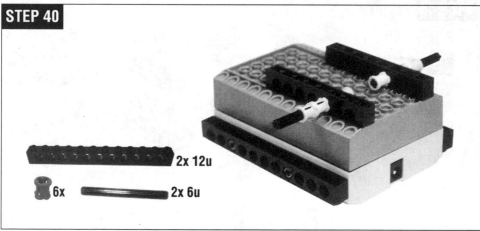

Attach the RCX on both sides as shown.

STEP 41

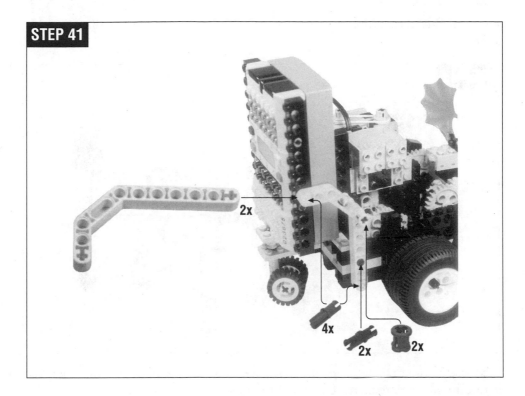

Wiring

First, attach the left motor, which powers the arm, to output A. Then use a wire brick to attach the right motor (the drive motor) to output C.

STEP 42

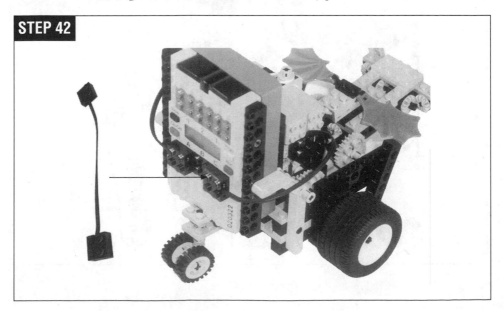

Attach the light sensor to the front of the arm. The wire attaches to Minerva's side as shown.

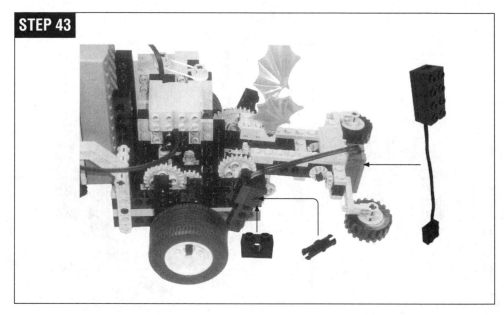

Next, use a wire brick to attach the touch sensor to the light sensor wire. Then use a longer wire brick to attach both wires to input 3.

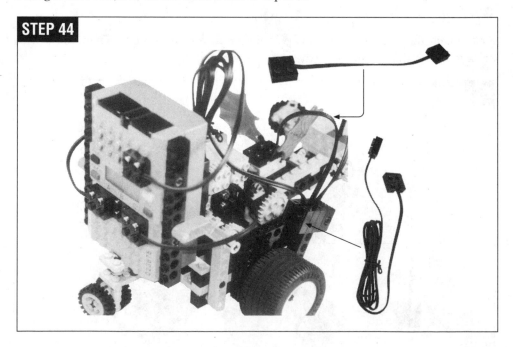

Programming

Minerva's basic program is straightforward:

```
find something to pick up
bring it back to the starting point
```

The program assumes that the objects to pick up will be dark and that the surface Minerva is driving on is light. To return to the starting point, Minerva measures how long it has to drive forward to pick something up. Then it turns around and drives back for the same amount of time. Here's a slightly exploded version of Minerva's program:

```
drive forward until the light sensor sees something dark
pick it up with the grabber
turn around
drive back to the starting point
drop whatever's in the grabber
```

I've written Minerva's program in NQC (see Chapter 4, *Not Quite C*). You could create a program in RCX Code (the environment that comes with RIS), but you wouldn't be able to implement some key features. In particular, Minerva's ability to drive back just as far as she drove forward is crucial. There's no way to do this in RCX Code. Minerva's program also does some sensor calibration that would also be impossible in RCX Code.

Here's the whole program:

```
#define TURNAROUND_TIME 425

int i;

task main() {
  // Arm limit sensor and grabber light sensor.
  SetSensor(SENSOR_3, SENSOR_LIGHT);
  SetPower(OUT_A + OUT_C, OUT_FULL);

  calibrate();
  i = 0;
  while (i < 5) {
    retrieve();
    i += 1;
  }
  Off(OUT_A + OUT_C);
}

#define NUMBER_OF_SAMPLES 10
int runningTotal;
int threshold;
```

```
sub calibrate() {
  // Take an average light reading.
  i = 0;
  runningTotal = 0;
  while (i < NUMBER_OF_SAMPLES) {
    runningTotal += SENSOR_3;
    Wait(10);
    i += 1;
  }
  threshold = runningTotal / NUMBER_OF_SAMPLES;
}

void grab() {
  // Run the motor until we hit the limit switch.
  OnFwd(OUT_A);
  until (SENSOR_3 == 100);
  // Back off from the switch.
  OnRev(OUT_A);
  until (SENSOR_3 != 100);
  Off(OUT_A);
}

void release() {
  // Run the motor until we hit the limit switch.
  OnRev(OUT_A);
  until (SENSOR_3 == 100);
  // Back off from the switch.
  OnFwd(OUT_A);
  until (SENSOR_3 != 100);
  Off(OUT_A);
}

int returnTime;

sub retrieve() {
  // Drive forward until we see something.
  OnFwd(OUT_C);
  ClearTimer(0);
  until (SENSOR_3 < threshold - 3);
  Wait(20); // Move up on it a little.
  returnTime = Timer(0);
  Off(OUT_C);

  grab();

  // Turn around (roughly).
  OnRev(OUT_C);
  Wait(TURNAROUND_TIME);

  // Drive back.
  OnFwd(OUT_C);
  ClearTimer(0);
  until (Timer(0) >= returnTime);
  Off(OUT_C);
```

```
    release();

    // Turn around.
    OnRev(OUT_C);
    Wait(TURNAROUND_TIME);
}
```

Let's look at the simple parts first. The `grab()` and `release()` inline subroutines take care of the grabber arm. All they do is run the arm motor in one direction until the limit sensor is pressed. Running the motor forward causes the arm to descend, the grabber to close, and the arm to lift again. Running the motor in reverse makes the arm descend, the grabber open, and the arm lift again. The mechanics of the arm take care of everything, as I'll explain later in the chapter. All we have to do is wait for the arm to lift, which presses the switch when it's finished. You might have noticed that the light sensor and the touch sensor are both attached to the same input. I'll talk about how this works later. For now, just be aware that it's necessary for `grab()` and `release()` to move away from the touch sensor to use the light sensor.

The `calibrate()` subroutine examines the values coming from Minerva's light sensor. It computes an average value, which is stored in the variable `threshold`. The `retrieve()` subroutine uses this value to figure out if it's looking at an object that should be picked up. Specifically, it tests if the light sensor value is a little less than the original average:

```
    until (SENSOR_3 < threshold - 3);
```

Calibrating the sensor in this way frees us from hard-coding a light sensor threshold value into Minerva's program. It also makes Minerva better able to deal with different lighting conditions.

The `retrieve()` subroutine is the heart of Minerva's program. It drives forward (by turning output C on) until it finds something dark to pick up. While it's driving forward, timer 0 is ticking away, measuring how long it takes until something is found:

```
    OnFwd(OUT_C);
    ClearTimer(0);
    until (SENSOR_3 < threshold - 3);
```

Once a dark object is found, Minerva moves forward a little farther to position the grabber over the object. She records the forward movement time for the return trip. Finally, Minerva turns off output C to stop the robot's forward motion:

```
    Wait(20); // Move up on it a little.
    returnTime = Timer(0);
    Off(OUT_C);
```

Having found something interesting, Minerva picks it up:

```
    grab();
```

Now she wants to turn around and return to her starting point. To turn around, she simply reverses the direction of output C for the duration given by TURNAROUND_TIME:

```
OnRev(OUT_C);
Wait(TURNAROUND_TIME);
```

Now she drives back to her starting point, using the `returnTime` value, which was saved earlier:

```
OnFwd(OUT_C);
ClearTimer(0);
until (Timer(0) >= returnTime);
Off(OUT_C);
```

Finally, the `retrieve()` subroutine drops the object that Minerva's carrying and turns around again:

```
release();

OnRev(OUT_C);
Wait(TURNAROUND_TIME);
```

The `main` task configures Minerva's inputs and then calls `retrieve()` five times in a row. If everything works perfectly, which it probably won't, Minerva finds five dark objects and brings them back to her starting point. In the next section, I'll explore some of the things that can confuse Minerva.

Try It Out!

To take Minerva out for a spin, I suggest using the back of the Test Pad that comes with RIS. It acts as a mostly uniform bright surface. Put the Test Pad on a hard, flat surface. Different surfaces will give you different results. In particular, you may need to adjust the TURNAROUND_TIME constant to make Minerva spin around 180°. Scatter some black blocks on the back of the Test Pad and start Minerva running. If you're lucky, she'll go pick up some blocks and bring them back to her starting point.

There are quite a few things that can go wrong:

1. Minerva may not "see" the dark blocks to pick them up. I found that I got better results after the RCX was on for a minute or two—the sensor values depend on the battery power, which stabilizes after the RCX is on for a while.

2. Minerva's wheels may stumble on the blocks, throwing her off course. Instead of driving and returning on a straight line, Minerva will now be pointing in a different direction. She probably won't bring blocks back to her original starting point.

3. The grabber doesn't always pick up the block Minerva is aiming for.

Some of the challenges Minerva faces are discussed later in this chapter. First, I'm going to talk about Minerva's amazing mechanical features.

Directional Transmission

Minerva uses a single motor to drive forward and to turn. This mechanical magic is accomplished with the aid of a *directional transmission*. A directional transmission does different things depending on whether you run a motor shaft forward or in reverse. Functionally, you can think of it as a box with an input shaft and two output shafts, as shown in Figure 5-2.

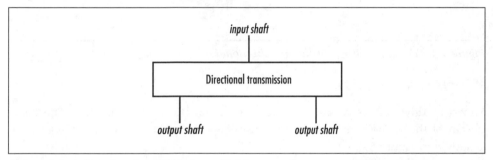

Figure 5-2. A directional transmission will drive one of two output shafts

If you rotate the input shaft clockwise, one of the output shafts will rotate. If you rotate the input shaft counterclockwise, the other output shaft rotates.

There are at least two ways to build a directional transmission with the parts included in your RIS. The first design uses a pair of gears on a swinging arm. The second design uses a worm gear. Minerva uses the worm gear design, but I'll briefly explain the fundamental ideas of both types of directional transmission.

Swing-Arm Design

A cutaway view of a swing-arm directional transmission is shown in Figure 5-3.

The bottom shaft is the input. A 24t gear mounted on this shaft drives another gear that is mounted on a beam that rotates on the input shaft. Depending on which direction the input shaft turns, the beam swings to the left or right; the top gear on the beam engages the gear on either the far left or far right. These gears are on the output shafts. You could create variations on this configuration, using different combinations of gears, but the idea is the same.

This design relies on friction to swing the arm in the right direction. In an ideal, frictionless world, this design would never work.

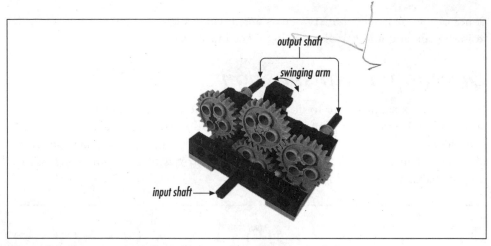

Figure 5-3. Cutaway view of a swing-arm directional transmission

Worm Gear Design

Minerva's drivetrain is based on a worm gear directional transmission. The basic design of the worm gear directional transmission is quite simple. A cutaway view is shown in Figure 5-4.

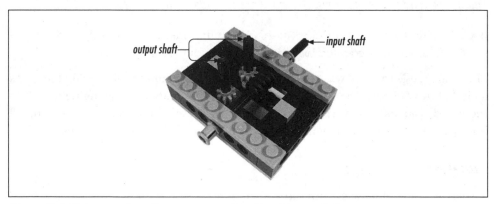

Figure 5-4. Cutaway view of a worm gear directional transmission

The input shaft drives the worm gear, which slides freely along the shaft. In fact, it's easier for the worm gear to slide on its shaft than to turn one of the output shafts. Depending on which way the input shaft turns, the worm gear slides as far as it can in one direction or the other. When it can't slide any more (because it's hit a beam), the worm gear will turn one of the output shafts.

Minerva actually uses a modified version of this design with four outputs. The worm gear engages two outputs at a time, as shown in Figure 5-5.

Figure 5-5. Minerva's directional transmission has four outputs

The basic directional transmission designs I've described are quite simple. Try to use one of these to drive a robot, however, and things get a little more complicated. Minerva, as you've seen, is a gear hog. The drivetrain alone sucks up all of the 8t gears, all of the 16t gears, and most of the 24t gears that come with RIS. If you decide directional transmissions are useful for your robot, you may want to have some extra gears handy from other sets.

Pulleys

Pulleys are an interesting alternative to gears. A pulley is simply a slotted wheel, like the ones used with outdoor clotheslines. The RIS comes with a handful of rubber bands that can be used to link pulleys together. This type of linkage is similar to using gears to transmit motion from one shaft to another. By using pulleys of different sizes, you can achieve the same power and speed tradeoffs as with gears. The only difference is that pulleys connected by a band turn in the same direction, while two gears meshed together turn in opposite directions. If you twist the band around once, you can get the pulleys to move in opposite directions, just as with gears. However, a twisted band will rub on itself, which may significantly reduce its life span. Pulleys also give you the flexibility to transmit motion between two perpendicular shafts. Figure 5-6 shows three different pulley arrangements.

One of the early designs of Minerva's drivetrain used pulleys to replace several gears. Although pulleys are useful for light-duty work, like the grabber arm, they don't work very well for drivetrains. Unless the band that connects two pulleys is very tight, it's likely to slip if it's used to do heavy work, like moving an entire robot.

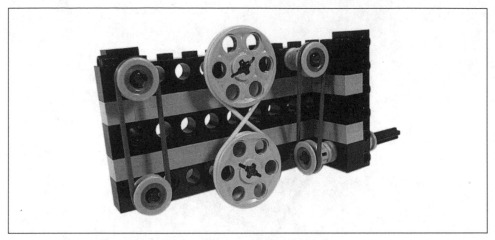

Figure 5-6. Linking shafts with pulleys and a band

On the other hand, you can use pulley slippage to your advantage. If part of your robot should have a limited range of motion, like a trap door that opens and closes, a pulley can be very useful. You can run the motor for longer than it actually takes to open or close the door—when the door has gone as far as it can go, the pulley band will simply slip.

In the final design, a pair of pulleys is used to link the arm motor to the arm worm gear shaft. You can see this arrangement on the top of Minerva—just look for the white band. Note that this band does not slip, in general. Its motion is geared down so far that the arm is likely to break apart before the pulley starts to slip.

Mechanical Design

Several thorny mechanical issues complicate the design and construction of Minerva. In this section, I'll talk about some of Minerva's more interesting mechanical features.

Grabber Arm

Minerva's grabber arm is operated by a single motor. If you run the motor in one direction, the arm lowers, the grabber grabs, and the arm rises again. Run the motor in the opposite direction and the arm lowers, the grabber relaxes, and the arm rises once again. This mechanical sorcery is based on the FetchBot, created by Ben Williamson (see the "Online Resources" section for details). A cutaway view of the arm is shown in Figure 5-7.

The entire arm is controlled by the main drive shaft. A motor linked to a worm gear drives the 40t gear on the main drive shaft.

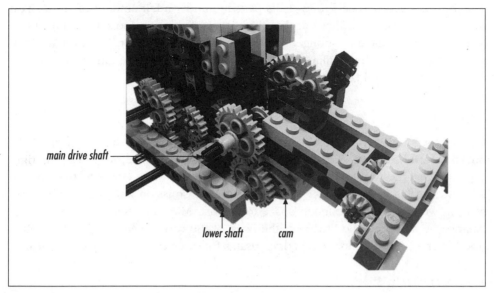

Figure 5-7. Cutaway view of the grabber arm

The key to understanding how the arm works is that it moves up and down for two separate reasons:

1. The cams on the lower shaft push the arm up and let it move back down.

2. When the grabber grips something, the geartrain that controls the grabber locks up. When the main drive shaft continues turning, it moves the entire arm up and down.

Suppose Minerva begins with her arm raised and the grabber open. When the main drive shaft starts turning counterclockwise, the lower shaft turns clockwise. The cams rotate down, allowing the arm to lower. (At the same time, the rotation of the main shaft closes the grabber a little bit.) As the main drive shaft continues turning, the grabber closes. When it is fully closed, either on an object or itself, the grabber geartrain becomes stationary with respect to the arm. The main drive shaft keeps rotating, raising the entire arm with the closed grabber.

A single touch sensor can be used to detect when the arm is fully raised, either with the gripper open or the gripper closed. Picking up an object is simply a matter of running the motor in the right direction and waiting for the touch sensor to be pressed. Releasing an object is just as simple.

The "fingers" of the gripper need to pick up objects. Ideally, they should be slightly pliable and tacky rather than smooth. Minerva uses two of the rubber wheels as fingers, which work reasonably well.

The arm also needs to be strong, as its parts are under a fair amount of stress. You may notice, as you use Minerva, that the pieces of the arm loosen up after time. You could make the arm stronger, but it would also be bulkier. See Ben Williamson's FetchBot (in the "Online Resources" section) for the original arm design, which is stronger and larger than Minerva's.

Balance

One of the fundamental issues Minerva faces is balance. The grabber arm sticks out in front of Minerva. Without some kind of counterbalance, Minerva falls right on her face. One way to fix this is to move the drive wheels closer to the front of Minerva. In this case, however, the directional transmission and the grabber arm gearing would not have enough space to coexist. Minerva solves the problem of balance by mounting the RCX near the back of the robot. The weight of the RCX (the batteries, mostly) more than compensates for the weight of the grabber arm.

Drivetrain

Although the directional transmission is relatively simple, Minerva's drivetrain is a little more complex. When the motor runs one way, the two drive wheels both turn forward. When the motor runs the other way, the drive wheels turn in opposite directions, causing Minerva to spin in place. Minerva uses a fairly complex system of gears to translate the outputs of the directional transmission into the correct wheel movements. Only one of the outputs drives a wheel directly.

Two Sensors, One Input

You might think that the RCX's three inputs limit you to designing robots with only three sensors. In this section, I'll describe one way to move beyond the three-input barrier: attaching more than one sensor to a single input. Minerva, for example, has a touch sensor and a light sensor attached to a single input. If you have ambitious plans (and parts) for expanding Minerva, you've got two inputs, not just one, with which to play.

There are two common variations on the theme of attaching multiple sensors to one input, both of which are discussed here.

Multiple Touch Sensors

The first and easiest possibility is to attach multiple touch sensors to a single input. With the input configured for a touch sensor, a press on any one of the attached sensors will produce a value of 1 on the input.

bFORTH

In Chapter 4, *Not Quite C*, I described how NQC allows you to get around many of the limitations of RCX Code, the programming environment that comes with RIS. Even NQC, however, has its limitations. Even though you finally have the use of variables, you're limited to 31 of them. Furthermore, you can't put your own data on the display, which would be very useful for debugging. In this chapter, I'll talk about pbFORTH (Programmable Brick Forth), a piece of software that gives greater access to the memory, display, and other resources in the RCX. pbFORTH allows you to program your robots using Forth, an established language that is suitable for small systems like the RCX.

This chapter will get you up and running with pbFORTH by covering the following topics:

- An overview of the pbFORTH software architecture
- Obtaining and installing pbFORTH
- A brief description of Forth
- Listings of RCX-specific words defined in pbFORTH
- Example programs

Replacement Firmware

Later, in Chapter 10, *legOS*, I'll talk about another popular programming environment. legOS and pbFORTH are both *replacement firmware*, which means they actually replace the software on the RCX. This is the next level of power and complexity beyond NQC. If you're considering this move, which should you choose? It all depends, of course, on what you're trying to do and what programming you've already done. Table 6-1 compares pbFORTH and legOS in several important areas.

This might be useful, for example, in a robot with a "skirt" touch sensor that runs around the entire robot. Different parts of the skirt might trigger different touch sensors. By putting all the skirt sensors on one input, you could easily detect any collision with the skirt, anywhere around the robot.

The downside, of course, is that you don't know which touch sensor is being pressed. There's a way around this problem, of course, but it involves using a soldering iron. I'll explain how it works in Chapter 11, *Make Your Own Sensors*.

Light and Touch

Minerva uses a light sensor and a touch sensor on one input. The input is configured for a light sensor. When the touch sensor is not pressed, it has no effect on the light sensor reading. When the touch sensor is pressed, the input gives a value of 100; the current value of the light sensor becomes irrelevant.

Usually the light sensor shows values in the range of 30 to 70, roughly speaking; the readings depend on the lighting conditions around the sensor. You'll rarely see a real light sensor reading of 100 unless you point some very bright light directly into the sensor. In general, it's safe to assume that readings of 100 correspond to the touch sensor being pressed.

Minerva's program must account for the two sensors being attached to one input. In particular, the touch sensor must normally be not pressed. In the `grab()` and `release()` subroutines, for example, the grabber arm motor is run forward or in reverse until the touch sensor is triggered. Then the motor must be run the other way briefly so the touch sensor is no longer pressed. This allows Minerva to observe values from the light sensor.

Where Am I?

You've probably discovered that Minerva gets lost easily. If she drives over anything, or if her wheels slip in any way, she can't find her way back to her starting point. Minerva, basically, is trying to answer the question "Where am I?" Unfortunately, she can't answer it very well.

Timing

Minerva uses a fairly unreliable technique, called *timing*, to determine her current position. She moves forward for some amount of time until she finds something to pick up. Then she turns around by spinning in place for a length of time defined in `TURNAROUND_TIME`. Then she drives back to her starting point by moving forward for as much time as she moved forward before. If Minerva drives forward for five seconds, she assumes she can reach her starting point by turning around and driving forward for five seconds again.

Timing is not a very accurate technique. Variations in battery power, the material Minerva is driving on, and other unpredictable factors will mess things up. Turning around, in particular, is not very reliable: Minerva almost never heads back precisely the way she came. Minerva's directional transmission makes things more complicated, as well, because it takes a little time for the transmission to shift from one direction to the other. This affects the timing of Minerva's forward motion, as the shifting time is also recorded.

Rotation Sensors

Ideally, Minerva should have some feedback about how far she's traveled and how far she's turned. You could, for example, buy some rotation sensors and attach them to inputs 1 and 2. If you put the rotation sensors on Minerva's two main wheels, you would know exactly how many times, and in what direction, each wheel had turned. By assuming that the wheels didn't slip on the ground, you could get a very accurate idea of where Minerva was, relative to her starting position. You wouldn't have to worry about the directional transmission any more.

Wheels do slip, sadly, so unexpected terrain like driving over blocks would likely throw this method of navigation off as well. Still, it's a step up from timing.

Navigation Tools

There are several generic navigation tools that you might consider attaching to your RCX to answer the question of location:

1. A magnetic compass would give a good indication of what direction Minerva was pointing. Feedback from the compass reading would allow Minerva to turn around with much better accuracy. The interface between the compass and Minerva's inputs, of course, is entirely up to you and would probably require a bit of electronics hacking.

2. *Triangulation* is a commonly used navigation technique. Suppose you mounted three radio transmitters around the area where Minerva was going to drive. By listening to the three signals, Minerva could determine her position relative to the radio transmitters. Again, this is pretty high-tech, serious electronics.*

---

* An obvious choice might be the Global Positioning System (GPS). Unfortunately, garden variety GPS is only accurate to 100 m or so. Unless you're the US military, or willing to spend some serious money, you won't get accurate enough information from GPS to help your robot navigate.

Why Should I Care?

Before you tear your hair out trying t⌐ about what you're trying to do. Do yo⌐ robot is? Using precise positioning and h⌐ are both techniques of the big-metal artificia⌐ robotics. The RCX is not very powerful. If you⌐ walls, build a bumper and back up when you hit⌐ bly won't be able to build a map of the world in y⌐ gramming environment you use.

Online Resources

Directional Transmission
http://www.sonic.net/~rci/transmission.htm

> This page, created by Michael Powell, describes the basic princ⌐ directional transmission with detailed photographs.

Ben's Lego Creations
http://www.pobox.com/~benw/lego/

> This page contains some fascinating robots created by Ben Williamson. A modified version of Ben's FetchBot arm was used as Minerva's grabber arm. These robots are mechanically superlative; check them out.

"Where am I?"—Systems and Methods for Mobile Robot Positioning
http://www-personal.engin.umich.edu/~johannb/position.htm

> Johann Borenstein's book about mobile robot navigation can be downloaded from this site as an Adobe Acrobat PDF file. The whole book is 13 Mb, which is a little hefty for my dial-up Internet connection, but a free book is a free book. It's gotten good reviews from the MINDSTORMS online community.

Table 6-1. pbFORTH and legOS Compared, Briefly

	pbFORTH	legOS
Programming language	Forth	C or C++
Interactive?	Yes	No
Development OS	Any	Unix, Linux, or similar
Programming tool	Terminal emulator	C compiler, either gcc or egcs

As a development environment, pbFORTH excels in two areas:

startup cost

There's a certain amount of pain, the *startup cost*, associated with learning and using a new development environment. For pbFORTH, this startup cost is low. The software tools you'll need on the PC side are simple and commonly available. Compare this with legOS, which requires some heavy-duty development tools that can be tricky to install and configure. pbFORTH is very open-ended; all you need is a terminal emulator or some other simple software that talks to the RCX's IR port. You can interact with pbFORTH from a Windows terminal emulator, a Java application running on Linux, or even a custom-developed application on a PalmPilot.

development cycle

A *development cycle* is the sequence of steps you need to follow to write and run a program. With pbFORTH, this sequence of steps is fairly short. Basically, you upload or type your program into pbFORTH via a terminal emulator running on your PC. The program is immediately available to run. With legOS, you need to compile the program on your PC and download the whole thing to the RCX, which takes a couple of minutes.

However, before you get all fired up about pbFORTH, remember some caution is in order. pbFORTH itself works well, especially considering it's relatively new software, but there are only a few good tools for working with it. As of this writing, you will have to put up with ugly-looking terminal sessions to program your RCX with pbFORTH.

pbFORTH Overview

Although I'm describing pbFORTH as a way around the limitations of NQC, it's not NQC that limits your robot programs; NQC just reflects the limitations of the RCX firmware. Remember, NQC is a replacement for software on the PC only. It generates bytecodes, just like RCX Code, that are downloaded and interpreted on the RCX itself. NQC's limitations are the result of the limitations of the bytecode interpreter on the RCX. To break through this barrier, you have to replace the RCX firmware itself. Figure 6-1 shows a block diagram, similar to Figure 4-1, that shows how pbFORTH replaces the RCX's firmware.

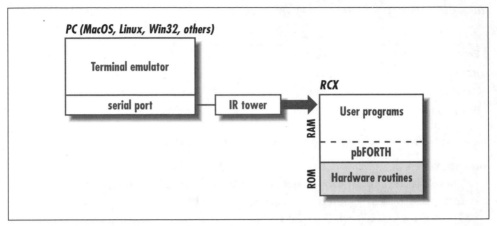

Figure 6-1. pbFORTH software architecture

Forth is an interpreted language, which means you can type commands to pbFORTH and have the robot respond immediately. You don't have to compile and download programs; you simply type them directly to the interpreter.

Installing pbFORTH

Installing pbFORTH is a simple process:

1. Obtain pbFORTH from *http://www.hempeldesigngroup.com/lego/pbFORTH/*. It's available as an archive that contains the pbFORTH replacement firmware, the source code, and example scripts.

2. Install pbFORTH on the RCX. To do this, you'll need a *firmware downloader*. The firmware downloader is a piece of software that knows how to transmit firmware over the IR link to the RCX. Two freely available firmware downloaders are `nqc` (described in Chapter 4) and `firmdl`, available in C source code at *http://graphics.stanford.edu/~kekoa/rcx/tools.html*. Downloading firmware to the RCX takes a couple of minutes, so be prepared to wait.

To download pbFORTH using `nqc`, for example, you use the `-firmware` option, like this:

```
nqc -firmware pbforth.srec
```

When the download is complete, your RCX's screen will go entirely blank. Although the RCX looks dead, don't be fooled. pbFORTH is running, and you will be able to talk to it as described in the next section.

pbFORTH will remain running on your RCX as long as the batteries are good. It replaces the regular MINDSTORMS firmware entirely, so you won't be able to program with RCX Code or NQC without reinstalling the regular firmware. To remove pbFORTH from your RCX, you'll need to remove the batteries to clear the memory. Then you can use `nqc` or `firmdl` to download a different set of firmware. If you want to reinstall the default firmware, you can use the RIS software.

Talking to pbFORTH

To interact with pbFORTH, you need to use a *terminal emulator* to exchange data with the RCX over the IR link.

Windows users can use the HyperTerminal application that comes with Windows. Linux users can use `minicom` or something similar. You'll need to point your emulator at whatever serial port has the IR tower attached. The other relevant settings are 2400 Baud, 8 data bits, 1 stop bit, and no parity.

Once you've got your emulator running, press **Enter** on your keyboard a couple of times. pbFORTH should respond with "ok" messages:

```
ok

ok
```

To get a quick start with pbFORTH, let's turn on one of the outputs. First, you'll need to initialize the RCX like this (the stuff you should type is shown in bold):

```
RCX_INIT
ok
```

To turn on an output, use the `MOTOR_SET` command, which will be covered later. Type the following:

```
7 2 0 MOTOR_SET
ok
```

Remember to press **Return** after you enter the whole line. Depending on your terminal settings, you will see the letters you type two or three times in a row, like this:

```
77 22 00 MMOOTTOORR__SSEETT
```

I have removed the extra letters in the examples in this chapter, for clarity. To minimize the repeated characters as you type in the examples, make sure "local echo" is disabled in your terminal emulator.

The `MOTOR_SET` line turns on output A (represented in the code by 0) in reverse (represented by 2) with full power (represented by 7). If your RCX is about to drive off your desk, you can turn off the output like this:

```
7 3 0 MOTOR_SET
ok
```

This is the same as the previous example, except the 2 is now a 3. The 3 tells pbFORTH to turn the output off. I'll get to the details of MOTOR_SET later, after I've introduced you to the Forth language itself.

Make sure you separate everything with spaces. pbFORTH reads different words by assuming that they're all separated by whitespace, either spaces or returns. If you miss a space, pbFORTH will get confused and complain that it can't find a word definition.

pbFORTH is also case sensitive. While MOTOR_SET is a defined word, Motor_Set is not, nor is motor_set or MOTOR_SEt.

Sending Files

For serious development, you'll want to create your source code in a text file and send the whole file to pbFORTH when you're ready to test. You can do this with many terminal emulators, although you have to set it up correctly.

First, the terminal emulator needs to know how long to wait after sending each character. In HyperTerminal (in Windows 95, 98, or NT), this setting is available in the **File > Properties** menu option. In the window that appears, choose the **Settings** tab and press the **ASCII Setup** button. You should set the **Line delay** to 100 milliseconds and the **Character delay** to 20 milliseconds, as shown in Figure 6-2.

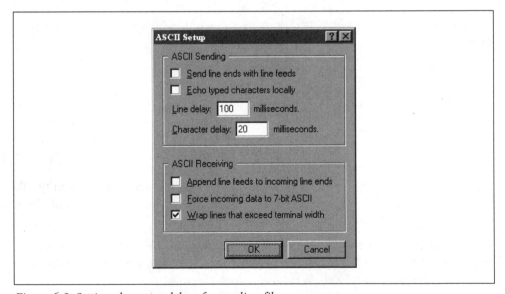

Figure 6-2. Setting character delays for sending files

To upload a file to pbFORTH, choose **Transfer** → **Send Text File** from the menu.

There are other options, as well. Appendix B, *A pbFORTH Downloader*, contains source code for a Java-based program downloader. Furthermore, the pbFORTH web site has pbFORTH tools written in Tcl/Tk.

About Forth

In this section, I'll briefly describe the Forth language itself. Then I'll detail pbFORTH's RCX-specific words and present some short examples of robotic programming with pbFORTH.

The Stack

Forth is a simple but powerful language. It is based around the idea of a *stack*. A stack is just what it sounds like, like a stack of trays in one of those spring-loaded carts at a cafeteria. You can add something to the stack or remove the top item. Adding an item to the stack is a *push*. Retrieving the top item is a *pop*. A pop always returns the last item that was pushed.

Assuming you've already gotten pbFORTH running on your RCX, let's see how this works. Let's begin by pushing a number on the stack. Type a number into your terminal emulator and hit return. pbFORTH responds with a friendly "ok":

77
ok

Now type a single period and press return. The period pops a value off the stack and prints it out to the console, along with that ubiquitous "ok":

.
77 ok

You can push multiple values on the stack by separating them with spaces. Similarly, you can pop more than one value off the stack with more than one period, like this:

77 12 55
ok
. .
55 12 ok
.
77 ok

If you understand the stack, you know almost everything there is to know about Forth.

Words and the Dictionary

The other important concept in Forth is the *dictionary*. This is simply a list of *words* and what they mean. A word is a simply a program with a name. To run it, you just type its name. Many programs expect to find input values on the stack and may place their results on the stack when they're done.

Built-in words

Forth has a number of simple words that are built in to the dictionary. DUP, for example, duplicates the top element of the stack. You can easily see how this works:

```
77
ok
DUP
ok
. .
77 77 ok
```

Table 6-2 lists some of the important built-in words in Forth. The table shows the stack before ("Initial Stack") and after ("Ending Stack") the word runs. By convention, the top is shown on the right. For example, x1 x2 shows a stack with x2 at the top and x1 as the second item. This seems confusing at first, but it makes sense after a while (and it's the convention in Forth documentation).

Table 6-2. Forth Built-in Words

Word	Meaning	Initial Stack	Ending Stack
DUP	Duplicates the top item on the stack	x	x x
OVER	Copies the second stack item	x1 x2	x1 x2 x1
PICK	Copies the nth stack item (n is zero-based)	... n	... xn
SWAP	Switches the top two stack items	x1 x2	x2 x1
ROT	Moves the third stack item to the top	x1 x2 x3	x2 x3 x1
DROP	Discards the top item on the stack	x	

Forth also supports mathematical operators, which operate on the top two items of the stack and leave their result at the top of the stack. For example, you can divide two numbers like this:

```
84 2 /
ok
.
42 ok
```

Bitwise operators are also defined: AND, OR, and XOR.

You can change the number base you're working in using the HEX and DECIMAL words. For example, if you wanted to work in hexidecimal (base 16), you would type HEX. Base 10 is represented by DECIMAL. Most of the numbers in this chapter will be base 16.

BASE is a word (a variable, which I'll talk about soon) that contains the current number base. To print out the current number base, for example, do this:

```
BASE @ .
 10 ok
```

Interestingly, the current base is printed in terms of the current base, so it will always be 10. Suppose you're working in base 8. If you print out the current base, 8, in base 8, it's expressed as 10. Retrieving the current base with BASE @ may seem like a pointless exercise, but it's useful if you want to save the current base away to be restored at some later time.

If you want to work in a number system other than HEX or DECIMAL, you can use BASE ! to store any base number. The following example shows two ways you can use Forth to convert numbers between different bases:

```
HEX 20 DECIMAL . (20 in base 16 is 32 in base 10)
 32 ok
8 BASE ! 20 DECIMAL . (20 in base 8 is 16 in base 10)
 16 ok
```

The open parenthesis (is used to indicate a comment. The pbFORTH interpreter simply ignores the rest of the line after it sees the (.

Defining words

Writing programs in Forth is a matter of defining your own words in the dictionary. Word definitions begin with a colon and end with a semicolon. Here's a simple example:

```
: threeTimes DUP DUP + + ;
 ok
```

The colon tells the Forth interpreter that the words that follow define a new word for the dictionary and should be stored to run later. The new word needs a name, threeTimes in this example, which is supplied immediately after the colon. Subsequent words will be executed when the new word is executed. The semicolon tells the interpreter that the new word definition has ended.

threeTimes duplicates the top item on the stack twice, so there are three copies of it, then adds them all together. Now that you've defined a new word, you can use it like any other Forth word:

```
5 threeTimes .
 15 ok
```

And you can, of course, use it in subsequent definitions:

```
: nineTimes threeTimes threeTimes ;
 ok
5 nineTimes .
 45 ok
```

Here's another simple example that demonstrates how to print messages from within a word. Be careful about the spacing: the actual string to be printed is framed by the . " and " words, which are separate from the string.

```
: helloWorld ." Hello, world. " ;
 ok
helloWorld
 Hello, world. ok
```

If you define a word that already exists, it will be redefined:

```
: helloWorld ." Tag, Welt. " ;
 redefine helloWorld ok
```

Constants and Variables

You can define words in Forth that represent numerical values. These words are called *constants*; you can use the word anywhere you really mean the number it represents. This is really handy for making programs more readable.

To define a constant, push its value on the stack. Then use the word CONSTANT and supply a name, like this:

```
7 CONSTANT FULL
 ok
```

You can then use FULL anywhere you really mean 7, like this:

```
FULL 2 0 MOTOR_SET
 ok
```

Variables are even easier to define. Just use the word VARIABLE and supply a name:

```
VARIABLE z
 ok
```

Values are stored in variables using the ! word, pronounced "store":

```
12 z !
 ok
```

The value of a variable can be retrieved and placed on the stack with the @ word:

```
z @ .
 12 ok
```

There's some tricky stuff going on here that I'll briefly discuss. A variable is really an address in memory. The ! word expects to find an address and a value on the stack; it stores the value at the specified address. Similarly, the @ word expects to find an address on the stack. It replaces the address with the value at that address. When you declare a variable with the VARIABLE word, all you're really doing is assigning an address (determined by the Forth interpreter) to a name.

Conditionals and Loops

Forth supports a standard IF statement, though the order is switched around from what you might be used to. The IF word comes in two different varieties:

condition IF body THEN

> The IF word looks at the condition on the stack. If the condition is true, the body between IF and THEN is executed. Table 6-3 lists some of the mathematical condition words that are available.

Table 6-3. Mathematical Condition Words

Word	Description
<	Compares the top two items on the stack; replaces them with true if the second item is less than the top item, false otherwise
=	Compares the top two items on the stack; replaces them with true if they are equal, false otherwise
>	Compares the top two items on the stack; replaces them with true if the second item is greater than the top item, false otherwise
0<	Replaces the top item of the stack with true if it is less than zero; false otherwise
0=	Replaces the top item of the stack with true if it is equal to zero; false otherwise

The following example prints out a message if the top item on the stack is less than 0:

```
: negative 0< IF ." less than zero " THEN ;
 ok
-2 negative
 less than zero ok
2 negative
 ok
```

The 0< word examines the top value on the stack. The result of this comparison is examined by the IF word. If it is true, the body of the IF is executed. The ." word tells pbFORTH to print text to the console, up until the " word. Finally, THEN marks the end of the body of the IF.

There's also a slightly more complicated IF word:

condition IF trueBody ELSE falseBody THEN

> This is the same as before, except words between ELSE and THEN will be executed if the condition is false.

Forth also includes some simple loops, including:

limit start DO words LOOP

> This loop performs the given words limit - start times. Internally, a loop index is given the value start. Each time through the loop, the index is increased by one. When it is equal to limit, the loop ends. You can put the

value of the loop index on the stack with the I word. For example, the following shows how to define a word that prints the numbers from 1 to 10.

```
: oneToTen 11 1 DO I . LOOP ;
 ok
oneToTen
 1 2 3 4 5 6 7 8 9 10 ok
```

limit start DO words delta +LOOP

This variation on the basic DO LOOP adds the given delta value to the loop index instead of always adding one. You can use this type of loop to count backwards by supplying a negative delta.

BEGIN body UNTIL

This loop performs its body until a false condition is left on the stack. The following example waits for the **View** button to be pressed (using some stuff we haven't covered just yet):

```
BUTTON_INIT
 ok
: waitForViewButton BEGIN RCX_BUTTON DUP BUTTON_GET @ 2 AND UNTIL ;
 ok
```

In the body of this loop we push RCX_BUTTON on the stack and duplicate it. Then we call BUTTON_GET, which retrieves the current state of the buttons into the RCX_BUTTON variable. Then the value of RCX_BUTTON is retrieved (with @) and compared to 2, which corresponds to the **View** button on the RCX. When this condition is true, the loop ends and waitForViewButton is done.

BEGIN body AGAIN

This variation on BEGIN UNTIL loops forever, executing its body each time through the loop.

pbFORTH Words

pbFORTH includes 34 words that perform RCX-specific functions. In this section, I'll describe them all for you. Each word's name is listed along with the starting and ending state of the stack, like this:

WORD_NAME (startStack -- endStack)

For example, the SWAP word would be listed like this:

SWAP (x1 x2 -- x2 x1)

The starting stack and ending stack are shown such that the top of the stack is shown on the right side. If you push x1 on the stack, then x2 and x3, then the stack would be shown like this: x1 x2 x3. The top of the stack is x3. The MOTOR_ SET word, for example, takes three values off the top of the stack:

MOTOR_SET (power mode index --)

After MOTOR_SET runs, the stack is empty. The first thing you need to push on the stack is power; the last thing is index. In your code, it comes out in the same order:

```
7 2 0 MOTOR_SET
```

In this case, 7 is power, 2 is mode, and 0 is index.

The very first pbFORTH word initializes the RCX:

RCX_INIT (--)

This word starts the input and output handlers, system timers, and performs other important initializations. After you load pbFORTH on the RCX, call this word before you try to do anything with the inputs, outputs, buttons, or other RCX services.

Output Control

One word is devoted to controlling the RCX's outputs:

MOTOR_SET (power mode index --)

This word turns an output on or off. It pops three parameters off the stack. The power parameter should be 1 to 7, where 7 is full power. The mode parameter indicates whether the output should be turned on going forward (1) or in reverse (2), or if it should be turned off in "brake" (3) or "float" (4) modes. In brake mode, the motor shaft resists turning; in float mode, it turns freely. The top parameter, index, should be 0, 1, or 2, representing output A, B, or C, respectively.

For example, to turn on output 3 in full reverse, do this:

```
7 2 2 MOTOR_SET
```

Remember that constants can make this kind of code a lot nicer. For example:

```
7 CONSTANT OUT_FULL
 ok
2 CONSTANT FORWARD 4 CONSTANT FLOAT
 ok
2 CONSTANT OUT_3
 ok
OUT_FULL FORWARD OUT_3 MOTOR_SET
 ok
OUT_FULL FLOAT OUT_3 MOTOR_SET
 ok
```

Front Panel Buttons

pbFORTH provides two words that allow you to examine which front panels are pressed.

BUTTON_INIT (--)

> This word initializes pbFORTH's button-handling system. Make sure to call it once before you try to call BUTTON_GET.

BUTTON_GET (address --)

> This word places the current button state into the variable **address**. pbFORTH provides a variable, RCX_BUTTON, that you can use for this purpose. The value placed in the variable tells which buttons are pressed and is a combination (boolean OR) of the values shown in Table 6-4.

Table 6-4. BUTTON_GET Return Values

Button Name	Value
Run	1
View	2
Prgm	4

> For example, if the **Run** and **Prgm** buttons are pressed simultaneously, the flags returned from BUTTON_GET will be 5.

Here's a word definition that retrieves the button state and places it on the top of the stack:

```
: buttonState RCX_BUTTON DUP BUTTON_GET @ ;
```

Building on this, here's a handy word definition that tests if the **Run** button is pressed:

```
: isRunButtonPressed buttonState 1 AND ;
```

Remember, you have to call BUTTON_INIT before you use this word; otherwise it won't work.

To test the state of the **On-Off** button, you'll need to use the POWER_GET word, described later in this chapter.

LCD Display Words

pbFORTH provides direct control of the RCX's display. This is exciting news because you can display the results of your programs or even intermediate values. Every segment of the LCD display can be controlled individually; this includes the "little man," the input and output arrows, the datalog indicators (which you might never have seen otherwise), and the large numbers in the center. Figure 6-3 shows the display with most of its segments lit up.

pbFORTH offers words that show and hide individual segments, display numbers, or clear the entire display. For changes to actually take effect, however, you must call LCD_REFRESH:

LCD_REFRESH (--)

Use this word after making changes to the display. The state of the display will not change until you call LCD_REFRESH.

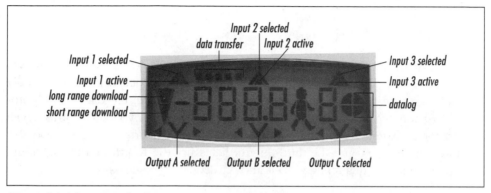

Figure 6-3. The RCX's display

pbFORTH can display a number from the stack with the following word:

LCD_NUMBER (decimal value signed --)

This word shows the number value on the display. The decimal parameter controls the location of the decimal point, if there is one, while the signed parameter determines whether value is shown as signed or unsigned. The acceptable values of decimal and signed are shown in Table 6-5 and Table 6-6.

Table 6-5. Values for the decimal Parameter of LCD_NUMBER

Value (in hexadecimal)	Description
3002	No decimal point
3003	One digit after the decimal point
3004	Two digits after the decimal point
3005	Three digits after the decimal point
any value	Single digit on the right of the display (use 3017 for signed)

Table 6-6. Values for the signed Parameter of LCD_NUMBER

Value (in hexadecimal)	Description
3001	Signed, no leading zeros
301F	Unsigned with leading zeros
3017	Single digit on the right of the display (ignores decimal)

For example, to display the number −4198, use the following:

```
3002 -1066 3001 LCD_NUMBER LCD_REFRESH
```

Note that we've specified the value in hexadecimal (–1066) but the display always shows decimal (–4198).

pbFORTH provides two words that show or hide individual display segments, basically everything except the numbers:

LCD_SHOW (segment --)

LCD_HIDE (segment --)

These words show or hide the given display segment. Valid values are shown in Table 6-7. The values that are flagged as a sequence can be repeatedly called to update the display automatically. For example, the datalog indicator (3018) consists of four quarters of a circle. The first time you show 3018, you'll see one quarter. Show 3018 again, and a second quarter lights up. Do this three more times, and the third quarter lights up, the fourth quarter lights up, and then all the quarters go blank and the sequence begins again.

Table 6-7. LCD Segment Numbers

Segment Number (hexadecimal)	Sequence?	Description
3006	no	Standing figure
3007	no	Walking figure
3008	no	Input 1 selected
3009	no	Input 1 active
300A	no	Input 2 selected
300B	no	Input 2 active
300C	no	Input 3 selected
300D	no	Input 3 active
300E	no	Output A selected
300F	no	Output A backward
3010	no	Output A forward
3011	no	Output B selected
3012	no	Output B backward
3013	no	Output B forward
3014	no	Output C selected
3015	no	Output C backward
3016	no	Output C forward
3018	yes (4)	Datalog indicator segments
3019	yes (5)	Data transfer segments (ascending)
301A	yes (5)	Data transfer segments (descending)
301B	no	Low battery indicator
301C	no	Short range download indicator

Table 6-7. LCD Segment Numbers (continued)

Segment Number (hexadecimal)	Sequence?	Description
301D	no	Long range download indicator
3020	no	All segments (LCD_SHOW only)

Conveniently, you can clear the entire display with a single word:

LCD_CLEAR (--)

This word clears the RCX's display so that no segments are lit.

Input Control Words

Before you configure inputs or read values from them, you should initialize pbFORTH's input system with the following word:

SENSOR_INIT (--)

This word initializes pbFORTH's input system. Call it once before working with inputs.

Configuring inputs

You probably remember that the RCX's inputs may be powered. The light sensor, for example, is powered from an input. These types of sensors are called *active*; all others are *passive*. In pbFORTH, the following words determine whether an input is active or passive:

SENSOR_ACTIVE (index --)
SENSOR_PASSIVE (index --)

These words set the input described by **index** to be active (powered) or passive. The **index** value should be 0, 1, or 2, corresponding to input 1, 2 or 3.

You can configure an input for a particular type and mode, just as in NQC:

SENSOR_TYPE (type index --)

This word sets the type of an input, which describes the electrical characteristics of the sensor you plan to attach. The values for **type** are shown in Table 6-8. As before, **index** should be 0, 1, or 2.

Table 6-8. Input Type Values

Value	Description
0	Raw
1	Touch sensor
2	Temperature sensor

Table 6-8. Input Type Values (continued)

Value	Description
3	Light sensor
4	Rotation sensor

SENSOR_MODE (mode index --)

This word sets the mode of the given input. An input's mode determines how the sensor values will be interpreted. The modes are shown in Table 6-9.

Table 6-9. Input Mode Values

Value (hexadecimal)	Description
0	Raw sensor value from 0 to 1023
20	Boolean, either 1 or 0
40	Counts transitions from 1 to 0 and vice versa (edge counting)
60	Counts transitions from 1 to 0 (pulse counting)
80	Percent from 0 to 100
A0	Celsius temperature
C0	Fahrenheit temperature
E0	Shaft angle, 16 counts per full revolution

The following example shows how you could configure input 3 for a light sensor:

```
2 CONSTANT INPUT_3
 ok
SENSOR_INIT
 ok
INPUT_3 SENSOR_ACTIVE
 ok
3 INPUT_3 SENSOR_TYPE
 ok
80 INPUT_3 SENSOR_MODE
 ok
```

Reading input values

Reading input values in pbFORTH is a two-step process. First, you need to tell pbFORTH to go and read the input values:

SENSOR_READ (index -- code)

This word tells pbFORTH to read the value of the specified input. The actual value can be retrieved with a call to SENSOR_GET, which is described later. A status code is placed on the stack. If code is 0, then the read was successful. Values other than 0 indicate that the RCX was busy and could not read the input value.

Having read an input value, you are now ready to retrieve it using one of the following words:

SENSOR_VALUE (index -- value)

This word returns the value of the given input. The range of the returned value is determined by the mode of the input.

SENSOR_RAW (index -- value)

Use this word to obtain the raw value of the input described by `index`. The raw value will always be in the range from 0 to 1023.

SENSOR_BOOL (index -- value)

This word returns the current value of the given input as a Forth-style boolean.

For example, to read the value of the sensor on input 3, you would do this:

```
: read 2 SENSOR_READ 2 SENSOR_VALUE . ;
```

Strictly speaking, of course, you should really check the return code from `SENSOR_READ` to make sure it was successful.

Finally, the current value of an input can be reset with the following word:

SENSOR_CLEAR (index --)

Some of the input modes count values, like the edge counting, pulse counting, and rotation modes. For these modes, the current count of an input can be reset to 0 using `SENSOR_CLEAR`.

RCX Timers

The RCX has 14 timers that you can use in your programs. Four of these timers count in tenth-of-a-second intervals. Each of these timers is identified by an index, from 0 to 3. The timers count up once every tenth of a second and have values from 0 to 7FFF (hexadecimal):

TIMER_SET (value index --)

This word sets the timer described by `index` to the supplied `value`.

TIMER_GET (index -- value)

This word places the current value of the timer described by `index` on the stack.

There are also 10 timers with a hundredth-second resolution. These timers have an index from 0 to 9; they count down instead of up and stop when they reach 0:

timer_SET (value index --)

This word sets the timer described by `index` to the supplied `value`.

timer_GET (index -- value)

This word places the current value of the timer described by `index` on the stack.

Power Management

pbFORTH includes a simple power management scheme that allows you to turn the unit off. It doesn't actually turn off completely; it just goes into a low power consumption mode until you press the **On-Off** button to turn it on. This is exactly the same behavior as with the default RCX firmware. Three words in pbFORTH are related to power:

POWER_INIT (--)

This word initializes pbFORTH's power management.

POWER_OFF (--)

Use this word to turn the RCX off. Note that this does not clear the display, turn off active inputs, or turn off running outputs. It does, however, put the interpreter in a kind of sleep mode; you should probably do this if you're going to stop using pbFORTH for a while, say overnight.

POWER_GET (address code --)

This word serves two purposes, depending on the value of **code**. The result is placed in the variable represented by **address**. pbFORTH provides the RCX_ POWER variable for use with this word. The possibilities are shown in Table 6-10.

Table 6-10. POWER_GET Code and Value Possibilities

Code (hexadecimal)	Value
4000	On-Off button state: 0 is pressed, 2 is not pressed
4001	Current battery level

The following example shows how to print out the current battery level:

```
RCX_POWER DUP 4001 POWER_GET @ .
11E ok
```

Sounds

Finally, pbFORTH can play the built-in beep sounds of the RCX, although it does not offer the possibility of playing arbitrary notes. The two words related to sound are:

SOUND_PLAY (sound code --)

This word plays the sound described by the **sound** parameter, which can have the values shown in Table 6-11.

Table 6-11. SOUND_PLAY Sounds

Sound Number	Description
0	Short beep
1	Two medium beeps

Table 6-11. SOUND_PLAY Sounds (continued)

Sound Number	Description
2	Descending arpeggio
3	Ascending arpeggio
4	Long low note
5	Quick ascending arpeggio (same as 3 but faster)

The sounds can be either *unqueued* or *queued*. Unqueued sounds will be played right away if no sound is currently playing. If a sound is currently playing (i.e., the sound system is already busy), then the unqueued sound will not be played at all. A queued sound, on the other hand, waits for the sound system to finish whatever it's doing and then plays. The value of code determines if a sound is queued (4003) or unqueued (4004).

SOUND_GET (address --)

This word returns the current state of the sound system to the given variable. You can use the pbFORTH-supplied variable RCX_SOUND for this word. A zero indicates that the sound system is not busy. Any other value means that the sound system is busy playing another sound.

Cooperative Multitasking

pbFORTH version 1.0.5 introduced words that support *cooperative multitasking*. Cooperative multitasking allows multiple tasks to appear to run simultaneously. reality, each task must voluntarily yield control to the next task in line. The other kind of multitasking, which you've seen in NQC and will see again in legOS called *preemptive multitasking*. With preemptive multitasking, the system give tle bits of time to each task, interrupting each task to give control to the next t

Cooperative multitasking is a little tricky to program because each task ne explicitly yield control to the other tasks. If your robot has a task that is g do any lengthy processing, the task needs to be structured so that it can yie trol frequently.

The pbFORTH web page has more information on cooperative multitask a look at the *tortask.txt* example, which is a good demonstration of t multiple tasks in pbFORTH.

The basic procedure for running a multitasking program has four steps:

1. First, you need to allocate space for each task using the ALLOT This includes space for user variables and space for a paramet stack. Here's a sample from *tortask.txt*:

```
0 32 CELLS 32 CELLS ALLOT_TASK MOTOR_TASK
```

The CELLS word simply converts a number on the stack from cells, which are the fundamental units of Forth memory, to bytes. The line above allocates no space for user variables and 32 cells each for the parameter stack and return stack. The name of the new task is MOTOR_TASK. In *tortast.txt*, three other tasks are allocated in the same way:

```
0 32 CELLS 32 CELLS ALLOT_TASK TIMER_TASK
0 32 CELLS 32 CELLS ALLOT_TASK SENSOR_TASK
0 32 CELLS 32 CELLS ALLOT_TASK DISPLAY_TASK
```

Notice how the name of the new task is specified after the ALLOT_TASK word, almost like a variable definition.

2. Next, each task must be built into a list. When one task voluntarily gives up control (*cooperates*), the next task in the list will get control. The BUILD word assembles tasks into a list:

```
MOTOR_TASK   BUILD
TIMER_TASK   BUILD
SENSOR_TASK  BUILD
DISPLAY_TASK BUILD
```

3. Next, you need to actually define what each task does. This is done with the ACTIVATE word, which can be used only inside a definition. Consider, for example, the MOTOR_TASK. Basically, we want it to look like this:

```
BEGIN UPDATE_MOTORS PAUSE AGAIN
```

The real work of the task is in UPDATE_MOTORS, a word that examines some other values in the system and sets the state of the motors. The PAUSE word is the key to cooperative multitasking—it passes control to the next task in the list. To associate this loop with MOTOR_TASK, we need another special word, ACTIVATE:

```
:NONAME MOTOR_TASK   ACTIVATE BEGIN UPDATE_MOTORS  PAUSE AGAIN ; EXECUTE
```

The ACTIVATE word associates MOTOR_TASK with the rest of the NONAME definition, which is simply the endless BEGIN AGAIN loop. To link the code into the task list, the NONAME definition is executed. (The combination of NONAME and EXECUTE allows you to execute a defined word just one time. Because it doesn't have a name, you can't execute the defined word again later.) The *tortast.txt* example sets up its other three tasks in the same way:

```
:NONAME TIMER_TASK   ACTIVATE BEGIN UPDATE_TIMERS  PAUSE AGAIN ; EXECUTE
:NONAME SENSOR_TASK  ACTIVATE BEGIN UPDATE_SENSORS PAUSE AGAIN ; EXECUTE
:NONAME DISPLAY_TASK ACTIVATE BEGIN UPDATE_DISPLAY PAUSE AGAIN ; EXECUTE
```

4. To actually start the tasks running, use AWAKE, like this:

```
DISPLAY_TASK AWAKE
SENSOR_TASK AWAKE
TIMER_TASK  AWAKE
MOTOR_TASK  AWAKE
```

To dive into this a little more, check out the whole *tortask.txt* example at the pbFORTH web site.

An Expensive Thermometer

This section contains an example that will help you get your feet wet with pbFORTH. We'll build a simple Celsius thermometer using a temperature sensor. Hook the sensor up to input 2 and enter the following (I've omitted pbFORTH's "ok" responses for clarity):

```
HEX

: buttonState RCX_BUTTON DUP BUTTON_GET @ ;

: isRunButtonPressed buttonState 1 AND ;

: showTemperature
  3003 SWAP 3001 LCD_NUMBER
  LCD_REFRESH
;

: clear LCD_CLEAR LCD_REFRESH ;

: thermometer
  RCX_INIT
  SENSOR_INIT
  BUTTON_INIT
  2 1 SENSOR_TYPE
  A0 1 SENSOR_MODE
  BEGIN
    BEGIN
      1 SENSOR_READ 0=
    UNTIL
    1 SENSOR_VALUE
    showTemperature
    isRunButtonPressed
  UNTIL
  clear
;
```

To run this program, use the **thermometer** word. The LCD display will show the temperature read by the sensor until you press the **Run** button.

The **isRunButtonPressed** word simply tests to see if **Run** has been pressed, using the **buttonState** word. This is how **thermometer** knows to stop running. **showTemperature** takes the top item on the stack and shows it on the display with the decimal point placed to show tenths. The **clear** word simply erases the entire display using the **LCD_CLEAR** word.

The main program, `thermometer`, begins by initializing the RCX and the input and button systems. It then configures input 1 for a temperature sensing using the temperature type (2) and the Celsius mode (A0).

The main part of `temperature` is a `BEGIN UNTIL` loop that reads a value from the input and shows it on the display. To retrieve the input value we first have to call `SENSOR_READ`. This call is inside its own `BEGIN UNTIL` loop that waits for `SENSOR_READ` to return 0, indicating success. Then the actual input value is read using `SENSOR_VALUE`. A call to `showTemperature` puts the input value on the display. Each time through the loop we call `isRunButtonPressed`; if the button is pressed, we fall out of the loop. A call to `clear` cleans up the display, and then `thermometer` is done.

If you bought LEGO's temperature sensor, you now have yourself a $225 digital thermometer. Chapter 11, *Make Your Own Sensors*, shows how you can build your own temperature sensor. You could use that code to make a digital thermometer for only about $202.

Minerva Revisited

To really put pbFORTH through its paces, let's rewrite Minerva's software in pbFORTH. (For a full description of this robot, see Chapter 5, *Minerva, a Robot with an Arm*.) As with any other language, the challenge with Forth is to break the large problem into pieces that are small enough to be understood easily. Here's a set of words that will run Minerva. They are defined in bottom-up fashion, such that the most sophisticated words are at the end.

```
HEX

: initialize
RCX_INIT
SENSOR_INIT
2 SENSOR_ACTIVE
3 2 SENSOR_TYPE
80 2 SENSOR_MODE
;

: showValue
3002 SWAP 3001 LCD_NUMBER
LCD_REFRESH
;

: sleep
0 0 TIMER_SET
BEGIN DUP 0 TIMER_GET = UNTIL
DROP
;
```

```
DECIMAL

42 CONSTANT TURNAROUND_TIME
10 CONSTANT NUMBER_OF_SAMPLES

VARIABLE threshold
VARIABLE returnTime

: sensorValue
  BEGIN DUP SENSOR_READ 0= UNTIL
  SENSOR_VALUE
;

: calibrate
  0
  NUMBER_OF_SAMPLES 0 DO
    2 sensorValue +
    1 sleep
  LOOP
  NUMBER_OF_SAMPLES /
  threshold !
  threshold @ showValue
;

: forward 7 1 2 MOTOR_SET ;
: spin 7 2 2 MOTOR_SET ;
: stop 7 3 2 MOTOR_SET ;

: armGrab 7 1 0 MOTOR_SET ;
: armRelease 7 2 0 MOTOR_SET ;
: armStop 7 3 0 MOTOR_SET ;

: grab
  armGrab
  BEGIN 2 sensorValue 100 = UNTIL
  armRelease
  BEGIN 2 sensorValue 100 < UNTIL
  armStop
;

: release
  armRelease
  BEGIN 2 sensorValue 100 = UNTIL
  armGrab
  BEGIN 2 sensorValue 100 < UNTIL
  armStop
;

: turnAround
  spin
  TURNAROUND_TIME sleep
  stop
;
```

```
: seek
  forward
  0 1 TIMER_SET
  BEGIN 2 sensorValue threshold @ 3 - < UNTIL
  2 sleep
  1 TIMER_GET returnTime !
  stop
;

: return
  forward
  returnTime @ sleep
  stop
;

: retrieve
  seek
  grab
  turnAround
  return
  release
  turnAround
;

: Minerva
  initialize
  calibrate
  5 0 DO
    retrieve
  LOOP
;
```

The pbFORTH implementation of Minerva's program closely resembles the NQC version of the program presented in Chapter 5.

By the time all the simpler words are defined, the more complex words are simply combinations of the earlier ones. Keep this in mind—I'll describe the words in Minerva's program starting at the end and returning to the beginning.

The main program word, Minerva, pretty much describes itself. It initializes the RCX, which includes configuring input 3 as a light sensor input. Then it calls calibrate to take an average reading of the light sensor. Finally, it loops five times, calling retrieve to go pick up something and bring it back.

The retrieve word is also pretty self-explanatory. It calls seek to drive forward and look for an object to pick up. Then grab is called to grab the object. Minerva turns around and heads back to her starting point with turnAround and return. Then she drops the object, with release, and turns around again with turnAround. With the simpler words defined correctly, retrieve is a highly readable piece of programming:

```
: retrieve
  seek
```

```
    grab
    turnAround
    return
    release
    turnAround
 ;
```

I won't describe every word in Minerva's program, but I do want to cover the more interesting ones. First, let's take a look at **seek** and **return**. The interesting thing about **seek** is that it uses one of the RCX's timers to figure out how long Minerva moves forward before finding something to pick up. Timer 1 is used for this purpose; the **sleep** word uses timer 0. **seek** first sets timer 1 to 0 like this:

```
0 1 TIMER_SET
```

Then Minerva moves forward until she "sees" something to pick up. The current timer value is recorded in a variable, **returnTime**, like this:

```
1 TIMER_GET returnTime !
```

When it's time for Minerva to drive back to her starting point, in **returnTime**, we just need to drive back for the stored amount of time:

```
: return
  forward
  returnTime @ sleep
  stop
;
```

Another interesting word is **calibrate**, which takes ten readings of the light sensor and calculates an average value. This value is used to determine if the light sensor "sees" something that can be picked up or not. We begin by pushing the current running total on to the stack. To begin with, the total is zero:

```
: calibrate
  0
```

Then we just run in a loop from 0 to the constant value NUMBER_OF_SAMPLES. Each time through the loop, we read the value of input 3 and add it to the running total on the stack. This is done every tenth of a second, by calling 1 **sleep**:

```
NUMBER_OF_SAMPLES 0 DO
  2 sensorValue +
  1 sleep
LOOP
```

Once this is done, calculating an average is a simple matter of division:

```
NUMBER_OF_SAMPLES /
```

Then the average value is stored in the **threshold** variable:

```
threshold !
```

Finally, as an added bonus, the average value is shown on the RCX's display:

```
threshold @ showValue
```

The average value, **threshold**, is used in the **seek** word to find a dark object to pick up. **seek** drives forward until the light sensor returns a reading that is 3 less than the average:

```
BEGIN 2 sensorValue threshold @ 3 - < UNTIL
```

Debugging

When you're writing your own programs, there are two things you should keep in mind when you are debugging:

1. The interactive nature of the pbFORTH interpreter can really help. You can, for example, make changes in a word by redefining it. With legOS (see Chapter 10), by contrast, you'd have to compile and download a whole new version of your software. With pbFORTH, you can simply make new definitions for the words that aren't working.*

   Furthermore, you can interactively test every word in your program. This makes it easy to drill down from the higher layers to the lower layers of your program to identify problems. Any word that is defined can be interactively tested. This is powerful medicine indeed.

2. On the other hand, you need to be very careful about endless loops. If you do get stuck executing an endless loop, there's no way to stop pbFORTH short of removing the batteries. In this case, you will have to use your firmware download utility to reload pbFORTH.

If you entered all of the Minerva source code, you can interactively test any of its words. For example, to show a number on the display, do something like this:

```
RCX_INIT
 ok
42 showValue
 ok
```

To pause for half a second, you could do this:

```
5 sleep
 ok
```

To test out the **calibrate** word, try this:

```
initialize
 ok
```

---

* Interestingly, new definitions don't replace the old ones, they just mask them out. If you want to return to an earlier definition, you should use the MARKER word. See the pbFORTH web site for details.

```
calibrate
ok
```

By now, you are probably getting a feel for this software. The main thing to keep in mind is to break your programs into small pieces that can be easily tested and debugged.

Interestingly, you can't retrieve a word definition from pbFORTH. The best way to program with pbFORTH is to put your program in a text file on your PC. When you're ready to give it a try, download the file to pbFORTH and test it out. You can modify the text source file to make changes or fix bugs and redownload the new word definitions each time you want to test the program.

Online Resources

Forth for Mindstorms
http://www.hempeldesigngroup.com/lego/pbFORTH/
> This is the center of the pbFORTH universe. Ralph Hempel, creator of pbFORTH, offers the current version of pbFORTH here. You can also get the source code, sample Forth programs (including *tortask.txt*), and helpful advice and pointers.

pbFORTH rcxTk GUI
http://www.hempeldesigngroup.com/lego/pbFORTH/rcxTkGUI.html
> This page describes some tools created by Ralph Hempel to make it easier to work with pbFORTH. The tools are based on Tcl/Tk.

Forth Interest Group Home Page
http://www.forth.org/
> This site is a good jumping-off point for all sorts of interesting information about the Forth language. If you want to learn more about Forth, this is a great place to start.

Tim Hendtlass's Real Time Forth Book
ftp://ftp.taygeta.com/pub/Forth/Literature/rtfv5.pdf
> This is one of the resources available from the Forth Interest Group Home Page (see the previous entry). It is a tutorial introduction to Forth. Although it describes a specific version in some detail, it's a good general introduction to the language itself (see its chapters 1 through 5).

NQC—Not Quite C
http://www.enteract.com/~dbaum/lego/nqc/index.html
> This is the home page for NQC. It's listed here because nqc can be used to download the pbFORTH firmware to the RCX.

firmdl.c

http://graphics.stanford.edu/~kekoa/rcx/firmdl.c

Another popular firmware downloader is firmdl. Written by Kekoa Proudfoot, the source code is available in C and should compile on most platforms.

LEGO World Shop

http://www.legoworldshop.com/

This online store offers various useful items like the temperature sensor used
in this chapter. You can also get touch sensors, light sensors, rotation sensors,
more motors, and extra RCX's.

7

A Remote Control for Minerva

In Chapter 5, *Minerva, a Robot with an Arm*, you read about a mechanically complex robot that could be built from one RIS kit. One of Minerva's shortcomings, however, is that she isn't very smart about searching out things to pick up. She simply drives forward, looking with her light sensor for something dark.

One way to improve Minerva's performance is to have a human being control her. This is called *teleoperation* or *telerobotics*. This chapter describes the construction and programming of a remote control for Minerva. It is based on a second RCX, which sends IR messages to Minerva. Minerva also needs a new program that will respond to incoming IR messages.

Two Heads Are Better Than One

If you're a MINDSTORMS enthusiast, you're probably always hoping to get more *stuff*: more motors, more sensors, and a better programming environment than RCX Code. A second RIS set is a great investment, if you can afford it or if you can convince somebody to buy it for you. If you're on a tighter budget, you can buy a single RCX, by itself, for about $120US. If you have a friend with a MINDSTORMS set, of course, you can always pool your resources.

There are several interesting things you can do with two RCXs:

1. Build a giant robot. The two RCXs can coordinate their actions by communicating over the IR port. With two RCXs, of course, you can build a robot with six outputs and six inputs.

2. Build leader and follower robots. One robot tells the other robot what to do by issuing commands over the IR port. This chapter illustrates this technique by describing how to build a remote control for Minerva.

3. Have a robot competition. In Chapter 9, *RoboTag, a Game for Two Robots*, I'll talk about one possible robot competition. There are many other types of competitions. You and a friend could build robots to accomplish a specific task. Then you could see whose robot performs better. The "Online Resources" section at the end of this chapter lists some existing competitions.

You might think that having three or more RCXs would be even better, but it actually complicates things considerably. Although IR communication between two RCXs is fairly straightforward, it gets messy with three or more RCXs. How do you know if an IR message is destined for a specific RCX? A simple solution is to assign a specific range of message values to various message pathways. For example, with three RCXs, named RCX1, RCX2, and RCX3, you might assign the message numbers as shown in Table 7-1.

Table 7-1. Sample Message Assignments for Three-way RCX Communication

Message Numbers	Message Pathway (Two-way)
0 to 9	RCX1 to RCX2
10 to 19	RCX1 to RCX3
20 to 29	RCX2 to RCX3

A more general solution may someday be supplied by the LEGO Network Protocol, a work in progress in the online MINDSTORMS community (see the "Online Resources" for more information).

The Allure of Telerobotics

Replacing the function of your robot's brain with that of a human brain is appealing in many situations. It's easy to program a robot to do the same task over and over again. However, if the task changes or if the environment changes, the robot may have a hard time adjusting. Humans are much better at adapting to new conditions.

On the other hand, telerobotics is a kind of cheating. Part of the point of autonomous mobile robots is that you can set them running and forget about them until they're done with whatever they're doing. If you build a robotic vacuum cleaner, you want to set it running and forget about it until it's done cleaning your floors. If you used a teleoperated robotic vacuum cleaner, you'd spend just as much time cleaning as with a conventional vacuum cleaner.

In the simplest form of telerobotics, the human can see the robot and can control it much as you might play with a radio control car. This is basically how the remote control for Minerva works: you can see Minerva and control it by sending IR messages from the remote control.

More sophisticated telerobots have a video camera that sends pictures back to a human operator. The operator can see what the robot sees and can send commands to control the robot.

Teleoperation does not work well if the human operator and the remote robot are separated by a very large distance, such as the distance between Mars and the Earth. In this case, the video signals from the robot take a long time to reach the operator, and the control signals from the operator take a long time to reach the robot. What the operator sees is really a second or two behind what's actually happening, so it's very hard to control the robot with any precision.

Fortunately, you don't have to worry about this with Minerva. Because the remote and the robot communicate with IR light, there must always be a line-of-sight between them. If you can control the robot, you can see it—there's no video connection to add confusion.

Building Instructions

The controls for the remote are built on the bottom of the RCX. This was a conscious design decision—it orients the IR port of the remote in the best place to broadcast commands to Minerva.

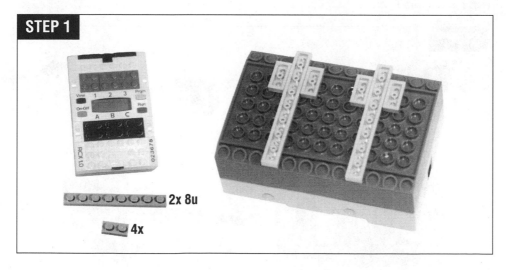

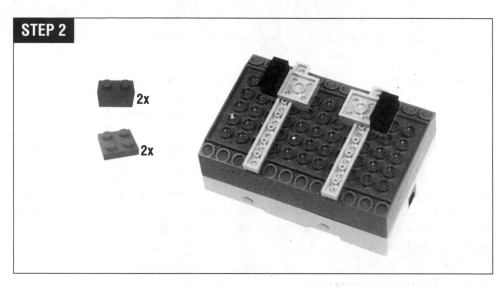

Attach the light sensor and wire bricks as shown. The light sensor goes on input 1, while the two wire bricks (which will be attached to the touch sensors) go to input 2 and input 3. If you get these two wires backwards, you'll know when you push the joystick backward and the robot moves forward. You can easily swap the two connectors later.

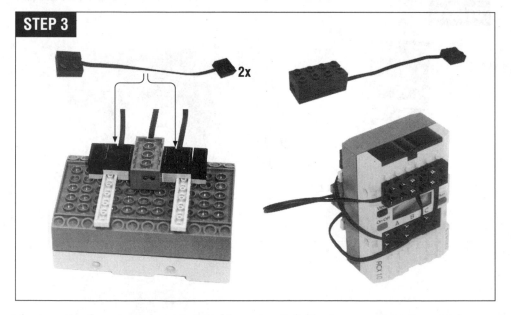

The two touch sensors are triggered by a joystick-like lever contraption. Only one of the sensors will ever be triggered at a time.

STEP 4

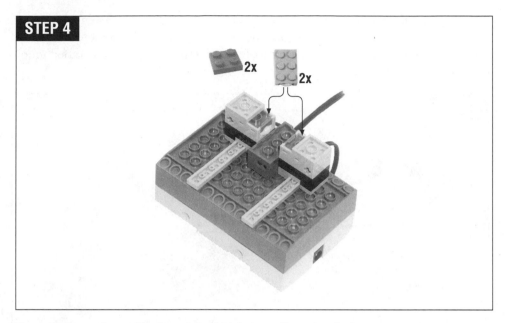

The next step shows the joystick, which is really a simple lever.

STEP 5

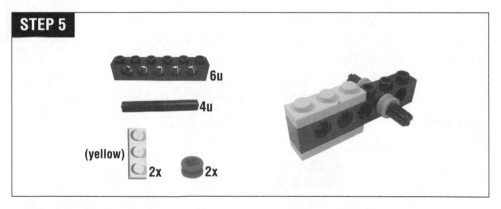

6u

4u

(yellow) 2x 2x

STEP 6

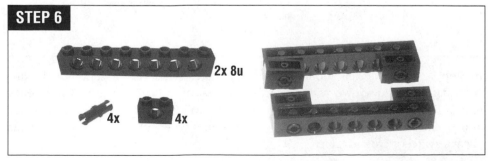

2x 8u

4x 4x

Put the joystick, from Step 5, into the assemblies from Step 6. Fasten it together with the two yellow plates. Then put the whole thing on the remote assembly. When you wiggle the joystick back and forth, it pushes one or the other touch sensor.

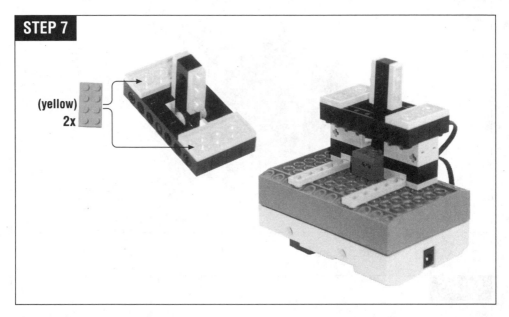

STEP 7

(yellow)
2x

Step 8 might not look like much, but it's important. It's the slider that controls Minerva's arm. It slides past the light sensor, presenting either a yellow or a black brick to the sensor. This is how the RCX knows if you've moved the slider.

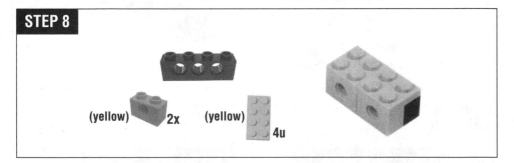

STEP 8

(yellow) 2x   (yellow) 4u

In Step 9, the slider gets mounted on the remote. Make sure it slides freely, and note that it's upside-down with respect to the rest of the construction. The orientation of the yellow and black bricks in the slider will make a difference in how the arm is controlled. If you don't like how it works when it's all together, you can always switch it around later.

STEP 9

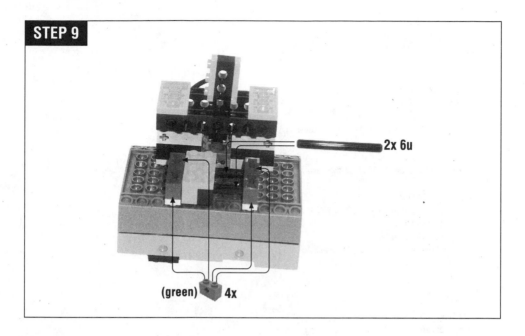

Programming the Remote Control

The remote control doesn't really have to do much. It responds to its sensors by sending commands to Minerva. The joystick control triggers the two touch sensors; the remote responds to these by telling Minerva to move forward or spin. The slider control is used to move Minerva's arm up or down.

One final feature is a "heartbeat"—a special message that the remote periodically sends to Minerva. If Minerva doesn't hear this message, it knows it has lost contact with the remote.

The remote uses three different tasks to get everything done. One task monitors the touch sensors, one task monitors the light sensor, and the third task sends the heartbeat signal. Here is the code for those tasks:

```
#define FORWARD_MESSAGE 16
#define SPIN_MESSAGE 17
#define STOP_MESSAGE 18
#define GRAB_MESSAGE 19
#define RELEASE_MESSAGE 20
#define HEARTBEAT_MESSAGE 21

#define HEARTBEAT_TIME 20

task main() {
  SetSensor(SENSOR_1, SENSOR_LIGHT);
  SetSensor(SENSOR_2, SENSOR_TOUCH);
  SetSensor(SENSOR_3, SENSOR_TOUCH);
```

```
      start lightWatcher;
      start touchWatcher;
      start heartbeat;
   }

   task touchWatcher() {
     while (true) {
       if (SENSOR_2 == 1) {
         SendMessage(FORWARD_MESSAGE);
         Wait(10);
         until (SENSOR_2 == 0);
         SendMessage(STOP_MESSAGE);
       }
       if (SENSOR_3 == 1) {
         SendMessage(SPIN_MESSAGE);
         Wait(10);
         until (SENSOR_3 == 0);
         SendMessage(STOP_MESSAGE);
       }
     }
   }

   #define TOLERANCE 3
   int current;
   int minimum;
   int maximum;
   int midline;

   int lastArmMessage;

   task lightWatcher() {
     minimum = 100;
     maximum = 0;

     while (true) {
       current = SENSOR_1;
       if (current < minimum) minimum = current;
       if (current > maximum) maximum = current;
       midline = minimum + (maximum - minimum) / 2;

       if (SENSOR_1 <= (midline - TOLERANCE) &&
           lastArmMessage != RELEASE_MESSAGE) {
         PlayTone(494, 10);
         PlayTone(660, 10);
         SendMessage(RELEASE_MESSAGE);
         lastArmMessage = RELEASE_MESSAGE;
       }
       if (SENSOR_1 >= (midline + TOLERANCE) &&
           lastArmMessage != GRAB_MESSAGE) {
         PlayTone(660, 10);
         PlayTone(494, 10);
         SendMessage(GRAB_MESSAGE);
         lastArmMessage = GRAB_MESSAGE;
       }
```

```
    }
  }

  task heartbeat() {
    while (true) {
      SendMessage(HEARTBEAT_MESSAGE);
      Wait(HEARTBEAT_TIME);
    }
  }
```

The **main** task configures the inputs on the remote control and starts up the other tasks.

The **touchWatcher** task is fairly straightforward. It listens for a touch on either touch sensor. When one is detected, the remote sends out an IR command to Minerva to go forward or to spin in place. Then the task waits for the touch sensor to be released and sends a stop command to Minerva.

The call to **Wait(10)** deserves more mention; it's an example of a technique called *debouncing*. Debouncing is a way of making touch sensors (and buttons in general) work reliably. The basic problem occurs just at the point where you press the touch sensor enough to make its state change from off to on. Tiny motions or electrical variations can cause the touch sensor's output to switch back and forth very quickly between on and off. This effect is called *bounce*, and it occurs while you're pressing or releasing the switch, between the steady states of off and on. Bounce can be eliminated with an electronic circuit or by special programming, as I've done here. The call to **Wait(10)** gives the touch sensor signal a chance to settle down before **touchWatcher** starts looking for the release of the touch sensor.

The slider on the remote changes the value of the light sensor. **lightWatcher** is the task that monitors the light sensor. If the sensor value changes from light to dark, the remote tells Minerva to release the grabber. A dark-to-light transition causes the remote to send a grab command to Minerva.

Just what exactly what "light" and "dark" are is a little tricky to define. I had originally hard-coded light values, but then the remote had to be reprogrammed depending on whether I was using it in daylight or at night. Instead, the remote uses a scheme to calibrate itself on the fly. It keeps track of its minimum and maximum light readings in the **minimum** and **maximum** variables, as shown here:

```
current = SENSOR_1;
if (current < minimum) minimum = current;
if (current > maximum) maximum = current;
midline = minimum + (maximum - minimum) / 2;
```

Then **lightWatcher** calculates the midpoint of the minimum and maximum values. This value is used to determine exactly what light and dark values cause the remote to fire commands to Minerva. **lightWatcher** also keeps track of the last grabber arm command it sent to avoid unnecessarily sending the same command twice.

To provide some feedback to the human operator, `lightWatcher` plays tones when it sends the grab or release commands.

The `hearbeat` task is very simple. It repeatedly sends the heartbeat command to the IR port.

Programming Minerva

Minerva's program, then, must listen for incoming messages on the IR port and respond to them. This is fairly simple, but it's complicated by two things:

1. Minerva should listen for the heartbeat commands from the remote. If she doesn't hear them, she should stop what she's doing until the IR link is established again.

2. The human operator should be able to change the direction of the arm as it is moving, without waiting for an entire grab or release cycle to be completed. This feature, however, should not interfere with Minerva's ability to stop the arm when it moves up as far as it can go.

Minerva's program is split into four primary tasks:

messageWatcher

>   The `messagewatcher` task examines the IR port for incoming messages. When one arrives, it is examined and the appropriate action is taken.

grab and *release*

>   The `grab` and `release` tasks are kicked off by `messageWatcher` to control Minerva's arm. They are separate tasks so that `messageWatcher` can continue to receive commands from the remote while the arm is moving. You could, for example, start driving forward while the arm was grabbing. `grab` and `release` have the ability to interrupt each other, so you can change the direction of the arm as it's moving.

heartbeatWatcher

>   This task keeps count of missing heartbeats. When `messageWatcher` receives a heartbeat, it subtracts one from a tally of missing heartbeats, kept in the `missedBeats` variable. The `heartbeatWatcher` adds one to this count; if it's ever more than one, `heartbeatWatcher` assumes it has lost contact with the remote. It then stops the `messageWatcher` task and shuts down the robot's motors. When the heartbeat is heard again, `heartbeatWatcher` starts up `messageWatcher` once again.

Here's the entire program. I'll describe more of the details after the listing.

```
#define FORWARD_MESSAGE 16
#define SPIN_MESSAGE 17
#define STOP_MESSAGE 18
#define GRAB_MESSAGE 19
#define RELEASE_MESSAGE 20
#define HEARTBEAT_MESSAGE 21

#define HEARTBEAT_TIME 20

int message;
int armLock;
int missedBeats;

task main() {
  SetSensor(SENSOR_3, SENSOR_LIGHT);
  armLock = 0;
  missedBeats = 0;

  start messageWatcher;
  start heartbeatWatcher;
}

task messageWatcher() {
  while (true) {
    message = Message();
    if (message == FORWARD_MESSAGE) {
      OnFwd(OUT_C);
      ClearMessage();
    }
    else if (message == SPIN_MESSAGE) {
      OnRev(OUT_C);
      ClearMessage();
    }
    else if (message == STOP_MESSAGE) {
      Off(OUT_C);
      ClearMessage();
    }
    else if (message == GRAB_MESSAGE) {
      start grab;
      ClearMessage();
    }
    else if (message == RELEASE_MESSAGE) {
      start release;
      ClearMessage();
    }
    else if (message == HEARTBEAT_MESSAGE) {
      missedBeats = missedBeats - 1;
      ClearMessage();
    }
  }
}

task grab() {
  until (armLock == 0);
```

```
    stop release;
    OnFwd(OUT_A);
    until (SENSOR_3 == 100);
    armLock = 1;
    OnRev(OUT_A);
    until (SENSOR_3 != 100);
    armLock = 0;
    Off(OUT_A);
}

task release() {
  until (armLock == 0);
  stop grab;
  OnRev(OUT_A);
  until (SENSOR_3 == 100);
  armLock = 1;
  OnFwd(OUT_A);
  until (SENSOR_3 != 100);
  armLock = 0;
  Off(OUT_A);
}

task heartbeatWatcher() {
  while (true) {
    if (missedBeats > 1) {
      PlaySound(SOUND_DOWN);
      stop messageWatcher;
      Off(OUT_C);
      until (armLock == 0);
      Off(OUT_A);
      until (Message() == HEARTBEAT_MESSAGE);
      PlaySound(SOUND_UP);
      missedBeats = 0;
      start messageWatcher;
    }
    missedBeats = missedBeats + 1;
    Wait(HEARTBEAT_TIME);
  }
}
```

Don't Break That Arm

The `grab` and `release` tasks, as I said, have the ability to interrupt each other. They use a variable, `armLock`, to avoid potentially dangerous situations. For example, suppose that `release` is running. It drives the arm motor in reverse until the arm is up and the limit touch sensor is pressed. Then the motor is run forward to release the touch sensor. Before the touch sensor is released, however, suppose `grab` starts up. It stops `release` and runs the motor forward until the touch sensor is pressed. It's already pressed, so `grab` starts running the motor in reverse, waiting for the touch sensor to be released. Since the arm is already at the top of its travel, running the arm motor in reverse creates pressure on the gears and will either break the arm apart or cause the gears to skip.

Using the `armLock` variable enables `grab` and `release` to complete the press–release cycle of the arm limit switch without being interrupted. Both `grab` and `release` wait for `armLock` to be 0 before interrupting the other task, like this:

```
until (armLock == 0);
```

The `grab` and `release` tasks set `armLock` to 1 before doing the sensitive press–release cycle. This means Minerva should never break her own arm.

Stayin' Alive

The `heartbeatWatcher` task also deserves some mention. It adds one to the `missedBeats` variable just as often as it expects the remote to send a heartbeat. Remember that just as `heartbeatWatcher` is adding to `missedBeats`, the `messageWatcher` task is subtracting from `missedBeats` every time it hears the heartbeat message. If `missedBeats` is ever greater than one, `heartbeatWatcher` shuts Minerva down. This shutdown is not as straightforward as you might think, however. First, a sound is played (the descending arpeggio). This lets the human operator know that contact with the remote has been lost. Then `heartbeatWatcher` shuts down the `messageWatcher` task and turns off Minerva's drive motor:

```
PlaySound(SOUND_DOWN);
stop messageWatcher;
Off(OUT_C);
```

`heartbeatWatcher` also wants to shut down Minerva's arm motor, but it respects the `armLock` variable so the arm is not left in an uncertain state:

```
until (armLock == 0);
Off(OUT_A);
```

Now `heartbeatWatcher` waits to regain the heartbeat signal from the remote. If it is regained, `heartbeatWatcher` plays another sound (the ascending arpeggio), resets `missedBeats`, and starts up `messageWatcher` again:

```
until (Message() == HEARTBEAT_MESSAGE);
PlaySound(SOUND_UP);
missedBeats = 0;
start messageWatcher;
```

Online Resources

LEGO Network Protocol

legOS : 180 [LEGO Network Protocol discussion thread]
http://www.lugnet.com/robotics/rcx/legos/?n=180&t=i&v=c
> Although the LEGO Network Protocol is not yet mature, you can view its genesis in the discussion groups at LUGNET. This URL points to a lengthy exchange from the middle of 1999.

Challenges and Competitions

Events
http://www.lugnet.com/robotics/events/
> This is the home page for the robotics events discussion group at LUGNET. To keep up on community activity related to challenges and competitions, check back here often or subscribe to the *lugnet.robotics.events* newsgroup.

Programs
http://www.thamesscience.org/program1.html
> The Thames Science Center, in Newport, Rhode Island, hosts monthly challenges for robot builders of all ages. Each challenge consists of an objective; to participate, you build a robot to accomplish the objective. Then bring in your robot and see how it compares to other designs. You can register online.

FIRST LEGO LEAGUE
http://www.legomindstorms.com/first/
> FIRST LEGO LEAGUE (FLL) is an organization for kids from 9 to 14. Teams can register to be a part of FLL, which includes a robotic challenge and competition.

RCX Challenge
http://home.connect.net/joel/Challenge.html
> Designed by Joel Shafer, the challenge is to build a robot that can navigate a room to pick up empty soda cans. If you're considering hosting your own robot competition, you might want to check out Joel's rules.

Lego Mindstorms Robot Arena
http://www.azimuthmedia.com/RobotArena/mainframe.html
> The Robot Arena is another robot competition in the San Francisco Bay area.

8

Using Spirit.ocx with Visual Basic

Part of the appeal of the programming environments described in Chapter 4, *Not Quite C*, and Chapter 6, *pbFORTH*, is that they don't tie you down to using Windows on your development PC. The programming environment that comes with RIS, RCX Code, is a Windows-only solution, which is distressing to people who prefer other operating systems. Aside from providing better capabilities than RCX Code, NQC and pbFORTH also allow you to develop RCX software using your operating system of choice.

In this chapter, I'll describe a Windows-only solution—programming your robots using Visual Basic (VB). Visual Basic is a language developed by Microsoft and included with many of their other products. The link between Visual Basic and your robots is a file called *Spirit.ocx*, which is installed as part of the standard RIS software. In this chapter, I'll show you how to use Visual Basic and *Spirit.ocx* to control and program your robots.

If you are running Windows, chances are good that you already have Visual Basic somewhere, as I'll describe in the next section. Because VB is so widespread in the Windows world, I won't attempt to describe the language itself. There are several good online tutorials, including information and examples at Microsoft's site. (See the "Online Resources" section at the end of this chapter for references.) Instead, this chapter focuses on how you can use VB to write programs for your RCX.

You May Already Have Visual Basic

Visual Basic is a programming language made by Microsoft. You can purchase it as a separate product. The "Learning Edition" is $109US. A "Professional Edition," with more bells and whistles, is available for $279US. If you have more money to burn, try the "Enterprise Edition," for $1299US.

Don't be alarmed by the price tags. You may already have Visual Basic without knowing it. The applications in the Microsoft Office software include a limited version of Visual Basic, called Visual Basic for Applications (VBA); Word, Excel, and Access all include VBA. In Word, for example, there's a **Visual Basic Editor** menu item in the **Macro** submenu of the **Tools** menu. The examples in this chapter were developed with VBA in Microsoft Word 97, but you could just as easily use one of the other incarnations of VB or VBA.

Even if you don't have VB or VBA, you can use a very similar environment called BrickCommand. BrickCommand allows you to program the RCX via *Spirit.ocx*, much the same way as you would using VB or VBA. Several similar packages are available online; see the "Online Resources" section for details.

About Spirit.ocx

Spirit.ocx is the glue that links Windows applications to the RCX. If you installed the software from the RIS kit, you already have *Spirit.ocx* on your computer. In essence, *Spirit.ocx* is a collection of functions that send commands to the RCX, ask the RCX for information, or create programs on the RCX. Figure 8-1 shows the software architecture, which is quite similar to Figure 4-1 in Chapter 4. *Spirit.ocx* can also be used from Visual C++ (VC++). If you're familiar with VC++, you can do this fairly easily. This chapter describes VB because it is simple and commonly available.

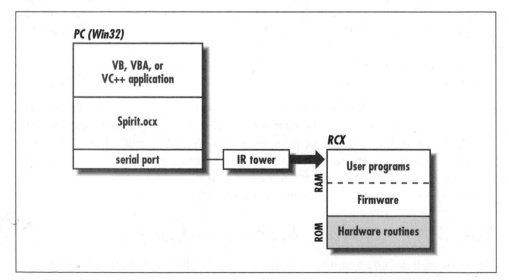

Figure 8-1. RCX software architecture

Like NQC, *Spirit.ocx* uses the default firmware that is loaded on the RCX and makes more features of the bytecode interpreter available than RCX Code. Unlike NQC, *Spirit.ocx* is a Windows-specific piece of software.

Calling Spirit.ocx Functions

The goal of this chapter is to enable you to call *Spirit.ocx* functions directly from VB or VBA with code like this:

```
.InitComm
.PlayTone 440, 10
.SetWatch Hour(Now), Minute(Now)
.On "01"
```

All you need to do is let VB know about the *Spirit.ocx* control. This process is described in the next few sections.

First Things First

To begin with, you should enter your VB or VBA environment. If you have a full version of VB installed, just start it up. If you have any of the Microsoft Office applications, you can use VBA. In Word, for example, choose **Tools > Macro > Visual Basic Editor**.

Showing Spirit.ocx in the Tool Palette

To reference *Spirit.ocx*, we first need to put it in a user form. Create a new form by choosing **Insert > UserForm**. A new form appears, along with a tool palette labeled **Toolbox**.

Spirit.ocx does not appear in the tool palette. To add it, choose **Tools > Additional Controls**. In the window that appears, scroll down to find **Spirit Control** in the list of available controls.* Click on the box to its left to select it, then click on **OK**. You only have to follow this procedure once. When you use VB again later, the *Spirit.ocx* control will automatically show up in your tool palette, as shown in Figure 8-2.

A new item with the familiar LEGO logo should now be in your tool palette. Select this item and place it on the form you just created. We won't use the form for anything except as a place to keep the *Spirit.ocx* control. Change the name to something like DummySpiritForm. The control itself has a default name of Spirit1, which is just fine for our purposes.

---

* The **Spirit Control** item appears in the list only if you have already installed the LEGO MINDSTORMS software. During this installation, *Spirit.ocx* is registered with the system in such a way that VB or VBA can find it later.

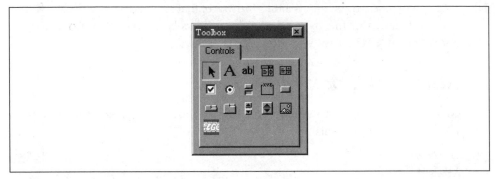

Figure 8-2. Spirit.ocx in the tool palette

You should glance over `Spirit1`'s properties to make sure they're set up properly. In particular, check the `ComPortNo` property to be sure you'll be talking to the right serial port.

Hello, Spirit

Now that you've placed a *Spirit.ocx* control on a form, let's write some code to use it. Choose the **Insert > Module** menu item to create a new code module. In the window that appears, type the following to create a new subroutine:

```
Sub HelloSpirit
```

To call functions in *Spirit.ocx*, you need to reference the control by name. The dummy form you created is `DummySpiritForm`. It contains a *Spirit.ocx* control called `Spirit1`. The full name of the control, then, is `DummySpiritForm.Spirit1`.

Fill out the body of the `HelloSpirit` subroutine as follows:

```
Sub HelloSpirit()
  DummySpiritForm.Spirit1.InitComm
  DummySpiritForm.Spirit1.PlaySystemSound 0
  DummySpiritForm.Spirit1.CloseComm
End Sub
```

To run this simple subroutine, make sure your RCX is on. Then click on the play button in the toolbar. If all goes well, you should hear your RCX play a simple beep.

It's a little cumbersome to always refer to the full name of the *Spirit.ocx* control. A simpler syntax, using `With`, looks like this:

```
Sub HelloSpiritII()
  With DummySpiritForm.Spirit1
    .InitComm
    .PlaySystemSound 0
    .CloseComm
  End With
End Sub
```

Immediate and Delayed Gratification

The functions in *Spirit.ocx* can be *immediate, delayed,* or both. An immediate function executes as soon as you call it. Delayed functions can be placed inside a program and executed later. For example, On is both an immediate and a delayed function. You can call it to turn on some outputs immediately, or you can call it to add it to a program that will be executed later.

The following subroutine plays a little song using the PlayTone function in its immediate mode:

```
Sub Charge()
  With DummySpiritForm.Spirit1
    .InitComm
    .PlayTone 392, 10
    .PlayTone 523, 10
    .PlayTone 659, 10
    .PlayTone 784, 20
    .PlayTone 659, 10
    .PlayTone 784, 20
    .CloseComm
  End With
End Sub
```

Instead of executing things on the RCX immediately, you can store them for later. The following subroutine redefines Program 5 on the RCX to play the same song:

```
Sub ChargeProgram()
  With DummySpiritForm.Spirit1
    .InitComm
    .SelectPrgm 4
    .BeginOfTask 0
      .PlayTone 392, 10
      .PlayTone 523, 10
      .PlayTone 659, 10
      .PlayTone 784, 20
      .PlayTone 659, 10
      .PlayTone 784, 20
    .EndOfTask
    Pause 1
    .CloseComm
  End With
End Sub

Sub Pause(ByVal duration As Integer)
  Start = Timer
  Do While Timer < Start + duration
  Loop
End Sub
```

When you run `ChargeProgram`, you won't hear anything. But when you select Program 5 and press the **Run** button, you'll hear the song. You have just downloaded a program to the RCX from Visual Basic!

This example uses `SelectPrgm` to select the RCX's current program number. `SelectPrgm` expects a zero-based number, from zero to four, representing the RCX's programs from one through five. Calling `SelectPrgm 4` tells the RCX to switch to Program 5.

The next unfamiliar *Spirit.ocx* function in this example is `BeginOfTask`. I'll explain more about tasks a little later; for now, just keep in mind that task 0 is run when you press the **Run** button on the RCX. Everything between the `BeginOfTask` and `EndOfTask` is stored as the task itself.

There's one final tweak I should mention. `ChargeProgram` uses a helper subroutine, `Pause`, to give *Spirit.ocx* a chance to download the program to the RCX before calling `CloseComm`. It simply waits for a second before shutting down the communication link to the RCX. Without this pause, the program does not get fully downloaded.

Programs, Tasks, and Subroutines

Each of the RCX's five programs is made up of one to ten tasks and zero to eight subroutines. This structure is dictated by the RCX firmware, and hence is exactly the same structure that I described for NQC in Chapter 4.

Subroutines are defined much the same way that tasks are defined, by framing some set of function calls with the `BeginOfSub` and `EndOfSub` functions. The same restrictions on subroutines in NQC apply here; subroutines cannot call other subroutines or themselves. Within a task, you can call a subroutine with the `GoSub` function.

As you learned in the last example, task 0 in a program is the task that is run when you press the **Run** button on the RCX. It's up to that task to start whatever other tasks you've defined. *Spirit.ocx* provides `StartTask`, `StopTask`, and `StopAllTasks` for controlling the execution of different tasks within a program.

The following example defines three tasks. Task 0 simply runs the other tasks, using `StartTask`. Task 1 sings a song, over and over, while task 2 runs the motors forward and reverse ad infinitum.

```
Sub MultiTaskingProgram()
  With DummySpiritForm.Spirit1
    .InitComm
    .SelectPrgm 3
    .BeginOfTask 0
      .StartTask 1
```

```
          .StartTask 2
        .EndOfTask
        .BeginOfTask 1
          .While 0, 0, 2, 0, 0
            .PlayTone 392, 10
            .PlayTone 523, 10
            .PlayTone 659, 10
            .PlayTone 784, 20
            .PlayTone 659, 10
            .PlayTone 784, 20
            .Wait 2, 80
            .Wait 2, 80
          .EndWhile
        .EndOfTask
        .BeginOfTask 2
          .On "02"
          .While 0, 0, 2, 0, 0
            .SetFwd "02"
            .Wait 2, 50
            .SetRwd "02"
            .Wait 2, 50
          .EndWhile
        .EndOfTask
        Pause 5
        .CloseComm
    End With
End Sub
```

Tasks 1 and 2 both use **While** and **EndWhile** to loop forever. Task 1 plays a song over and over, while task 2 runs the outputs in forward and reverse.

Tips

You've already seen a lot of the functionality of *Spirit.ocx* exposed in NQC. Although the syntax in Visual Basic is different, the basic functions are the same. LEGO's official Technical Reference Document (see the "Online Resources") does a good job describing the syntax of *Spirit.ocx* commands; I won't attempt to duplicate that work. Instead, this section contains down-to-earth information on using *Spirit.ocx*.

Retrieving Input and Timer Values

Although the Technical Reference Document makes it clear how to reset timer values and how to configure the RCX's inputs, you may be left wondering how to retrieve the value of an input or timer. The answer is a versatile function called **Poll**. **Poll** can return many values from the RCX, including input values (in several different forms), timer values, variable values, the current status of the RCX's outputs, and the last value received over the IR port.

`Poll` accepts a `Source` and a `Number` that, taken together, describe the value you want to retrieve. The key to understanding `Poll` is the Parameter Table in the Technical Reference Document. This table simply lists out the possible values for `Source` and `Number` and how they are interpreted. For example, a call to `Poll 9, 1` would return the value of input 2. A call to `Poll 0, 11` would return the value of the twelfth variable.

Using Constants

As you might have guessed, symbolic constants in your Visual Basic code can make `Source` and `Number` values a lot easier to read. The Technical Reference Document even includes a set of constant definitions, *RCXDat.bas* (also available online). You can incorporate this file as part of your Visual Basic project, but the constant names are not very descriptive (`SENVAL` and `VAR`, for example).

You can easily define your own constants in the `(Declarations)` section of your code module. For example, you might add the following definitions (the lines beginning with a single quotation mark are comments):

```
' Sources
Public Const VARIABLE = 0
Public Const SENSOR_VALUE = 9
' Sensor names
Public Const SENSOR_1 = 0
Public Const SENSOR_2 = 1
Public Const SENSOR_3 = 2
```

Using these constants, the above `Poll` functions could be rewritten like this:

```
With DummySpiritForm.Spirit1
  ' ...
  Result = .Poll(SENSOR_VALUE, SENSOR_2)
  Result = .Poll(VARIABLE, 11)
  ' ...
End With
```

It's a lot more readable with the symbolic constants. If you ever have to look at the code at some later date, you'll really appreciate knowing what's going on.

Using If and While

The Parameter Table is likewise the key to understanding the `If` and `While` functions. In essence, `If` compares two `Poll` values, each described by a `Source` and a `Number`. In the following example, the `If` statement tests to see if the value of input 3 is less than the constant value 100:

```
If 9, 2, 1, 2, 100
```

The value of input 3 is represented by the first **9, 2**; the constant value 100 is represented by **2, 100**. What's that **1** in the middle? That's the operator that's used for comparison. The available operators are shown in Table 8-1. As you might have guessed, you can define constants to make these easier to understand.

Table 8-1. Operators for If and While

Number	Meaning
0	>
1	<
2	=
3	!= (not equal)

A good set of constants makes the `If` statement a lot easier to read:

```
' Sources
Public Const VARIABLE = 0
Public Const CONSTANT = 2
Public Const SENSOR_VALUE = 9
' Sensor names
Public Const SENSOR_1 = 0
Public Const SENSOR_2 = 1
Public Const SENSOR_3 = 2
' Operators
Public Const GREATER = 0
Public Const LESS = 1
Public Const EQUAL = 2
Public Const NOT_EQUAL = 3

Sub UsingConstants()
  With DummySpiritForm.Spirit1
    .InitComm
    ' ...
    .If SENSOR_VALUE, SENSOR_3, LESS, CONSTANT, 100
      ' Do stuff here.
    .EndIf
    ' ...
    .CloseComm
  End With
End Sub
```

Once you've mastered `If`, the `While` loop is easy. Like `If`, it compares two values using an operator. The body of the `While` (until an `EndWhile`) is executed until the comparison is false. The body of the following loop, for example, would be executed as long as the value of input 3 was less than 100:

```
While SENSOR_VALUE, SENSOR_3, LESS, CONSTANT, 100
  ' Loop body
EndWhile
```

Other Nuggets

Spirit.ocx offers some interesting capabilities that go beyond even NQC. One of these is the ability to turn off the RCX, using `PBTurnOff`. Interestingly, this function can be executed either immediately or inside a program. The following Visual Basic code defines an RCX program that turns itself off:

```
Sub TurnOffProgram()
  With DummySpiritForm.Spirit1
    .InitComm
    .SelectPrgm 2
    .BeginOfTask 0
      .PBTurnOff
    .EndOfTask
    Pause 1
    .CloseComm
  End With
End Sub
```

By itself, of course, it's a pretty silly program. You can imagine how it might be useful, though: shouldn't your robot turn itself off when it's accomplished its mission, to conserve battery power?

You can also use *Spirit.ocx* to query the RCX for the current battery charge. The `PBBattery` function returns the current battery voltage in milliVolts (mV). For fresh batteries, you should get a reading of 9000. The following example shows how you can retrieve and display the current battery power level:

```
Sub ShowBattery()
  With DummySpiritForm.Spirit1
    .InitComm
    battery = .PBBattery()
    .CloseComm
    MsgBox (battery)
  End With
End Sub
```

Retrieving the Datalog

Back in Chapter 4, I described the *datalog*, a special set of data in the RCX that your programs can use. It's easy to create a datalog and add values to it in NQC, but how to you get that data back? Although you can retrieve the datalog using a tool like **nqc** or RCX Command Center, it may not be in exactly the format you'd like. In this section I'll show you how to write a program in Visual Basic to extract the datalog from the RCX. You can modify this program to suit your needs.

The main part of the program is a subroutine, `SaveDatalog`. It opens up communications with the RCX, extracts the datalog values, and writes them into a file of comma-separated values. It's all pretty straightforward, except that the RCX will only upload fifty datalog values at a time. If you have a larger datalog, it must be uploaded in pieces.

The relevant *Spirit.ocx* function is `UploadDatalog`, which takes a starting index and a length. The first (zero-th) item of the datalog contains the length of the datalog. It's the first thing `SaveDatalog` reads:

```
data = .UploadDatalog(0, 1)
length = data(2, 0) - 1
```

The actual data length is one less than the reported length, because the zeroth item is not a data point.

The data returned from `UploadDatalog` is an array. Each datalog item is represented by three numbers. The first two numbers indicate the *source* and *number* of the value; *source* and *number* have exactly the same meaning here as they do for `Poll`. The third number is the actual value stored in the datalog.

`SaveDatalog` writes the source, number, and value for each datalog item out to a text file. Each line of the text file represents one item from the datalog. On each line, the source, number, and value of the item are separated by commas. This example interprets the source of each value, then converts it to a descriptive string before writing it out to the file. The output file will look something like this (depending, of course, on the contents of the datalog):

```
Variable, 1, 2
Timer, 0, 543
Variable, 2, 8
Variable, 8, 368
Sensor value, 1, 33
Watch, 0, 7
```

A plain text file of comma-separated values is usually pretty easy to import into a spreadsheet or statistical analysis program. You can use your robot to gather data, use this example program to upload it to your PC, and then use some other program to analyze or graph the data. Some people have built optical scanners based on RIS using these techniques.

The example is comprised of three parts. The `SaveDatalog` subroutine does most of the work. It uses the `min` function to calculate a minimum and the `getTypeString` function to convert the datalog item source number to a descriptive string:

```
Sub SaveDatalog(filname As String)
    Dim data As Variant
    Dim index, length, stepSize As Integer
    Dim line As String

    With DummySpiritForm.Spirit1
```

```
        ' Open the output file.
        out = FreeFile
        Open filename For Output As #out

        .InitComm
        ' First get item zero, which describes the length of the datalog.
        data = .UploadDatalog(0, 1)
        length = data(2, 0) - 1

        ' Now upload 50 items at a time.
        index = 0
        While (index < length)
            ' Find the smaller of the remaining items or 50.
            stepSize = min(length - index, 50)

            ' Get the data.
            data = .UploadDatalog(index + 1, stepSize)

            ' Write it out to a file.
            For i = 0 To stepSize - 1
                line = getTypeString(data(0, i)) + "," + _
                    Str(data(1, i)) + "," + _
                    Str(data(2, i))
                Print #out, line
            Next i

            index = index + stepSize
        Wend

        .CloseComm

        ' Close the file.
        Close #out
    End With
End Sub
Function min(n1 As Integer, n2 As Integer) As Integer
    If n1 < n2 Then
        min = n1
    Else
        min = n2
    End If
End Function
Function getTypeString(ByVal code As Integer) As String
    getTypeString = Switch( _
        code = 0, "Variable", _
        code = 1, "Timer", _
        code = 2, "Constant", _
        code = 3, "Motor status", _
        code = 4, "Random", _
        code = 8, "Program number", _
        code = 9, "Sensor value", _
        code = 10, "Sensor type", _
        code = 11, "Sensor mode", _
        code = 12, "Sensor raw", _
```

```
        code = 13, "Sensor boolean", _
        code = 14, "Watch", _
        code = 15, "IR message" _
    )
End Function
```

This example, of course, is really just a jumping-off point. You may want to make the following enhancements:

- Integrate `SaveDatalog` into a form to create a user-friendly application.

- Modify the output file format to suit your own needs.

Online Resources

LEGO Programmable Bricks Reference Guide
http://www.legomindstorms.com/sdk/

> This official document from LEGO describes *Spirit.ocx* in detail. Although LEGO calls it a Software Development Kit (SDK), it's not really a big deal. There's a PDF file of the Technical Reference Document, which is 112 pages of reference material describing every function in *Spirit.ocx*. There are also some Visual Basic files that you can download and experiment with, including a file of handy constant definitions.

LEGO on my mind: Roboworld
http://homepages.svc.fcj.hvu.nl/brok/legomind/robo/

> This is the robotics area of Eric Brok's excellent site. There are actually two relevant resources here. The first is an outstanding introduction (the "Spirit programming" link) to using *Spirit.ocx* from Visual Basic. The second resource is "Mind Control," a programming environment that interprets Visual Basic–like programs and can download them to the RCX.

Lego Robotics Course
http://emhain.wit.ie/~p98ac25/

> This tutorial, created as a course handbook at the Waterford Institute of Technology in Ireland, provides a gentle introduction to Visual Basic and programming with *Spirit.ocx*. It's available as a PDF file, either in one big chunk or in separate pieces. The document describes how to work in the Visual Basic environment, how to use VB to talk to the RCX, and even includes several sets of instructions for building robots that you then program with VB.

Bot-Kit
http://www.object-arts.com/Bower/Bot-Kit/Bot-Kit.htm

> Bot-Kit, developed by Andy Bower, is glue that allows you to program your RCX using Smalltalk, a popular object-oriented programming language. To use Bot-Kit, you will need Dolphin Smalltalk, which is a Smalltalk implementation for Windows. Links are provide on the Bot-Kit web site for obtaining Dolphin

Smalltalk, which is available for free. Bot-Kit itself is free, although you'll need to join a related mailing list in order to install the software. As with VB, you can write Smalltalk programs that run on your PC and control the RCX, or you can write Smalltalk programs and download them to the RCX. If you are interested in learning Smalltalk, this would certainly be a fun way to do it. The documentation is excellent.

The BrainStorm Web Page
http://www.netway.com/~rmaynard/

BrainStorm is a version of the Logo programming language adapted to work with MINDSTORMS robots. Developed by Richard Maynard, BrainStorm is a work in progress and currently stands at version 0.1. Richard wrote BrainStorm using Visual C++ to communicate with *Spirit.ocx*. The source code is available.

IGUANO Entertainment Lego Page [BrickCommand]
http://www.geocities.com/Area51/Nebula/8488/lego.html

BrickCommand is a programming environment for MINDSTORMS that is similar to Visual Basic. It opens up the full power of *Spirit.ocx* for your programming pleasure. It includes other goodies like a piano keyboard for playing music on the RCX, an interactive motion controller, and the ability to call single *Spirit.ocx* functions interactively.

BotCode RCX Development System
http://www.desktopmusic.com/botcode.htm

BotCode is another alternative to VB. It opens up the power of *Spirit.ocx* but doesn't have as many extras as BrickCommand. Furthermore, it's shareware ($20US), whereas BrickCommand is entirely free.

LEGO MINDSTORMS: GORDON'S BRICK PROGRAMMER
http://www.umbra.demon.co.uk/gbp.html

Gordon's Brick Programmer is yet another alternative to VB. Like BrickCommand and BotCode, it's a programming environment built on top of *Spirit.ocx*.

9

RoboTag, a Game for Two Robots

RoboTag is a game for two robots. The robots drive around in a simple arena; the edge of the arena is marked by a black line. When one robot bumps into the other robot, it shouts "Tag!" by sending a message out its IR port. The tagged robot must sit still for a while, and then the game continues.

The two robots are identical. Each has two motor-driven treads. Each robot has a bumper on its front and a downward pointing light sensor. The light sensor is used to detect the edge of the playing arena. When the light sensor "sees" the edge, the robot backs up and turns to stay inside the arena.

When the bumper is triggered, the robot assumes it bumped into the other robot and shouts "Tag!" It waits for an acknowledgement from the other robot (in the form of another IR message). If the acknowledgment is received, the robot adds one to its current score.

When one of the robots receives the "Tag!" message from the other robot, it is obliged to send an acknowledgement and then sit still for a short time. Then it starts up again, wandering around to tag the other robot.

RoboTag is the creation of Matthew Miller, who teamed up with a friend, Paul Stauffer, to build and program the first RoboTag contestants. In this chapter, I'll use RoboTag as a way to explain *subsumption architecture*, an important paradigm in robotics programming.

Building Instructions

STEP 1

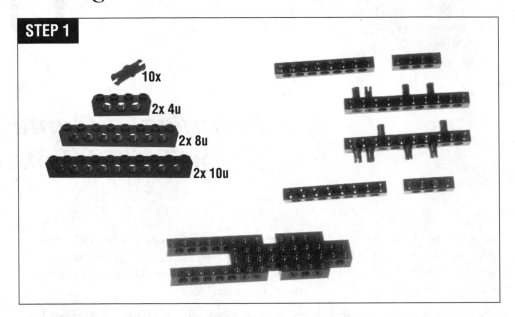

STEP 2

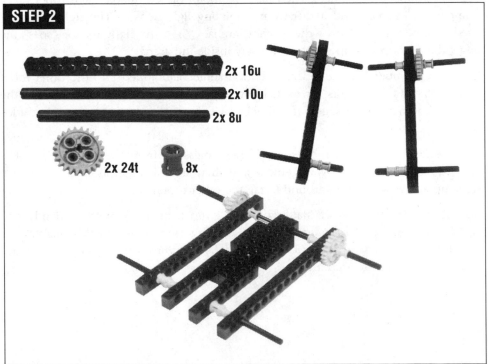

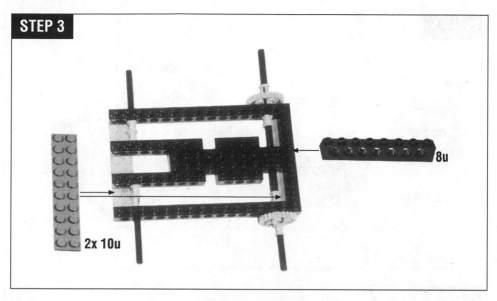

The 16t gears are nestled inside the tread wheels.

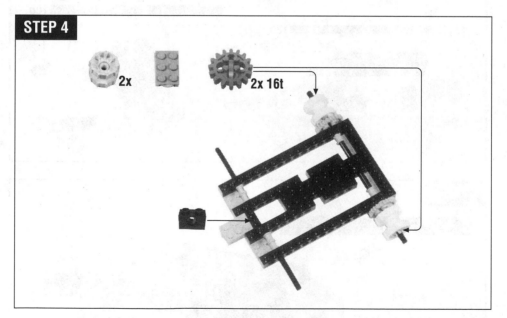

STEP 5

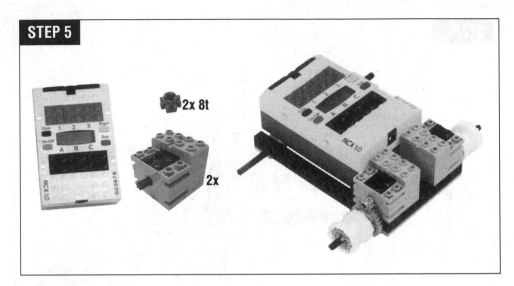

STEP 6

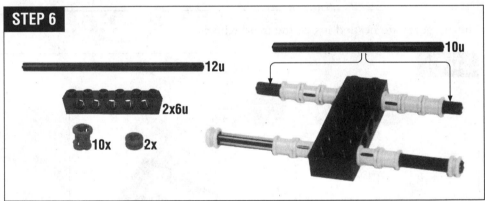

STEP 7

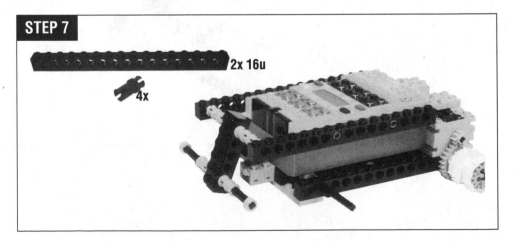

STEP 8

4x 6u

6x 2x

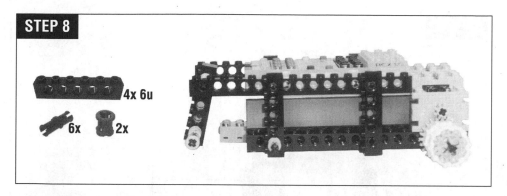

STEP 9

(yellow) 2x

6u

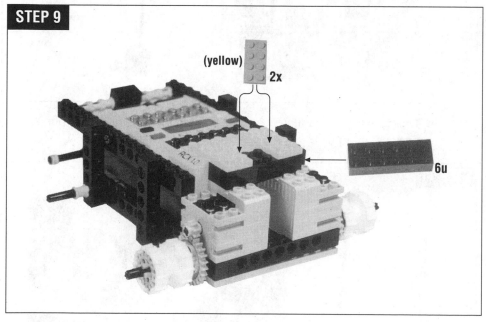

Attach the motors to output A and output C as shown.

STEP 10

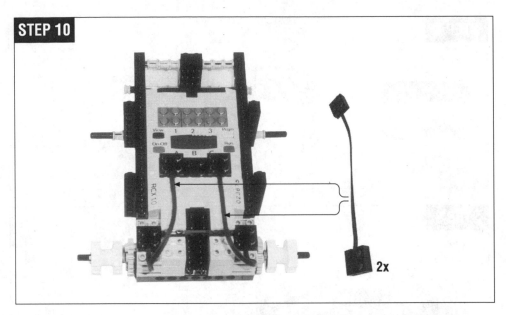

The light sensor, which is mounted on the bumper, is attached to input 2. The touch sensor goes on input 1.

STEP 11

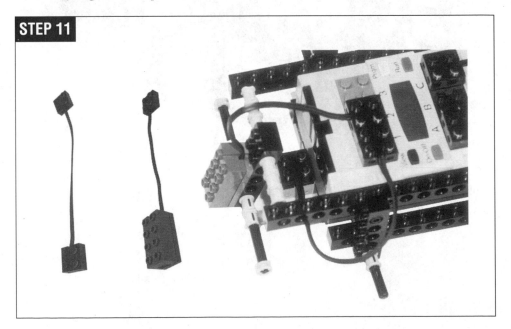

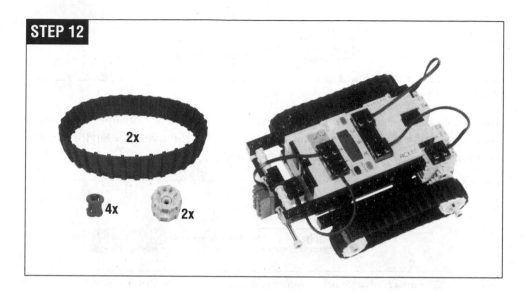

Subsumption Architecture

The traditional approach to robot programming has been to emulate human thought processes. First, the robot processes its sensor data. Based on the sensor data, the robot constructs or updates a model of the world. Then it decides how to act. This deliberative approach is very complicated; it requires heavy-duty processing power and may not work properly anyway.

Overview

Subsumption architecture is a radically different paradigm for robot programming developed by Rodney Brooks at MIT in the late 1980s. In this reactive approach, several robot behaviors run at the same time. Input from sensors is used to determine which behavior controls the robot at any given time. Depending on the sensor values, higher-level behaviors completely take over control of the robot, *subsuming* (replacing) lower-level behaviors. As you'll see, subsumption architecture is simple enough to be implemented on inexpensive hardware, including the RCX.

A basic example will clarify the concept. Imagine a robot that has a bumper (a touch sensor) on its front. When the robot bumps into something, it should back up and turn around. With subsumption architecture, the robot will use two behaviors. The first behavior is `cruise` and simply moves the robot forward. Figure 9-1 shows a diagram of this behavior. It controls the motors to make the robot move forward.

To avoid obstacles, the robot needs another behavior, `avoid`. This behavior will become active when it detects a bump on the touch sensor. It will completely take

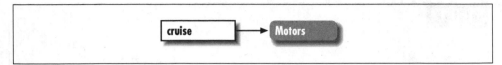

Figure 9-1. Cruise, a simple robot behavior

over control of the robot. Figure 9-2 shows a diagram with both the `cruise` and `avoid` behaviors. The circle with an "S" indicates that the `avoid` behavior can take control of the motors from the `cruise` behavior.

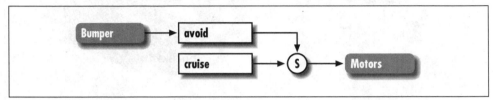

Figure 9-2. The avoid behavior takes control of the robot when the bumper is pressed

There won't always be a one-to-one relationship between inputs and behaviors. It's entirely possible that one behavior will be triggered by some combination of inputs. Likewise, a single input might trigger multiple behaviors, depending on the input's value.

Implementation

It's fairly easy to implement subsumption architecture on a system that includes preemptive multitasking. As you'll recall, the RCX's default firmware supports this feature. Our implementation of subsumption architecture is written in NQC.

The basic idea is that each behavior is a separate task. The behaviors all run simultaneously, trying to control the robot according to their own rules. One additional task decides which behavior is in charge and then sends its commands to the motors.

RoboTag behaviors

The robots in RoboTag actually need four different behaviors, shown in Figure 9-3. The basic `cruise` behavior is the same as before—it moves the robot forward. If one robot collides with the other robot, the bumper is pressed. This causes the `tag` behavior to take control of the robot. If the robot drives over the edge of the . playing field, the reading from the light sensor causes the `avoid` behavior to assert itself. Finally, the top level behavior is `tagged`. This behavior is triggered if the robot has been tagged by the other robot.

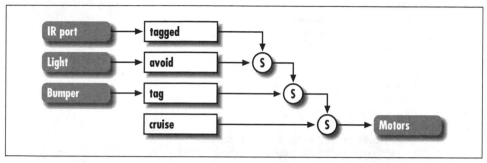

Figure 9-3. RoboTag behaviors

I'll start by examining the NQC code for each behavior. Then I'll talk about how a behavior is selected and how the motors are controlled. In the next section, I'll present the entire source code for RoboTag.

The `cruise` behavior is simple:

```
int cruiseCommand;

task cruise() {
  cruiseCommand = COMMAND_FORWARD;
  while (true) Wait(100);
}
```

`cruise` sets the `cruiseCommand` variable to the value `COMMAND_FORWARD` and then loops forever.* Each behavior (task) has an associated command variable that holds the desired motor output. `cruise`, for example, uses the `cruiseCommand` variable to hold the desired motor output. In this simple case, `cruise` always wants the robot to move forward. Later on, I'll show you how this variable is used to determine what actually happens to the robot.

The next behavior is `tag`. Like `cruise`, `tag` has its own motor output variable, `tagCommand`:

```
int tagCommand;

task tag() {
  while(true) {
    if (BUMP_SENSOR == 1) {
      // Say tag!
      SendMessage(MESSAGE_TAG);
      // Coast to a stop.
      tagCommand = COMMAND_FLOAT;
      Wait(20);
      // Check to see if we got an acknowledgement.
      if (Message() == MESSAGE_ACKNOWLEDGE) {
```

---

* The endless loop isn't strictly necessary, but it makes `cruise` look more like the other behaviors.

```
        PlaySound(3);
        SetPower(OUT_B, score);
        On(OUT_B);
        if (score < 7) score = score + 1;
    }
    else PlaySound(2);
    ClearMessage();
    // Back up.
    tagCommand = COMMAND_REVERSE;
    Wait(50);
    // Turn left or right for a random duration.
    if (Random(1) == 0) tagCommand = COMMAND_LEFT;
    else tagCommand = COMMAND_RIGHT;
    Wait(Random(200));
    tagCommand = COMMAND_NONE;
    }
    else tagCommand = COMMAND_NONE;
  }
}
```

tag acts only if the bumper is pressed. Otherwise, it sets tagCommand to a special value, COMMAND_NONE, which indicates that tag is not interested in controlling the robot.

When the bumper is pressed, tag sends out an IR message, using Send-Message(), to the other robot. Then it waits for a reply by repeatedly calling Message(). The robot also backs up and turns to the left or right to move around the robot it has just tagged. This movement is accomplished by setting the tagCommand variable.

If tag receives an acknowledgement from the other robot, it adds one to its score. There's a bit of a hack here to keep score. The power setting of output B is used to contain the robot's current score. The initialization code for RoboTag (presented later) tells the RCX to view the output B setting:

```
SelectDisplay(5);
```

All tag does is set the power of output B to show the current score on the display:

```
SetPower(OUT_B, score);
On(OUT_B);
if (score < 7) score = score + 1;
```

Of course, the counter runs from only 1 to 7, so the maximum score is 7.

If tag sends out a tag message but doesn't receive a reply, it doesn't do anything. The lack of a reply can mean two things: either the other robot did not receive the IR tag message, or the robot bumped into an obstacle, not the other robot. In the original RoboTag by Matthew Miller, the arena contained no obstacles, so it was safe to assume that the other robot didn't "hear" the tag message. The tagging robot would then spin in place shouting "Tag!" repeatedly, hoping to get in range of the other robot's IR port.

In our design, `tag` doesn't do anything if a reply is not received. This opens up the possibility of adding physical obstacles to the arena. If the robot bounces into something that doesn't respond to the tag message, it must be an obstacle.

The next behavior is `avoid`, which helps the robot to avoid the edge of the playing arena. It is triggered by the light sensor. This behavior backs up and turns to move away from the edge, much like `tag`.

```
int avoidCommand;

task avoid() {
  while(true) {
    if (LIGHT_SENSOR < averageLight - 3) {
      // Back away from the border.
      avoidCommand = COMMAND_FLOAT;
      Wait(20);
      avoidCommand = COMMAND_REVERSE;
      Wait(50);
      // Turn left or right for a random duration.
      if (Random(1) == 0) avoidCommand = COMMAND_LEFT;
      else avoidCommand = COMMAND_RIGHT;
      Wait(Random(200));
      avoidCommand = COMMAND_NONE;
    }
  }
}
```

The highest-level behavior is `tagged`, which is triggered when the IR port receives notification that the robot has been tagged. This behavior tells the robot to send an IR acknowledgement, play a sad sound, and sit still for eight seconds.

```
int taggedCommand;

task tagged() {
  while(true) {
    if (Message() == MESSAGE_TAG) {
      taggedCommand = COMMAND_STOP;
      SendMessage(MESSAGE_ACKNOWLEDGE);
      PlaySound(4);
      Wait(800);
      ClearMessage();
      taggedCommand = COMMAND_NONE;
    }
  }
}
```

Arbitration

As mentioned earlier, an additional task is needed to link the robot's behaviors to its motors. In this implementation, a task called `arbitrate` examines the output command variable of each behavior. If it is not `COMMAND_NONE`, it is used to set the current motor command.

```
int motorCommand;

task arbitrate() {
  while(true) {
    if (cruiseCommand != COMMAND_NONE) motorCommand = cruiseCommand;
    if (tagCommand != COMMAND_NONE) motorCommand = tagCommand;
    if (avoidCommand != COMMAND_NONE) motorCommand = avoidCommand;
    if (taggedCommand != COMMAND_NONE) motorCommand = taggedCommand;
    motorControl();
  }
}
```

Note that the order is important. The commands in the end of the list will over-write the value of `motorCommand` and are thus higher-level behaviors. For example, if both the `cruise` and `tagged` behaviors are attempting to control the robot, the `tagged` behavior takes precedence by subsuming the lower-level behavior, `cruise`.

In this implementation, if no behavior asserts control, then `motorCommand` will be unchanged, and the robot will just continue doing whatever it did before. This isn't an issue, since `cruiseCommand` is always `COMMAND_FORWARD`. However, in a different program, you might want to set `motorCommand` to a default action at the beginning of the `while` loop in `arbitrate()`.

Where the rubber meets the road

The `arbitrate` task hands off the actual dirty work of controlling the motors to a subroutine called `motorControl()`. All `motorControl()` has to do is examine the value of `motorCommand` and set the motors accordingly. Here it is:

```
sub motorControl() {
  if (motorCommand == COMMAND_FORWARD)
    OnFwd(OUT_A + OUT_C);
  else if (motorCommand == COMMAND_REVERSE)
    OnRev(OUT_A + OUT_C);
  else if (motorCommand == COMMAND_LEFT) {
    OnRev(OUT_A);
    OnFwd(OUT_C);
  }
  else if (motorCommand == COMMAND_RIGHT) {
    OnFwd(OUT_A);
    OnRev(OUT_C);
  }
  else if (motorCommand == COMMAND_STOP)
    Off(OUT_A + OUT_C);
  else if (motorCommand == COMMAND_FLOAT)
    Float(OUT_A + OUT_C);
}
```

The relationship between `arbitrate` and `motorControl` is important. At first glance, you might think it makes sense to implement `motorControl` as a separate task. However, if you do this, the robot "jiggles" badly. The problem is that `arbitrate` changes the value of `motorCommand` several times each time it loops. As the value changes, `motorControl` responds by changing the motors' directions.

We're really interested only in the value of `motorCommand` at the end of each loop in `arbitrate`. Therefore, `motorControl` is implemented as a subroutine and is called once each time at the end of the `arbitrate` loop.

The RoboTag Program

Once you get through the details of implementing subsumption architecture, the rest of the programming is pretty simple. The RoboTag program uses its `main` task to start up all the behavior tasks and, of course, `arbitrate`. It also uses the light sensor initialization code from Minerva (see Chapter 5, *Minerva, a Robot with an Arm*) to calculate a baseline value for the light sensor. When the light sensor reads lower than the average, the RoboTag robot can assume it's reached the edge of the arena.

Here is the entire code for RoboTag. You should download this program to both of the robots that will be playing.

```
// Motor commands.
#define COMMAND_NONE -1
#define COMMAND_FORWARD 1
#define COMMAND_REVERSE 2
#define COMMAND_LEFT 3
#define COMMAND_RIGHT 4
#define COMMAND_STOP 5
#define COMMAND_FLOAT 6

// IR messages.
#define MESSAGE_TAG 33
#define MESSAGE_ACKNOWLEDGE 6

#define BUMP_SENSOR SENSOR_1
#define LIGHT_SENSOR SENSOR_2

int score;
int averageLight;

int cruiseCommand;

task cruise() {
  cruiseCommand = COMMAND_FORWARD;
  while (true) Wait(100);
}

int tagCommand;

task tag() {
```

```
    while(true) {
      if (BUMP_SENSOR == 1) {
        // Say tag!
        SendMessage(MESSAGE_TAG);
        // Coast to a stop.
        tagCommand = COMMAND_FLOAT;
        Wait(20);
        // Check to see if we got an acknowledgement.
        if (Message() == MESSAGE_ACKNOWLEDGE) {
          PlaySound(3);
          SetPower(OUT_B, score);
          On(OUT_B);
          if (score < 7) score = score + 1;
        }
        else PlaySound(2);
        ClearMessage();
        // Back up.
        tagCommand = COMMAND_REVERSE;
        Wait(50);
        // Turn left or right for a random duration.
        if (Random(1) == 0) tagCommand = COMMAND_LEFT;
        else tagCommand = COMMAND_RIGHT;
        Wait(Random(200));
        tagCommand = COMMAND_NONE;
      }
      else tagCommand = COMMAND_NONE;
    }
}

int avoidCommand;

task avoid() {
  while(true) {
    if (LIGHT_SENSOR < averageLight - 3) {
      // Back away from the border.
      avoidCommand = COMMAND_FLOAT;
      Wait(20);
      avoidCommand = COMMAND_REVERSE;
      Wait(50);
      // Turn left or right for a random duration.
      if (Random(1) == 0) avoidCommand = COMMAND_LEFT;
      else avoidCommand = COMMAND_RIGHT;
      Wait(Random(200));
      avoidCommand = COMMAND_NONE;
    }
  }
}

int taggedCommand;

task tagged() {
  while(true) {
    if (Message() == MESSAGE_TAG) {
      taggedCommand = COMMAND_STOP;
```

```
            SendMessage(MESSAGE_ACKNOWLEDGE);
            PlaySound(4);
            Wait(800);
            ClearMessage();
            taggedCommand = COMMAND_NONE;
        }
    }
}

int motorCommand;

task arbitrate() {
  while(true) {
    if (cruiseCommand != COMMAND_NONE) motorCommand = cruiseCommand;
    if (tagCommand != COMMAND_NONE) motorCommand = tagCommand;
    if (avoidCommand != COMMAND_NONE) motorCommand = avoidCommand;
    if (taggedCommand != COMMAND_NONE) motorCommand = taggedCommand;
    motorControl();
  }
}

sub motorControl() {
  if (motorCommand == COMMAND_FORWARD)
    OnFwd(OUT_A + OUT_C);
  else if (motorCommand == COMMAND_REVERSE)
    OnRev(OUT_A + OUT_C);
  else if (motorCommand == COMMAND_LEFT) {
    OnRev(OUT_A);
    OnFwd(OUT_C);
  }
  else if (motorCommand == COMMAND_RIGHT) {
    OnFwd(OUT_A);
    OnRev(OUT_C);
  }
  else if (motorCommand == COMMAND_STOP)
    Off(OUT_A + OUT_C);
  else if (motorCommand == COMMAND_FLOAT)
    Float(OUT_A + OUT_C);
}

task main() {
  initialize();

  cruiseCommand = COMMAND_NONE;
  tagCommand = COMMAND_NONE;
  avoidCommand = COMMAND_NONE;
  taggedCommand = COMMAND_NONE;

  start cruise;
  start tag;
  start avoid;
  start tagged;

  start arbitrate;
}
```

```
sub initialize() {
  SetSensor(BUMP_SENSOR, SENSOR_TOUCH);
  SetSensor(LIGHT_SENSOR, SENSOR_LIGHT);
  ClearMessage();
  score = 0;
  Fwd(OUT_B);
  SelectDisplay(5);
  calibrateLightSensor();
}

#define NUMBER_OF_SAMPLES 10
int i;
int runningTotal;

void calibrateLightSensor() {
  // Take an average light reading.
  i = 0;
  runningTotal = 0;
  while (i < NUMBER_OF_SAMPLES) {
    runningTotal += LIGHT_SENSOR;
    Wait(10);
    i += 1;
  }
  averageLight = runningTotal / NUMBER_OF_SAMPLES;
}
```

Online Resources

mattdm's Mindstorms stuff
http://www.mattdm.org/mindstorms/

This is the original RoboTag web page, created by Matthew Miller. It contains the original source code and a couple of movies of RoboTag in action.

Brooks' Subsumption Architecture
http://ai.eecs.umich.edu/cogarch3/Brooks/Brooks.html

This page has some background on subsumption architecture. If you really want to learn more, however, you should look up Brooks' papers; they're an excellent read.

10

legOS

legOS is the most powerful development tool available for the RCX.[*] If programming environments were cars, RCX Code would be a plastic tricycle, NQC would be a comfortable sport/utility vehicle, and pbFORTH would probably be an eco-conscious alcohol-burning car with a Grateful Dead bumper sticker. legOS would be a fire-breathing, smoke-snorting monster truck with a roaring engine and no muffler. legOS offers you the ability to program your RCX in assembly language, C, or C++. If you've been wanting to implement a neural network on your RCX, here's your chance. With legOS, you have direct control of the inputs and outputs, display, IR port, and memory of the RCX. There's a lot of power here.

The flip side, of course, is that legOS is harder to use than any of the other programming environments. Unless you're already running Linux and using GNU development tools, you'll have to spend some time configuring your system to support legOS development.

In this chapter, I'll talk about what software you need to develop legOS programs and what alternatives are available. I'll describe the legOS services and present some sample code. I won't attempt to describe C, which is well-documented in other publications. If you don't already know C, you might want to work your way through a tutorial before reading this chapter.

About legOS

legOS is replacement firmware that completely replaces the default RCX firmware that LEGO gives you. Like pbFORTH, it offers full control of the RCX. If you're already familiar with C, you may be more comfortable running legOS than pbFORTH.

---

[*] For updated information on legOS, please see *http://www.oreilly.com/catalog/lmstorms/*.

legOS is more of a library than an OS, in some ways. The programs you write are compiled with the legOS source code to produce a firmware. To run your program you need to download the whole thing to the RCX. This makes for a clumsy development cycle: even though you're only changing your own code, you need to recompile with legOS and download the whole firmware each time. pbFORTH, by contrast, is an interpreter. You only have to download it once to the RCX; after that, you can program it using a terminal emulator.

As time passes, someone will probably write a rudimentary set of tools so that you can leave legOS on the RCX and download new user programs to it. For now, though, no such facility exists.

Figure 10-1 shows the architecture of legOS. On the PC side, some kind of cross compiler compiles your code with the legOS code to produce a firmware. To get your program on the RCX, you need to use a firmware downloader tool, like nqc or firmdl. Once downloaded, the firmware lives in the RAM of the RCX, running whatever program you have created.

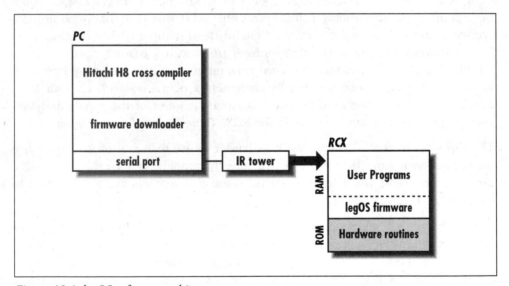

Figure 10-1. legOS software architecture

Development Tools

You'll need some heavy-duty tools to work with legOS. (There is another possibility, as described in the sidebar, "An Innovative Alternative.") The good news is that the tools are free. The basic tool you need is a cross compiler, a tool that runs on one platform but produces executable files for another. In this case, you want a cross compiler that runs on your PC and produces firmware for the RCX.

legOS is built using **egcs**, the open-source successor to the GNU **gcc** compiler. To build legOS, you'll also need GNU's **binutils** package. These tools are present on most Linux systems, but they must be reconfigured to support cross-compilation for the RCX. I'll explain this process soon.

If you're not running Linux, don't despair. On a Unix-like operating system, you can probably build **egcs** and **binutils** yourself, or find someone who has binaries for your platform. See the "Online Resources" section later in this chapter for information on obtaining **egcs** and **binutils**.

Cygwin

What if you're not running Linux or a Unix-like operating system? If you have Windows instead, there is a way to make Windows act like Linux. The Cygwin package from Cygnus Solutions is a port of many GNU tools to Windows 95, 98, and NT. Like lots of GNU stuff, it's a little bulky. A full download is about 13 MB, compressed. If you're a Linux enthusiast trapped in a Microsoft world, though, you'll definitely want to check this out. (The "Online Resources" section has more information on obtaining Cygwin.)

Setting Up egcs

To compile legOS, you're going to need to configure **egcs** as a cross compiler for the RCX. There are two ways to do this:

1. You can recompile **egcs** itself to make it into a cross compiler.
2. You can download someone else's binary version of the **egcs** cross compiler.

Obviously, the second option is a lot easier, if you can find somebody who's created the cross compiler for your particular platform. The "Online Resources" section at the end of this chapter lists web sites that contain instructions for recompiling **egcs** as well as the locations of popular binaries of the cross compiler.

Oh, and Perl Too

Part of compiling legOS involves running some Perl. You'll need to have Perl installed on your computer to make legOS programs. As before, Linux users probably have Perl lying around already. If you've installed Cygwin on your Windows machine, you'll need to go get Perl. See "Online Resources" for more information.

Downloading Firmware

Once you have successfully compiled something in legOS, you will need to download it to your RCX to run it. To do this, you need a small utility that's called a *firmware downloader.* This piece of software uses the IR tower to transfer firmware to your RCX.

Two firmware downloaders are readily available. Dave Baum's `nqc`, described in Chapter 4, *Not Quite C,* is capable of downloading firmware files to the RCX, using the `-firmware` option. Another option is Kekoa Proudfoot's `firmdl`, which is available as a C source file.

An Innovative Alternative

If the complexity of setting up tools for legOS is making you sad, there's a creative solution. Two kind individuals have set up web-based legOS compilers. All you do is submit your source code. Across the Internet, a machine compiles the code and sends you the result, which you can then download to your RCX. This completely sidesteps the whole problem of obtaining a cross compiler. This solution is useful even for platforms that don't support the GNU tools. As long as you have a web browser, you can compile legOS programs.

The web-based cross compilers are here:

> *http://www.dwarfrune.com/web-legOS.html*

> *https://vheissu.mersenne.com/~dhm/compile-legOS.html*

There are some downsides to this approach, as well:

1. You have to fit your program into a single source file.

2. You have to depend on someone else to keep the compiler running.

3. You can't apply patches and tweak other things yourself.

Hello, legOS

Let's begin with something simple. This will allow you to verify that your tools are working and give you a first taste of programming with legOS. The following program displays "Hello" on the RCX's display briefly:

```
#include "conio.h"

int main(void) {
  cputs("Hello");
  lcd_refresh();
  delay(1000);
  return 0;
}
```

To run this example, first compile it. If you have the cross compiler installed locally, you just need to edit the legOS *Makefile* so that the TARGET line points to your source code.* For example, if you saved the source code above in a file called */projects/HellolegOS.c*, you would edit the *Makefile*'s `TARGET` line like this:

```
TARGET=/projects/HellolegOS
```

Then type **make** at the command line. If everything is installed correctly, you'll end up with a *HellolegOS.srec* file in the same directory as the source file.

Trouble with Make

If you can't make *HellolegOS.c,* and you're starting to curse at your computer, take a deep breath. legOS has a strong online community; people will help if you ask. The "Online Resources" section of this chapter has pointers to helpful sites. One of the best things you can do is look at LUGNET, *http://www.lugnet.com/*, and search through the discussion group archives for the particular problem you're having. There are at least as many messages about configuring the legOS development tools as there are about actually programming in legOS.

If you're using one of the online compilers, just copy the source into the web page and press the compile button. If there are no errors, you will get back an *.srec* file representing your compiled legOS program.

Regardless of how the source file is compiled, you will then need to download the *.srec* file to the RCX, using either **nqc** or **firmdl**.

When the download is complete, your RCX will display the string "legOS" to indicate that legOS is running. To actually run the program you just wrote, press the **Run** button. The display will show "Hello" for a second or so, then show two zeros. The left number shows the result returned from our **main()** function. Control has now returned to legOS; you can use the **On-Off** button to switch the RCX off and on. When the RCX is on, you can press **Run** again to see the "Hello" message again. Show your friends and family; they will be awed and inspired.

Function Reference

Once you've seen one RCX development environment, you've seen them all—to some degree, at least. If you've been reading through this book in order, you've probably noticed that NQC and pbFORTH have similar commands but different syntax. Likewise, legOS has a set of functions that looks a lot like pbFORTH and

---

* Make sure you've edited *Makefile.common*. The TOOLPREFIX and LEGOS_ROOT lines should point to the appropriate directories on your system, as described in the comments. Make sure you put a trailing slash on the LEGOS_ROOT directory.

NQC, but the syntax and usage is slightly different. In this section, I'll describe the important functions of legOS and demonstrate how they are used.

There are, of course, different levels at which you can use legOS. I'll describe the "user-level" functions, meaning the functions you can call without knowing much about what's inside legOS. If you're looking for even more power, the full source code of legOS is freely available; you can read it, debug it, or reprogram it as much as you'd like.*

Using the Display

legOS is surprisingly capable when it comes to managing the display on the RCX. Aside from just displaying numbers, you can ask legOS to approximate a text string using the display, as we did in the *HellolegOS.c* example.

Numbers and symbols (rom/lcd.h)

Most of the useful display functions are defined in *rom/lcd.h*. The first function you should learn is `lcd_refresh()`:

void lcd_refresh(void)
> This is the function that makes it all happen. After you call any other display function, you must call `lcd_refresh()` to actually update the display.

To display a number, use `lcd_number()`:

void lcd_number(int i, lcd_number_style n, lcd_comma_style c)
> Use this function to show a number, `i`, on the display. The number style is one of `sign`, `unsign` or `digit`. Signed and unsigned numbers are shown in the main display area, while `digit` shows a single digit on the right side of the display. The comma style is `digit_comma` (for use with the `digit` number style), `e0`, `e_1`, `e_2` or `e_3`, indicating the number of digits to the right of the decimal point.

In many cases, you won't need to call `lcd_number()` directly; *rom/lcd.h* includes definitions for four macros that simplify the process of displaying numbers:

lcd_int(i)
> Use this macro to display a signed integer. Values over 9999 are shown as 9999.

lcd_unsigned(u)
> This macro displays an unsigned value. Leading digits are padded with zero if necessary—for example, 123 is shown 0123.

---

* The source code is subject to the Mozilla Public License (MPL), which is fully described at the following URL: *http://www.mozilla.org/MPL/.*

lcd_clock(t)

> This macro simulates showing a digital clock on the display. The supplied number is shown as a time, with the decimal point between the first two and last two digits.

lcd_digit(d)

> Use this macro to display a single digit on the right side of the display.

The RCX's display contains many symbols, as well—indicators for the outputs, inputs, datalog, battery level, download status, and others. Each display segment can be controlled individually:

void lcd_show(lcd_segment segment)

> Show a single display segment with this function. The `lcd_segment` enumeration is defined in *rom/lcd.h*; the comments in that file describe each segment type. To show the low battery indicator, for example, you would do this:

```
lcd_show(battery_x);
lcd_refresh();
```

void lcd_hide(lcd_segment segment)

> This function hides a specific display segment.

Finally, to clean up when you're done playing, use `lcd_clear()`:

void lcd_clear(void)

> This function clears the entire display. (You still have to call `lcd_refresh()` afterwards.)

As your program is running, legOS will try to animate the running man. Keep this in mind as it may modify your display unexpectedly.

Text, kind of (conio.h)

The *conio.h* file defines several functions that are handy for displaying text on the RCX:

*void cputs(char *s)*

> This function displays the supplied string, as nearly as possible. Only the first five characters of the string are shown. Letters like "w" and "m" don't come out very well, but overall this is a great function for debugging.

void cputc(char c, int pos)

> Use this method to display a character at the given position. Valid positions are 0 through 4, where 0 is the right-most position (the single digit at the right of the display) and 4 is the left-most position.

void cputw(unsigned word)

> This function displays the supplied value as four hexadecimal digits.

Controlling Outputs (direct-motor.h)

Controlling the outputs with legOS is very easy. All you need to do is give the output a direction and a speed.

void motor_a_dir(MotorDirection dir)
void motor_b_dir(MotorDirection dir)
void motor_c_dir(MotorDirection dir)

> These functions set the direction of the RCX's outputs. The `dir` value can be `fwd`, `rev`, `brake`, and `off`. The `off` mode is the same as `Float()` in NQC.*

void motor_a_speed(unsigned char speed)
void motor_b_speed(unsigned char speed)
void motor_c_speed(unsigned char speed)

> These functions set the speed for the outputs. Of course, the speed only really matters when the output direction is `fwd` or `rev`. Values range from 0 to 255. You can use the handy constants `MIN_SPEED` and `MAX_SPEED` if you wish.

To set outputs A and C running forward at top speed, do this:

```
motor_a_dir(fwd);
motor_c_dir(fwd);
motor_a_speed(MAX_SPEED);
motor_c_speed(MAX_SPEED);
```

Working with Inputs (direct-sensor.h)

In legOS, support for inputs is rudimentary. Remember all that nice input value processing in NQC and pbFORTH? In legOS, you have to deal with the raw input values, except for light and rotation sensors. The following macros return the raw value of the inputs:

SENSOR_1
SENSOR_2
SENSOR_3
BATTERY

> Use these macros to retrieve the raw value of the corresponding input. `BATTERY` returns an indication of the battery level. The raw values are in the range from 0x0000 to 0xffff.

Don't expect sensors to use the full range of raw input values. You might think a touch sensor would produce a value of 0x0000 when it's pressed and 0xffff when it's not pressed, but the actual values are not as extreme. The rule of thumb for testing touch sensors is to test if the value falls below 0xF000, like this:

---

* If you're accustomed to working with NQC, don't get confused here: `off` in legOS is the same as `Float()` in NQC, while `brake` in legOS is the same as `Off()` in NQC.

```
if (SENSOR_1 < 0xf000) {
  // Touch sensor is pressed.
}
```

If you're working with light or rotation sensors, legOS does offer some help. First, you can set inputs to be active or passive:

void ds_active(unsigned* const sensor)
void ds_passive(unsigned* const sensor)

> Use these functions to set the specified sensor to active or passive mode. The light and rotation sensors are active sensors; the touch and temperature sensors are passive.

The argument to these functions is the address of one of the sensor values. For example, to set input 2 to be active, you would do this:

```
ds_active(&SENSOR_2);
```

Processed light sensor values can be retrieved with the following macros:

LIGHT_1
LIGHT_2
LIGHT_3

> These macros process raw input values to produce a light sensor reading in the range from 0 to approximately `LIGHT_MAX`.

legOS also supports rotation sensors with the following functions:

void ds_rotation_on(unsigned* const sensor)
void ds_rotation_off(unsigned* const sensor)

> These functions turn on or off rotation counting for the specified input.

void ds_rotation_set(unsigned* const sensor, int pos)

> This function sets the current rotation count of the given input.

Once you get the input set up for rotation, you can retrieve the rotation value with one of the following macros:

ROTATION_1
ROTATION_2
ROTATION_3

> These macros return the rotation count for each of the inputs.

Setting up input 3 for a rotation sensor, then, looks something like this:

```
ds_active(&SENSOR_3);
ds_rotation_on(&SENSOR_3);
ds_rotation_set(&SENSOR_3, 0);
```

To actually read the rotation value, you would just use the `ROTATION_3` macro.

The rotation sensor code does not work in the March 30, 1999 build of legOS 0.1.7.

Using the Buttons (direct-button.h)

legOS provides one function and some other handy definitions to describe the state of the front panel buttons:

int button_state(void)

This function returns a value that indicates the state of the RCX's four buttons. Use the following macros to interpret the returned value.

PRESSED(state, button)
RELEASED(state, button)

These macros return a boolean value indicating if the specified button was pressed or not. To use these macros, pass the result of `button_state()` as the `state` parameter and the name of a button for `button`. Buttons names are `BUTTON_ONOFF`, `BUTTON_RUN`, `BUTTON_VIEW`, and `BUTTON_PROGRAM`.

For example, the following code tests the state of the **View** button:

```
if (PRESSED(button_state(), BUTTON_VIEW)) {
  // View button is pressed.
}
```

To test the state of more than one button, it makes sense to store the result of `button_state()`, like this:

```
int state;
state = button_state();
if (PRESSED(state, BUTTON_VIEW)) {
  // View button is pressed.
}
if (PRESSED(state, BUTTON_PROGRAM)) {
  // Program button is pressed.
}
```

The Infrared Port (direct-ir.h)

To send data out the IR port, just use the `dir_write()` function:

size_t dir_write(void const buf, size_t len)*

This function writes `len` bytes of data from the supplied buffer out the IR port. It returns the number of bytes written or –1 if there is an error.

s not work in the March 30, 1999

eci()), and

g data from the IR port:

functions:

f data into the supplied buffer. It returns the
ere is an error.

(ms).

o" and

to be

s, and

iich means incoming data is placed in a buffer.
available to dir_read(). To force the contents of
able to dir_read(), first call dir_fflush().

n-and-ir.c. This program listens for incoming IR data
splay. You can type into a terminal emulator on your
p on the display.

OS (unistd.h and sys/tm.h)

rted in legOS through a reduced version of the standard
idea is to set up some number of tasks using the execi()
manager itself must be started with a call to tm_start().

_start)(int, char**), int argc, char **argv,
ze_t stack_size)

arts the task described by code_start. Don't worry about the
syntax above; all you have to do is pass the name of a function.
information to the task using the argc and argv parameters. The
the given priority and stack size. Lower priorities take precedence
priorities. In general, you can pass 0 for the priority and DEFAULT_
E as the stack size. This function returns a process identification
ID). You can stop a task, as you'll see later, using this number.

If the stack size you pass to execi() is too small, all sorts of weird
behavior results. If your program crashes, this is one of the first
things you should check. Remember, a function's return addresses
and automatic variables (declared in the scope of the function) are
stored on the stack. If you have many levels of function calls, or
many automatic variables, or large arrays as automatic variables, you
may overrun your stack.

void tm_start(void)

Use this function to start up the task manager.

Once the task manager is running, new tasks can be started (with **ex**
running tasks can be stopped with this function:

void kill(pid_t pid)

Use this function to stop the task represented by pid.

You can suspend tasks for a given amount of time with the following two

unsigned int sleep(unsigned int sec)

This function suspends execution for the given number of seconds.

unsigned int msleep(unsigned int msec)

This function suspends execution for the given number of milliseconds

Here is a simple example that uses two tasks. The first task shows "Hel
"nurse" on the display. The second task just waits for the **Run** button
pressed. When it is pressed, the first task is stopped, the second task end
control returns to legOS.

```
#include "conio.h"
#include "direct-button.h"
#include "unistd.h"
#include "sys/tm.h"

pid_t pid;

int display_task(int argc, char **argv) {
  while(1) {
    cputs("Hello");
    lcd_refresh();
    sleep(1);
    cputs("nurse");
    lcd_refresh();
    sleep(1);
  }
  return 0;
}

int stop_task(int argc, char **argv) {
  msleep(200);
  while (!PRESSED(button_state(), BUTTON_RUN))
    ;
  kill(pid);
  return 0;
}

int main() {
  pid = execi(&display_task, 0, NULL, 0, DEFAULT_STACK_SIZE);
  execi(&stop_task, 0, NULL, 0, DEFAULT_STACK_SIZE);
```

```
    tm_start();

    return 0;
}
```

Let's start at the bottom and work our way up. The `main()` method uses `execi()` to start the two tasks: `display_task()` and `stop_task()`. The process ID of the display task is saved away in the `pid` variable so that it can be stopped later. The last thing `main()` does is call `tm_start()` to start the task manager, which actually handles running the tasks.

The `stop_task()` waits for the **Run** button to be pressed. When the button is pressed, `stop_task()` calls `kill()` to stop the display process. What's that call to `msleep()` at the beginning of `stop_task()`? When legOS first boots on the RCX, it's waiting for the **Run** button to be pressed. As soon as it is, your program is started. It's very possible that `stop_task()` will already be running before you have a chance to take your finger off the **Run** button. The call to `msleep()` simply delays a little while to give you a chance to release the **Run** button.

The `display_task()` is straightforward. It alternates between displaying "Hello" and "nurse" on the display, looping forever until it is killed by `stop_task()`.

Waiting (unistd.h)

For a cleaner way to wait for specific events, consider `wait_event()`:

*wakeup_t wait_event(wakeup_t (*wakeup)(wakeup_t), wakeup_t data)*

Use this function to wait for a specific event. The function pointed at by **wakeup** is called, with **data** as a parameter, until it returns a non-zero result. At this point, `wait_event()` will return.

It's not hard to use `wait_event()`, but it's certainly not obvious. It helps to look at some of the examples that come with legOS. The following is a rewrite of the previous example that uses `wait_event()` instead of a `while` loop:

```
#include "conio.h"
#include "direct-button.h"
#include "unistd.h"
#include "sys/tm.h"

pid_t pid;

int display_task(int argc, char **argv) {
  while(1) {
    cputs("Hello");
    lcd_refresh();
    sleep(1);
    cputs("nurse");
    lcd_refresh();
```

```
      sleep(1);
    }
    return 0;
}

wakeup_t button_press_wakeup(wakeup_t data) {
    return PRESSED(button_state(),data);
}

int stop_task(int argc, char **argv) {
    msleep(200);

    wait_event(&button_press_wakeup, BUTTON_RUN);

    kill(pid);
    return 0;
}

int main() {
    pid = execi(&display_task, 0, NULL, 0, DEFAULT_STACK_SIZE);
    execi(&stop_task, 0, NULL, 0, DEFAULT_STACK_SIZE);

    tm_start();

    return 0;
}
```

All that happened in this code was that the `while` loop from the previous example was replaced with a call to `wait_event`. The given function, `button_press_wakeup()`, does the dirty work of checking the state of the button.

Memory (stdlib.h)

You can request chunks of memory in the RCX using the familiar `malloc()` and `calloc()` functions. legOS, by itself, takes up about 5K or 6K of the RCX's 32K of RAM. You should have about 26K left for your program and its data.

void *malloc(size_t size)
> This function allocates a chunk of memory of the given size (in bytes). A pointer to the memory is returned. If the memory cannot be allocated, `NULL` is returned.

void *calloc(size_t nmemb, size_t size)
> This function allocates enough memory for `nmemb` chunks of memory, each `size` bytes long. It also sets each byte of the allocated memory to zero. Like `malloc()`, it returns `NULL` if something goes wrong.

void free(void *ptr)
> When you are done with memory you've allocated, you should free it using this function.

Sound (rom/sound.h and direct-sound.h)

You can play one of the RCX's built-in "system" sounds with the following function:

void sound_system(unsigned nr)

This function plays one of the system sounds of the RCX. The **nr** parameter describes the sound; it can be any of the values shown in Table 10-1.

Table 10-1. sound_system() Sound Numbers

Sound Number	Description
0	Short beep
1	Two medium beeps
2	Descending arpeggio
3	Ascending arpeggio
4	Long low note
5	Quick ascending arpeggio (same as 3 but faster)

Furthermore, you can play any sound you want using this function:

*void ds_play(unsigned char *sample, unsigned length)*

This function plays the sound data described by **sample**, using **length** bytes of data. The sample data should be 1 bit, 8 kHz data.

Unfortunately, neither **sound_system()** nor **ds_play()** works in the March 30, 1999 build of legOS 0.1.7.

Other Goodies

legOS has a grab-bag of other interesting features. In this section, these functions are organized by the header file in which they are defined.

In stdlib.h

legOS supports a simple random number generator with the following two functions:

long int random(void)

This function returns a pseudorandom number.

void srandom(unsigned int seed)

Use this function to provide a new seed for the pseudorandom number generator.

In string.h

There are also functions for working with text strings:

char* strcpy(char *dest, const char *src)
int strlen(const char *s)
int strcmp(const char *s1, const char *s2)
    These are the standard string copy, length, and compare functions.

In time.h

You can retrieve the number of milliseconds since the RCX was powered up using the **sys_time** variable. It's got a limited range; the count resets once every 49.7 days.

In rom/system.h

Your programs have tremendous power in legOS. You can turn the RCX off or even obliterate legOS and your program from memory, using these functions:

void power_off(void)
    This function puts the RCX into its low power consumption "off" mode.

void rom_reset(void)
    This function resets the RCX to its out-of-the-box state, essentially blowing away legOS and your program. This is really only useful if you want to load some new firmware on the RCX. Use with care!

New Brains for Hank

In this section I'll present a longer example program. It's a program for a slightly modified version of Hank, the robot from Chapter 2, *Hank, the Bumper Tank*. All you need to do is mount the light sensor on the front of Hank and attach it to input 2. This light sensor will allow Hank to search for light, while the bumpers allow him to avoid obstacles. Figure 10-2 shows a picture of Hank, newly fitted with the light sensor.

Hank's new legOS program will be implemented using subsumption architecture. The basic structure of the program is similar to the subsumption architecture example presented in Chapter 9, *RoboTag, a Game for Two Robots*, although the syntax is somewhat different.

Hank's light-seeking proclivity is produced by the interaction of three behaviors:

* **cruise**, as in the RoboTag program, constantly tries to move forward.
* **seek_enlightenment()** examines the values of the light sensor. If the values are decreasing, generally speaking, this behavior attempts to turn Hank back toward the light.

Figure 10-2. Hank, retrofitted with a light sensor

- **avoid()** is the highest-level behavior. It is triggered by the bumpers and does the standard back-up-and-turn.

Convincing Hank to seek light is surprisingly hard. You can, of course, implement your own algorithm in **seek_enlightenment()**. It's a neat feature of subsumption architecture that you can concentrate solely on light-seeking behavior in **seek_ enlightenment()**. The obstacle avoidance behavior is already programmed in a different behavior and will subsume the light-seeking behavior as necessary.

Without further ado, here's the entire program, *LightSeeker.c*:

```
#include "conio.h"
#include "direct-button.h"
#include "direct-motor.h"
#include "direct-sensor.h"
#include "unistd.h"
#include "sys/tm.h"

#define MAX_TASKS 32
pid_t pid[MAX_TASKS];
int task_index;

#define BACK_TIME 500
#define TURN_TIME 800

// Motor commands.
#define COMMAND_NONE -1
#define COMMAND_FORWARD 1
```

```
#define COMMAND_REVERSE 2
#define COMMAND_LEFT 3
#define COMMAND_RIGHT 4
#define COMMAND_STOP 5

int avoid_command;

int avoid(int argc, char **argv) {
  avoid_command = COMMAND_NONE;
  while(1) {
    if (SENSOR_1 < 0xf000) {
      avoid_command = COMMAND_REVERSE;
      msleep(BACK_TIME);
      avoid_command = COMMAND_RIGHT;
      msleep(TURN_TIME);
      avoid_command = COMMAND_NONE;
    }
    if (SENSOR_3 < 0xf000) {
      avoid_command = COMMAND_REVERSE;
      msleep(BACK_TIME);
      avoid_command = COMMAND_LEFT;
      msleep(TURN_TIME);
      avoid_command = COMMAND_NONE;
    }
  }
  return 0;
}


#define RAW_DARK 0x7c00
#define RAW_LIGHT 0x6000

int process_light(int raw) {
  long big = 100 * ((long)raw - RAW_LIGHT);
  long percent = big / (RAW_DARK - RAW_LIGHT);
  return 100 - (int)percent;
}


int seek_command;

#define FUDGE 5

int wait_for_better(int baseline, unsigned long milliseconds) {
  int current;
  int saved_time = sys_time;
  do {
    msleep(50);
    current = process_light(SENSOR_2);
    lcd_int(current * 100 + baseline);
    lcd_refresh();
  } while (sys_time < (saved_time + milliseconds)
      && current < (baseline + FUDGE));
  if (current >= (baseline + FUDGE)) return current;
  return -1; // Timed out.
}
```

```
int seek_enlightenment(int argc, char **argv) {
  int baseline, current, loop_count, result;

  seek_command = COMMAND_NONE;

  // Get a baseline.
  baseline = process_light(SENSOR_2);

  loop_count = 0;

  while(1) {
    msleep(50); // Slow things down a little.
    // Every so often, increase the baseline.
    if (++loop_count == 5) {
      if (baseline < 100) baseline++;
      loop_count = 0;
    }
    current = process_light(SENSOR_2);
    lcd_int(current * 100 + baseline);
    lcd_refresh();
    // If the current value is somewhat less than the baseline...
    if (current < (baseline - FUDGE)) {
      // Set the baseline from the current value.
      baseline = current;
      // Search for something better.
      if (sys_time % 2 == 0) seek_command = COMMAND_LEFT;
      else seek_command = COMMAND_RIGHT;
      result = wait_for_better(baseline, 1000);
      if (result == -1) {
        // If that timed out, search back the other direction.
        if (seek_command == COMMAND_LEFT) seek_command = COMMAND_RIGHT;
        else if (seek_command == COMMAND_RIGHT) seek_command = COMMAND_LEFT;
        result = wait_for_better(baseline, 2000);
        if (result != -1) baseline = result;
        // If there's nothing better, bail.
      }
      // Set the new baseline.
      else baseline = result;
    }
    // Relinquish control.
    seek_command = COMMAND_NONE;
  }
  return 0;
}

int cruise_command;

int cruise(int argc, char **argv) {
  cruise_command = COMMAND_FORWARD;
  while (1) sleep(1);
  return 0;
}
```

```
int motor_command;

void motor_control() {
  motor_a_speed(MAX_SPEED);
  motor_c_speed(MAX_SPEED);

  switch (motor_command) {
    case COMMAND_FORWARD:
      motor_a_dir(fwd);
      motor_c_dir(fwd);
      break;
    case COMMAND_REVERSE:
      motor_a_dir(rev);
      motor_c_dir(rev);
      break;
    case COMMAND_LEFT:
      motor_a_dir(rev);
      motor_c_dir(fwd);
      break;
    case COMMAND_RIGHT:
      motor_a_dir(fwd);
      motor_c_dir(rev);
      break;
    case COMMAND_STOP:
      motor_a_dir(brake);
      motor_c_dir(brake);
      break;
    default:
      break;
  }
}

int arbitrate(int argc, char **argv) {
  while(1) {
    if (avoid_command != COMMAND_NONE) cputc('a', 0);
    else if (seek_command != COMMAND_NONE) cputc('s', 0);
    else if (cruise_command != COMMAND_NONE) cputc('c', 0);
    else cputc(' ', 0);
    lcd_refresh();

    if (cruise_command != COMMAND_NONE) motor_command = cruise_command;
    if (seek_command != COMMAND_NONE) motor_command = seek_command;
    if (avoid_command != COMMAND_NONE) motor_command = avoid_command;
    motor_control();
  }
}

int stop_task(int argc, char **argv) {
  int i;

  msleep(200);
  while (!PRESSED(button_state(), BUTTON_RUN))
    ;
  for (i = 0; i < task_index; i++)
```

```
        kill(pid[i]);
    return 0;
}

void exec_helper(int (*code_start)(int,char**)) {
    pid[task_index++] = execi(code_start, 0, NULL, 0, DEFAULT_STACK_SIZE);
}

int main() {
    task_index = 0;

    exec_helper(&avoid);
    exec_helper(&seek_enlightenment);
    exec_helper(&cruise);

    exec_helper(&arbitrate);

    execi(&stop_task, 0, NULL, 0, DEFAULT_STACK_SIZE);

    tm_start();

    return 0;
}
```

LightSeeker.c is a relatively large program, but it consists of easily understandable pieces. As before, I'll start at the bottom and work backwards through the source code.

The **main()** function simply serves to start the other tasks in the program. A helper function, **exec_helper()**, is used to start the three behavior tasks, **avoid()**, **seek_enlightenment()**, and **cruise()**. **exec_helper()** is also used to start the **arbitrate()** task, which examines the output of the three behaviors and sends the appropriate command to the motors. The **exec_helper()** function simply starts each task using **execi()** and stores the returned process ID in an array. Back in **main()**, **stop_task()** is also started. When the **Run** button is pressed, **stop_task()** simply goes through the process ID array that **exec_helper()** built and kills each process.

arbitrate() examines the output commands of each behavior. If the command is not **COMMAND_NONE**, the current motor command is set from the behavior. The later behaviors, of course, will overwrite the motor command. The last behavior, **avoid()**, is at the highest level. If it chooses to control the robot, **seek_enlightenment()** and **cruise()** have nothing to say about it.

To make it clearer what's going on while the robot is running, **arbitrate()** writes a character to the display that indicates which behavior is currently active. A "c" on the right side of the display indicates that **cruise()** has control, an "s" stands for **seek_enlightenment()**, and an "a" shows that the **avoid()** behavior is controlling the robot.

When `arbitrate()` has determined the motor command, it uses `motor_control()` to interpret the command and to actually set the direction and speed of the outputs. This design is very similar to the design of the NQC RoboTag program, from Chapter 9.

The `cruise()` behavior is simple; it just sets its command variable to `COMMAND_FORWARD` ad infinitum.

The next behavior, `seek_enlightenment()`, is not so simple. The basic idea, however, goes like this:

```
if I'm seeing darker stuff than I've just been seeing
   look to either side for something brighter
```

`seek_enlightenment()` implements this with the idea of a baseline. The initial baseline is taken straight from the light sensor reading:

```
baseline = process_light(SENSOR_2);
```

The behavior then enters an endless loop, examining the value of the light sensor. If it falls too far below the baseline, `seek_enlightenment()` asserts control and searches for brighter light:

```
current = process_light(SENSOR_2);
if (current < (baseline - FUDGE)) {
```

To search for brighter light, `seek_enlightenment()` first sets a new baseline from the current light value:

```
baseline = current;
```

Then the robot turns left or right, more or less randomly using the system clock:

```
if (sys_time % 2 == 0) seek_command = COMMAND_LEFT;
else seek_command = COMMAND_RIGHT;
```

A helper function, `wait_for_better()`, is used to wait for a brighter light than the new baseline:

```
result = wait_for_better(baseline, 1000);
```

It's entirely possible that the robot will not find any brighter light. In this case, it times out (after 1000 milliseconds) and returns -1. In this case, the robot will turn back in the opposite direction and search for brighter light:

```
if (result == -1) {
   if (seek_command == COMMAND_LEFT) seek_command = COMMAND_RIGHT;
   else if (seek_command == COMMAND_RIGHT) seek_command = COMMAND_LEFT;
```

The `wait_for_better()` helper function is again used with a longer timeout:

```
result = wait_for_better(baseline, 2000);
```

In either search, if a better value is found, it is used as the new baseline:

```
    if (result != -1) baseline = result;
  }
  else baseline = result;
}
```

That's the basic algorithm. There is one extra feature that makes everything run a little smoother: every so often the baseline value is incremented. This means that if the robot is stuck in a dark corner, it will eventually get dissatisfied (because of the increasing baseline) and look for something better.

To communicate with the outside world about what's going on, seek_ enlightenment() shows the current light value as well as the current baseline on the display. The current value is shown in the first and second digits of the display, while the baseline is shown in the third and fourth digits. (Remember that the letter on the right side of the display tells you which behavior is currently active.) You can actually see the baseline increasing slowly as the program runs.

I've implemented my own light sensor processing in process_light(). I didn't use legOS's LIGHT_2 macro because the values I was getting from it were not in the range from 0 to 100. Perhaps this is a bug that will be fixed in an upcoming release. At any rate, I implemented my own sensor data processing to produce a value from 0 to 100. You may need to adjust the RAW_DARK and RAW_LIGHT constants for your particular light sensor.

The avoid() behavior is very simple. It just checks the touch sensors on inputs 1 and 3. If one of the touch sensors is pressed, avoid() backs the robot up and turns it a little.

Development Tips

legOS has serious programming power, but it has its rough spots, too. This section contains some helpful advice based on my own experience developing with legOS.

Development Cycle

legOS's development cycle is a little clumsy. You write a program, compile it with the legOS source code, then download the whole thing to the RCX. It's the downloading that takes a long time. Here are some tips to make things go smoother:

1. Always include code that terminates your own program. If your program can stop itself, control returns to legOS. When legOS has control, you can turn the RCX on and off and even reinitialize the firmware, as described next.

2. When legOS has control of the RCX, you can press and hold the **Prgm** button, then press the **On-Off** button. This blows away legOS (and your program) and returns control of the RCX to the ROM. You'll need to do this before you can download a new set of firmware to the RCX.

3. If your program doesn't stop itself and give control back to legOS, you'll need to erase the firmware by removing a battery. If your program has a bug and does not terminate, you'll need to remove a battery to reset the RCX.

4. Sometimes, through a bug in legOS or in your program, the RCX cannot be initialized by removing the batteries for just a few seconds. You will need to remove the batteries from your RCX and wait for a minute or so before the firmware is erased. Some circuitry keeps the RCX's memory alive; in some cases, you need to wait for the circuitry to drain completely before the firmware will be erased.

If the endless code–compile–download–reset cycle is getting you down, you might consider using an *emulator*. An emulator is a special program that runs on your development PC but acts like an RCX. You can test your programs on the emulator much faster than you can test them on an actual RCX. Currently one legOS emulator exists; see the "Online Resources" section for details.

Debugging

The display is your best friend when it comes to debugging. legOS offers an impressive array of display functions. You can show words that indicate which part of your program is executing or display the contents of variables. Of course, there's not a lot of space to work with, but you could easily display a series of values for a short time. You could even write debugging code that lets you cycle through data by pressing a button.

Unexpectedly Static Variables

One of the craziest things about legOS development is that global variables retain their value from one time you run your program to the next. This is very important—it means that variables you initialize at declaration time are initialized only once, when your program is first loaded on the RCX. Use the following program to convince yourself:

```
#include "conio.h"

int x = 44;

int main(void) {
  lcd_int(x);
  lcd_refresh();
```

```
    x++;
    delay(1000);
    return 0;
}
```

The value shown on the display will be 44 the first time the program is run, but it goes up by one each subsequent time, even when you turn the RCX off and on again. This interesting property was the source of several bugs in the original *LightSeeker.c* program.

If you really want to initialize a variable each time your program is run, you should do it explicitly in the code somewhere, like this:

```
#include "conio.h"

int x;

int main(void) {
  x = 44;
  lcd_int(x);
  lcd_refresh();
  x++;
  delay(1000);
  return 0;
}
```

If you look back at *LightSeeker.c*, you'll see that all the variable initialization is done explicitly. In general, it should ring a warning bell in your head when you see variables that are initialized at declaration time.

Online Resources

legOS

legOS
http://www.noga.de/legOS/

> This is the official home page of legOS, written by Markus Noga. You can download files, browse the documentation, see installation instructions, and browse related web pages.

LegOS HOWTO
http://arthurdent.dorm.duke.edu/legos/HOWTO/HOWTO.html

> Luis Villa has created a comprehensive set of information about legOS at this site. It covers the tools you'll need, where to get them, and how to install them. It also talks about programming in legOS and includes useful links to the online MINDSTORMS community.

Another Low-level Tool

RCX Tools

http://graphics.stanford.edu/~kekoa/rcx/tools.html

This page contains a link to `librcx`, a C library for interacting with the RCX's ROM routines. It was developed by Kekoa Proudfoot, who did most of the original reverse engineering work on the RCX.

Development Tools

egcs project home page

http://egcs.cygnus.com/

This is the home page for `egcs`, the compiler you'll need for legOS. The full package is 11 MB (compressed!).

Binutils—GNU Project—Free Software Foundation (FSF)

http://www.gnu.org/software/binutils/binutils.html

This is the home page for `binutils`, which you'll also need to compile legOS. Compressed, it's about 5 MB; uncompressed, it's around 25 MB.

Cygwin

http://sourceware.cygnus.com/cygwin/

If you want to make Windows look like Linux, try the Cygwin package from Cygnus Solutions. Like `egcs` and `binutils`, it's free.

Perl.com—Acquiring Perl Software

http://www.perl.com/pub/language/info/software.html

This is the place to visit if you need Perl for your system. It has links to versions of Perl for most platforms.

emulegOS

http://www.geocities.com/~marioferrari/emulegos.html

Originally developed by Mario Ferrari, this legOS emulator has been enhanced by Mark Falco and Marco Beri. It comes in two versions. The Windows version requires Borland's C++ Builder 3.0. The Linux version uses Tcl/Tk. Like legOS, this is not for the faint of heart, but it looks like it could be very useful.

Installation Help for Windows Users

Lego Knees

http://www.beesknees.freeserve.co.uk/lego/

Gavin Smyth wrote this helpful page about installing the legOS development tools under Windows 95, 98, or NT. It includes links to various files you'll need.

Installing legOS—the unauth, unofficial Lego RCX firmware
http://ex.stormyprods.com/lego/legOS.html

This page, created by Brain Stormont, also details the steps you'll need to follow to install a legOS development environment under Windows 95. It includes useful links to the relevant software.

Web-Based Cross Compilers

Web-LegOS 0.1
http://www.dwarfrune.com/web-legOS.html

This page, maintained by Shawn Menninga, compiles your source code. The resulting *.srec* file can be displayed as HTML or emailed to you.

Compile legOS RCX code
https://vheissu.mersenne.com/~dhm/compile-legOS.html

This is Dave Madden's web-based legOS compiler.

Firmware Downloaders

firmdl.c
http://graphics.stanford.edu/~kekoa/rcx/firmdl.c

One popular firmware downloader is `firmdl`. Written by Kekoa Proudfoot, the source code is available in C and should compile on most platforms.

NQC—Not Quite C
http://www.enteract.com/~dbaum/lego/nqc/index.html

This is the home page for NQC. It's listed here because `nqc` can be used to download legOS programs.

11

Make Your Own Sensors

If you're not afraid of a soldering iron, you can create your own robot sensors. Although you can buy the "official" sensors from the LEGO online store or LEGO DACTA (see the Appendix A, *Finding Parts and Programming Environments*), there's not a very wide selection. Furthermore, they are expensive—$10US for the touch sensor, $20US for a light sensor, $15US for the rotation sensor, and $25US for the temperature sensor. Building your own sensors is a great way to expand your robot's capabilities without spending a lot of money.

This chapter describes different ways of fitting sensors into LEGO bricks, provides discussions of various types of sensors you can build, and considers some innovative possibilities for putting multiple sensors on one RCX input.

Mounting

The first thing you should think about is how you are going to attach your new sensors to the LEGO world. There are two goals to consider here:

1. The sensor, ideally, should be a LEGO brick itself so you can easily attach it to your robots. The sensors that come with RIS exhibit this property: the touch sensors and the light sensor are simply specialized bricks.

2. The sensor needs to connect electrically to the RCX. Somehow the electrical connections from the sensor circuit will need to mate with the RCX's input connections.

There are four basic approaches—cut wire, copper tubing, machine screws, and a conductor plate—which are described in the following sections.

Cut Wire

The simplest approach to attaching a new sensor is to cut one of the wire bricks that comes with RIS. Figure 11-1 shows half of one of these wire bricks.

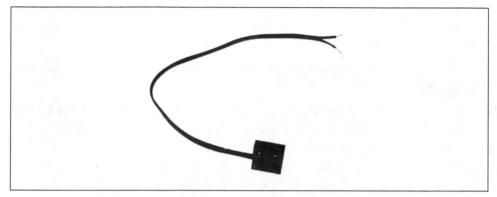

Figure 11-1. A wire brick yields two connectors like the one shown here

You can wire the cut end directly to your sensor. Each wire brick therefore yields two connectors that you can use to make your sensors compatible with the RCX. If you don't want to ruin your perfect set, you can order additional wires from Pitsco LEGO DACTA (800-362-4308), although you'll pay dearly for them.

Copper Tubing

The studs (or "bumps") on LEGO bricks are exactly 3/16 inch in diameter. You can use 3/16" copper tubing, available at hobby stores, to replace studs in a regular LEGO brick. In essence, the tubing acts as an electrically conductive LEGO stud. Using the tubing, you can build a sensor into a brick and use the regular "wire bricks" that come with RIS to attach the sensor to the RCX.

The basic procedure is to drill out two of the studs in a regular brick. Then you push the tubing through the holes up as far as a regular stud. The sensor or sensor circuit can be soldered to the part of the tubing that's inside the brick. You should place the tubing in diagonally opposite studs; this ensures that an electrical connection is made no matter which way the sensor is attached to the RCX.

Michael Gasperi's excellent web site describes this technique clearly. For details, see the "Online Resources" section at the end of this chapter.

Machine Screws

Using machine screws is a variation on the copper tubing method. Instead of replacing studs with tubing, you replace them with 4/40 machine screws, which have a head that is 3/16" in diameter. You can use pan head or round head machine screws, but the pan head is shaped more like a LEGO stud. Instead of drilling out the stud, just shave off the top of it, so that it's level with the surface of the brick. Then you can drill a hole and thread the screw down into the brick. An example of this technique is shown at *http://www.kabai.com/lego/lego.htm*. Again, you should replace diagonally opposite studs so that the sensor will be connected to the RCX, regardless of the orientation of the wire brick.

You'll see an example of this technique later. In the meantime, here are some construction tips:

1. Begin by shaving off two diagonally opposite studs on the brick. A hobby tool like a Dremel™ rotary tool or Black and Decker Wizard™ works well for this purpose if you have cutting disks for it.

2. Now make sure the screw heads are the right size. Some 4/40 machine screws have heads that are larger than a LEGO stud. You can adjust the diameter of the screw by mounting it in a drill (with the head facing out). Turn on the drill and use a file to reduce the diameter of the head. With round head machine screws, you may also need to flatten the top of the head. You can test your modifications by trying to place the head of the screw in the bottom of a wire brick. You should only have to push it a little bit to get it to fit.

3. Solder a short wire to the tip of each screw before you put the screws in the brick. There are two very good reasons for this. It takes a lot of heat to solder on to the screws, so you don't want to either melt the plastic around the screws by soldering them in-place, or burn out the sensor you're mounting by soldering it directly to the screws.

4. Thread the wires you just soldered to the screws into the holes in the top of the brick. Now turn the screws into the brick—they should thread nicely into the holes.

5. Now you're ready to mount your sensor in the brick and solder its leads to the screw wires from Step 3. Make sure to use heat sinks so you don't undo your previous work or damage the sensor.

Conductor Plate

Another technique for attaching sensors to the RCX's inputs is based on special conductive plates. These plates are available as an accessory pack, #5037, from the LEGO Shop-at-Home service (800-453-4652). The kit, which is $6.75US, comes with several plates to which you can attach your sensor electronics. This technique is fully described at: *http://www.akasa.bc.ca/tfm/lego_temp.html*.

Passive Sensors

There are several simple passive sensors that attach directly to the inputs of the RCX. These are the simplest do-it-yourself sensors because you don't need any interface circuitry to make their output comprehensible to the RCX.

A Peaceful Demonstration

To really understand passive sensors, it's helpful to see a diagram of one input of the RCX in passive mode:

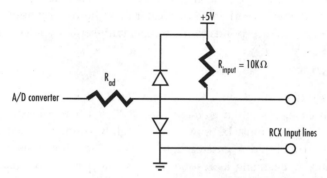

In passive mode, the sensor connected to the input is essentially a resistance. It forms a voltage divider with R_{input}. The A/D converter in the RCX converts the analog voltage to a digital raw input value from 0 to 1023. The A/D converter itself has a resistance, R_{ad}, but it's so small you probably don't have to worry about it. The two diodes limit the voltage that can be seen by the A/D converter; this makes it hard to damage the RCX by hooking something up incorrectly.

Touch Sensors

Touch sensors are the easiest kind of sensors to make. Any kind of contact switch is appropriate, and no special circuit is necessary. All you need to do is attach the switch leads to the input somehow.

Browse the pages of a catalog from Jameco (800-831-4242) or Digi-Key (800-344-4539) and you'll find a dizzying array of contact switches.

Another interesting possibility is using a *mercury switch* as a touch sensor. A mercury switch has a sealed bulb that contains a drop of mercury. When the switch is oriented the right way, the mercury drop connects the two switch leads together. Figure 11-2 shows a photograph of a mercury switch; you may have seen ones with clear bulbs in your thermostat. The LEGO brick is shown for scale.

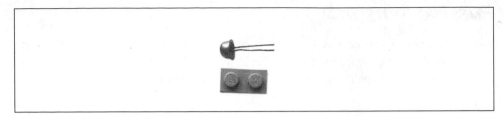

Figure 11-2. A mercury switch

The mercury switch works just like a contact switch. When the switch is correctly oriented, the two leads are shorted together. It's basically a primitive angle sensor. In a thermostat, for example, the mercury switch is used to indicate two states: either it's less than the desired angle or greater than the desired angle. The desired angle in a thermostat corresponds to the temperature setting you've chosen.

Light Sensors

The light sensor that comes with RIS is a powered device; it emits light using an LED, and senses light with a *phototransistor*. The phototransistor responds to changes in light, but it must be powered. A slightly simpler device, a *photoresistor*, can be used to build a passive light sensor. The photoresistor responds to changes in light by changing its resistance. This is a perfect candidate for an RCX sensor. Basically all you have to do is hook up the leads of the photoresistor to one of the RCX inputs.

Radio Shack sells Cadmium Sulfide (CdS) photoresistors that work well as robot sensors. Figure 11-3 shows a photograph of one such photoresistor mounted in a brick using the machine screw mounting method.

Figure 11-3. A CdS photoresistor mounted in a brick

The machine screws were mounted on the brick as described previously. All that remained was to mount the photoresistor itself in the brick. To do this, two holes were made for the leads of the photoresistor. Then the leads were threaded through to the inside of the brick and soldered to the wires that were already there. These wires were previously attached to the screws. The extra wire can be pushed up inside the brick. Figure 11-4 shows a photograph of the bottom of the same photoresistor sensor.

Figure 11-4. A bottom view of the CdS photoresistor sensor

You can make holes for the sensor leads using a small drill. If you don't have one of these, you can heat a wire with a soldering iron and push it through the side of the brick, creating a small hole.

Although LEGO's light sensor is a powered device, the CdS photoresistor is a passive device. This means that you can't blindly configure the photoresistor input as a light sensor input. You should, instead, make sure the sensor is not powered and read the raw input values.

In NQC, for example, you can configure the input as follows:

```
SetSensorType(SENSOR_1, SENSOR_TYPE_TOUCH);
SetSensorMode(SENSOR_1, SENSOR_MODE_RAW);
```

You'll have to experiment to find out what kind of values you get for different lighting conditions. Darker lighting will produce higher sensor readings, while bright lighting produces lower sensor readings.

Temperature Sensors

A simple device called a *thermistor* can be used to make a temperature sensor. The thermistor has a resistance that changes according to the temperature. By measuring the resistance of the thermistor, you can figure out the temperature.

Thermistors are widely available and cost only a couple of dollars each. Chances are, however, that your device won't have the same electrical characteristics as the official temperature sensor. Thus, your temperature readings will be off slightly. If you are concerned about correct temperature readings, rather than just sensing increases and decreases in temperature, you may want to convert raw sensors readings into temperature values yourself.

Powered Sensors

It's a little harder to attach a powered circuit to the RCX. Remember, there are only two wires connecting the RCX to each of its sensors. For powered sensors, these wires alternately power the sensor and read its value.

Active Sensor Magic

The designers of the RCX pulled some magic out of their electrical engineering bag to enable active sensors. The following figure shows a diagram of an RCX input in active mode:

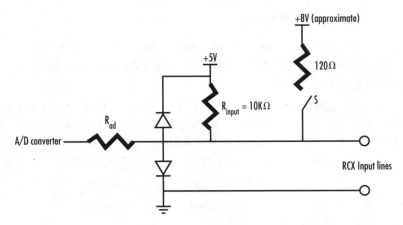

The active mode circuit looks a lot like the passive mode circuit, except for the 8V power supply. Conceptually, at least, there's a switch S that closes for three milliseconds at a time to supply power to the sensor. At the end of every power interval, the switch opens for 0.1 millisecond, and the RCX takes a reading from the input.

The 8V that is supplied to the active sensor is an approximate number; the actual value depends on the juice in your batteries. The difference between fresh and used batteries can produce any voltage in the range from about 6.5V to 8.5V. Many electronic circuits are happy with 5V or more, so this may not be an issue for you. But it's something you should be aware of.

Signal Splitter

The input wires carry power and sensor signals at the same time. Furthermore, the polarity of the signals may be reversed, depending on how the sensor is attached to the RCX. Remember how the direction of the motors depended on how they were attached to the RCX? The same problem applies to sensors and sensor circuits, but a special circuit makes it irrelevant which way the sensor is hooked up.

Six diodes are sufficient to separate out the power and signal on an input. These six diodes make up a circuit called a *signal splitter*. The circuit makes sure that all the electrons go in the right directions so your sensor circuit gets power and the RCX gets a sensor reading. Diodes are used to steer the electrons the correct way so that it doesn't matter which way the active sensor is attached to the input on the RCX. Figure 11-5 shows how to set up the diodes.[*]

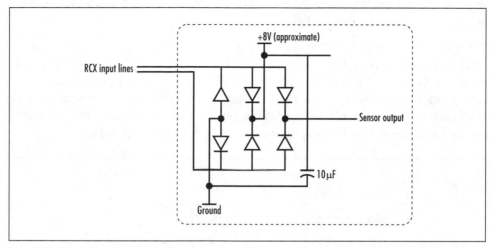

Figure 11-5. A signal splitter

Remember, power is only applied for 3 ms at a time, punctuated by .1 ms sensor readings. You will need to smooth out the power supply with a capacitor, as shown in Figure 11-5.

The Touchless Touch Sensor

This section describes how to build an interface circuit for a *Hall effect sensor*. A Hall effect sensor is triggered by the presence of a magnetic field. If you place a small magnet near the sensor in the proper orientation, it will trigger. The sensor itself is very small and looks like a transistor. Figure 11-6 shows a photograph of a Hall effect sensor.

Figure 11-6. A Hall effect sensor

---

[*] The signal splitter is really a combination of two circuits, a *bridge rectifier* and a *current router*. The bridge rectifier ensures that power is correctly supplied to the active sensor; it consists of the left four diodes in Figure 11-5. The current router ensures that the sensor signal is supplied with the correct polarity to the input on the RCX. The right two diodes in Figure 11-5 make up the current router.

Not all Hall effect sensors are created equal. Some have on-board circuitry that processes the sensor's signal and converts it to a boolean electrical signal. Some respond to one polarity of magnetic field; some respond to both. Read the fine print closely when you buy a Hall effect sensor.

The circuit presented in this section is built around a "sticky" Hall effect sensor (Digi-Key part number DN6847SE-ND). This sensor responds to both magnetic polarities. One polarity turns the sensor on, and the other turns it off. The on or off setting "sticks" until the opposite magnetic field is applied. The processing circuitry is all built into the sensor. Hooking up the sensor to the RCX is a matter of applying the signal splitter circuit from the previous section, as shown in Figure 11-7.

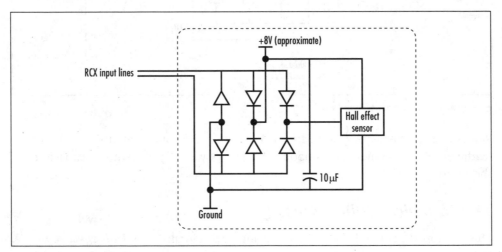

Figure 11-7. A Hall effect sensor circuit

Once the sensor is hooked up, you can read boolean values from the appropriate input. Remember, though, you need to configure the input for a powered sensor. In NQC, it looks like this:

```
SetSensorType(SENSOR_3, SENSOR_TYPE_LIGHT);
SetSensorMode(SENSOR_3, SENSOR_MODE_BOOL);
```

How you use this sensor is, of course, up to you. You could build the Hall effect sensor and the signal splitter circuit into a large LEGO brick. Then you could build small permanent magnets into other LEGO bricks. This would give you a flexible system, suitable for building limit switches, counters, or anything you can imagine.

Touch Multiplexer

No matter what software you're running, the RCX still has only three inputs and three outputs. Short of using another RCX, what can you do if you want to use more than three inputs or outputs? On the input side, at least, there are some tricks. Chapter 5, *Minerva, a Robot with an Arm*, describes some ways of putting more than one sensor on a single input. It's possible to put multiple switches on a single input, but you can't tell which of them was pressed when a touch occurs.

A simple circuit allows you to hook up four switches to a single input and detect them individually. This circuit is called a *touch multiplexer*, because it mashes three input signals into one. This idea was originally suggested by Paul Haas; one implementation is documented nicely at Michael Gasperi's web site.

Note that this method uses regular switches, not the LEGO touch sensors. The touch sensors that come with RIS provide a varying resistance as they are pressed. A garden variety switch is much more of a binary device, which is better suited to our touch multiplexer.

The touch multiplexer is based on a fundamental concept in electronics: the combination of different resistances. Michael Gasperi's design combines resistors in parallel. The touch multiplexer I'll describe here combines resistors in series, which simplifies the math.[*] The basic circuit is shown in Figure 11-8.

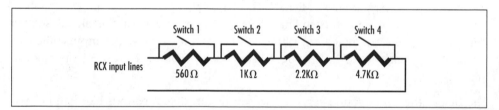

Figure 11-8. The touch multiplexer circuit

Pressing a single switch shorts out the corresponding resistance, which reduces the raw input value. Because each touch sensor has a different resistance, the touch sensors each reduce the raw input readings by recognizable amounts. Note that the resistors roughly double in value as you move from left to right. This makes it easier to interpret the results of the touch multiplexer.

Each combination of switches produces a unique resistance, which results in a unique raw input value. By examining the raw input values in your robot's program, you can figure out which touch sensors were pressed.

You can convert the raw value to a resistance with the following equation, where *raw* is the raw input value:

$$R = \frac{10000\,raw}{(1023 - raw)}$$

---

[*] John Tamplin deserves the credit for this idea.

Once you've got the resistance, and assuming you have a binary progression of resistors, you can convert the input resistance to a bitmask of switch presses with this equation:

$$bitMask = (int)\left(\frac{R}{R1} + \frac{1}{2}\right)$$

The `bitMask` will contain four bits of information, one for each switch. Each bit is 0 when the switch is closed (pressed) and 1 otherwise.

The raw input value depends on the battery voltage. As the batteries drain, the raw reading will become lower, which means that the calculated value of R becomes lower. Adding 1/2 in the previous equation (and rounding to an integer) helps compensate for this and allows the touch multiplexer to work until the batteries are about half-drained.

Other Neat Ideas

This chapter has presented some simple sensors you can build yourself, but there are many other possibilities. Michael Gasperi's web site (listed in the "Online Resources") has several outstanding ideas. Once you've built the signal splitter (Figure 11-5), you can attach any old electronic circuit to the RCX's inputs. Michael Gasperi has built several interesting sensors based around the use of operational amplifiers (op amps).

The first of these is a sound sensor. This sensor can detect sounds like hand claps; you can program your robot to respond to sound. Basically, this circuit uses an op amp to amplify the signal from a microphone.

Michael has also built a *differential light sensor*. This sensor actually contains two photoresistors and some circuitry. The circuitry interprets the signals from the two photoresistors and sends a signal to the RCX that indicates the balance of light between the two photoresistors. This process allows you to easily build a robot that seeks light.

What About Actuators?

I've talked a lot about building sensors; why not build actuators too? LEGO only offers two actuators: motors and lights. The lights aren't very practical and usually serve only a decorative purpose, although it's possible you could use them to signal other robots.

Outside the tidy world of LEGO MINDSTORMS, however, robots have all sorts of different actuators. Three good possibilities for do-it-yourself actuators are servo motors, solenoids, and Shape Memory Alloy (SMA) wire:

servo motors

Servo motors are special motors that are used in radio controlled cars and airplanes. They are actually an assembly of a motor, some gearing, and some electronics. In response to an electronic signal, they rotate an output shaft to a certain angle. Interfacing a servo motor to the RCX is a matter of making the RCX produce the right signal. You'll probably also need a power supply for the servo.

The bottom line, however, is that you can get just as much done with a LEGO motor and a LEGO rotation sensor. The whole point of a servo is that it rotates to a precise angular position; but that's just as easy to do with a motor coupled to a rotation sensor. As a matter of fact, the LEGO-only solution is more flexible. While a servo has only a limited range of angular motion, the motor and rotation sensor have no such constraints.

solenoids

A solenoid converts electrical power into a small linear motion. You can harvest solenoids from discarded fax machines and cassette players, or buy them new from a supplier like Jameco.

SMA wire

Shape Memory Alloy is a special kind of metal that changes shape dramatically when it's heated. You can buy wires that contract when they are heated. Conveniently, you can heat SMA wires by passing current through them. SMA wire should be simple to interface to the RCX's outputs. Note, however, that heated SMA wire can melt LEGO bricks—mounting the SMA wire may be a challenge.

Online Resources

General Information

Mindstorms Sensor Input
http://www.plazaearth.com/usr/gasperi/lego.htm

This is the definitive online resource on the inputs of the RCX. It contains a wealth of information about the inputs themselves, the official LEGO sensors, and sensors you can build yourself. It's full of schematic diagrams, graphs, explanations, and links to other people's RCX sensor web pages.

Toy building block with electrical contacting portions (US4552541)
http://www.patents.ibm.com/details?pn=US04552541__

This is the patent that describes the clever scheme used by the input and output connectors on the RCX, the sensors, the motors, and the wire bricks. Did you ever wonder why you can attach wires and sensors in any orientation and still make a connection? This patent explains the system.

Mounting Methods

Homebrew Temperature Sensor
http://www.plazaearth.com/usr/gasperi/temp.htm

Michael Gasperi's temperature sensor uses the copper tubing method of sensor mounting. This page has a clear description of the technique. Putting the tubing on diagonally opposite studs would make this sensor more generally useful. However, the basic technique is very well illustrated.

LEGO
http://www.kabai.com/lego/lego.htm

This page has brief instructions for building a sound sensor for the RCX. It demonstrates the machine screw mounting method. However, the screws are not mounted on diagonally opposite studs, which would make them more useful.

TFM's Lego Page - Lego Mindstorms Compatible Temperature Sensor
http://www.akasa.bc.ca/tfm/lego_temp.html

This page describes the construction of a temperature sensor using the conductor plate mounting method.

Tools

Black and Decker
http://www.blackanddecker.com/powertools.htm

Black and Decker makes a tool called the Wizard. With a cutting disk, it's useful for shaving the studs off LEGO bricks.

Welcome to Dremel International
http://www.dremel.com/

Dremel makes hand tools that are good for working with small things like LEGO bricks.

Electronics Parts Suppliers

Jameco Electronics: Home
http://www.jameco.com/

> This is the web site of Jameco, where you'll find goodies like switches, Hall effect sensors, bend sensors, diodes, resistors, and other great stuff.

Digi-Key Corporation Home Page
http://www.digikey.com/

> If there's something you can't find at Jameco (thermistors, for example), try Digi-Key instead. They have a huge selection and good service.

Mouser Electronics, Distributor of Electronic Components
http://www.mouser.com/

> Here's another good supplier; their web site is a little easier to use than Digi-Key's.

Finding Parts and Programming Environments

You can order sensors, motors, and other robot parts from several sources. Although you can probably find the Robotics Invention System (RIS) at a local toy store, you'll hardly ever see extra motors and sensors.

LEGO Sources

Table A-1 lists three places where you can get RIS accessories.

Table A-1. Sources for LEGO Parts

Name	Telephone	Web Site
LEGO World Shop	-	*http://www.legoworldshop.com/*
LEGO Shop-at-Home Service	(800) 453 - 4652	-
Pitsco LEGO DACTA	(800) 362 - 4308	*http://www.pitsco-legodacta.com/*

Pitsco LEGO DACTA sells LEGO's educational products, including RIS, a programming environment called ROBOLAB, classroom packages, and a fine assortment of spare parts.

Parts

Table A-2 lists the parts you may wish to buy along with their prices at the three sources shown in Table A-1. This information is current as of mid-1999. (LWS is LEGO World Shop, S@H is LEGO Shop-at-Home Service, and Pitsco is Pitsco LEGO DACTA.) Note that the Shop-at-Home Service does not charge extra for shipping, so the list is not exactly comparing apples to apples.

Table A-2. Parts and Prices, in US Dollars

Part	Item	Pitsco Item	LWS	S@H	Pitsco
Robotics Invention System	9719	N979719	$219.00	$219.00	$219.00
RoboSports expansion set	9730	-	$49.99	$54.00	-
Extreme creatures expansion set	9732	-	$49.99	$54.00	-
RCX	9709	N979709	$129.99	$129.00	$120.00
IR cable for Macintosh	-	4119830	-	-	$15
Light sensor	9758	N979890	$19.99	$19.75	$27.75
Touch sensor	9757	-	$9.99	$11.00	-
Touch sensor (two wire bricks)	-	N779911	-	-	$11.00
Temperature sensor	9755	N979889	$24.99	$24.00	$27.75
Rotation sensor	9756	N979891	$14.99	$16.50	$27.75
Geared motor	5225	N775225	$18.25	$17.50	$15.75
Micro motor	5119	N775119	-	$11.00	$10.00
Standard motor	5114	N775114	-	$17.50	$15.75
Train motor	5300	-	-	$27.50	-
Remote control	9738	-	$19.99	$19.75	-
Electric plates	5037	N779886	-	$6.75	$6.00
Wire brick, 128 cm	5111	-	-	$4.50	-
Wire brick set	-	N779897	-	-	$12.50
Large turntables	-	N779876	-	-	$9.75

Other Suppliers

Table A-3 lists suppliers for electronics parts. These are useful sources for the electronics described in Chapter 11, *Make Your Own Sensors.*

Table A-3. Sources for LEGO Parts

Name	Telephone	Web Site
Jameco	(800) 831 - 4242	*http://www.jameco.com/*
Digi-Key	(800) 344 - 4539	*http://www.digikey.com/*
Mouser	(800) 346 - 6873	*http://www.mouser.com/*

Programming Environments

Table A-4 summarizes the development environments that are available for the RCX.

Table A-4. RCX Development Environments

Name	URL	Language	Replacement Firmware?	Price	Host OS	Tools Needed[a]
RCX Code	-	(visual)	no	-	Win32[b]	-
Not Quite C (NQC)	http://www.enteract.com/~dbaum/lego/nqc/	NQC	no	free	MacOS, Linux, Win32	-
MacNQC	http://www.enteract.com/~dbaum/lego/nqc/macnqc/	NQC	no	free	MacOS	-
ROBOLAB	http://www.lego.com/dacta/robolab/defaultjava.htm http://www.ceeo.tufts.edu/graphics/robolab.html	(visual)	no	$50	MacOS, Win32	-
pbFORTH	http://www.bempeldesigngroup.com/lego/pbFORTH/	Forth	yes	free	Any	Terminal emulator
legOS	http://www.noga.de/legOS/	C, C++	yes	free	Linux, Unix, Win32	GNU egcs and binutils, Perl
BrainStorm	http://www.netway.com/~rmaynard/	UCBLogo	no	free	Win32	UCBLogo (suggested)
Bot-Kit	http://www.object-arts.com/Bower/Bot-Kit/	Smalltalk	no	free	Win32	Dolphin Smalltalk
TclRCX	http://www.demailly.com/tcl/rcx/	Tcl	no	free	MacOS, Linux, Unix, Win32	Tcl
BrickCommand	http://www.geocities.com/Area51/Nebula/8488/lego.html	VB-like[c]	no	free	Win32	-

a. This column assumes you've installed the RIS software. Most of the Win32 packages work with *Spirit.ocx*, which is installed with the RIS software.

b. Win32 means Windows 95, 98, or NT.

c. VB-like means similar to Visual Basic. Function names are modeled on *Spirit.ocx*.

Table A-4. RCX Development Environments (continued)

Name	URL	Language	Replacement Firmware?	Price	Host OS	Tools Needed[a]
Gordon's Brick Programmer	http://www.umbra.demon.co.uk/gbp.html	VB-like	no	free	Win32	-
MindControl	http://homepages.svc.fcj.bvu.nl/brok/legomind/robo/mindcontrol.html	VB-like	no	free	Win32	-
PRO-RCX	http://prelude.psy.umontreal.ca/~cousined/lego/robot/rcx/rcx_command/	VB-like	no	free	Win32	-
BotCode	http://www.desktopmusic.com/botcode.htm	VB-like	no	$20	Win32	-

a. This column assumes you've installed the RIS software. Most of the Win32 packages work with *Spirit.ocx*, which is installed with the RIS software.

b. Win32 means Windows 95, 98, or NT.

c. VB-like means similar to Visual Basic. Function names are modeled on *Spirit.ocx*.

B

A pbFORTH Downloader

pbFORTH is a interesting, funky programming environment, but there are not many tools available for it. This appendix contains source code for a program downloader, written in Java. A program downloader enables you to develop your pbFORTH programs in a text editor and download them all at once to the RCX. This means you have a saved copy of your program that is easy to browse and modify.

The program downloader presented here is a "smart" one; it analyzes the responses from pbFORTH to see if any errors occur as the download is progressing. If pbFORTH complains about something, the downloader tells you about it.

System Requirements

To compile and run this program, you'll need the Java Development Kit (JDK) version 1.1 or later (see *http://java.sun.com/products/jdk/1.2/* for the latest version). You'll also need the Communications API, a standard extension API that enables Java programs to use the serial and parallel ports of a computer (see *http://java. sun.com/products/javacomm/*).

Usage

The program downloader is called `Download`. It's very simple to use—you just need to supply the name of the Forth source code file. For example, you can download a file like this:

```
C:\>java Download thermometer.f
...........................
C:\>
```

Download prints a period for each line of the file it downloads to the RCX. If there's an error, you'll hear about it like this:

```
C:\>java Download thermometer.f
....
Line 5: Error: redefine isRunButtonPressed  RbuttonState ? undefined word
C:\>
```

By default, Download uses the COM1 port. If you are not running Windows, or if you have your IR tower attached to a different port, you can tell Download to use a different port like this:

```
C:\>java Download -port COM3 thermometer.f
```

Source Code

```java
import java.io.*;
import java.util.*;

import javax.comm.*;

public class Download {
  public static void main(String[] args) {
    String filename = args[args.length - 1];
    String portName = "COM1";

    for (int i = 0; i < args.length - 2; i++) {
      if (args[i].equals("-port")) portName = args[i + 1];
    }

    try { new Download(filename, portName); }
    catch (NoSuchPortException nspe) {
      System.out.println("Sorry, I don't know about the " +
          portName + " port.");
    }
    catch (PortInUseException piue) {
      System.out.println("Sorry, somebody else is using " +
          portName + ".");
    }
    catch (UnsupportedCommOperationException ucoe) {
      System.out.println(ucoe);
    }
    catch (IOException ioe) {
      System.out.println("An IOException occurred: " + ioe);
    }
  }

  private SerialPort mPort;
  private Reader mFileIn;
  private Writer mOut;
  private PortListener mPortListener;

  private static final int kCharSleep = 20;
```

```
        private static final int kTimeOut = 800;

        public Download(String filename, String portName)
            throws NoSuchPortException, PortInUseException,
            UnsupportedCommOperationException, IOException {
          initialize(portName);
          mFileIn = new FileReader(filename);
          run();
        }

        protected void initialize(String portName)
            throws NoSuchPortException, PortInUseException,
            UnsupportedCommOperationException, IOException {
          CommPortIdentifier id =
              CommPortIdentifier.getPortIdentifier(portName);
          mPort = (SerialPort)id.open("Download", 1000);
          mPort.setSerialPortParams(
              2400,
              SerialPort.DATABITS_8,
              SerialPort.STOPBITS_1,
              SerialPort.PARITY_NONE
          );
          Reader in = new InputStreamReader(mPort.getInputStream());
          mPortListener = new PortListener(in);
          mOut = new OutputStreamWriter(mPort.getOutputStream());
        }

        public void run() {
          int c, n = 1;
          try {
            sendReturn();
            sendReturn();
            while ((c = mFileIn.read()) != -1) {
              if (c == '\r') {
                sendReturn();
                if (mPortListener.isComplete() == false) {
                  throw new DownloadException("Timed out waiting " +
                      "for a response from the RCX.");
                }
                else if (mPortListener.isError() == true) {
                  throw new DownloadException("Error: " +
                      mPortListener.getLastLine());
                }
                System.out.print(".");
                n++;
              }
              else if (c != '\n') {
                mPortListener.reset();
                mOut.write(c);
                mOut.flush();
                Thread.sleep(kCharSleep);
              }
            }
            sendReturn();
```

```
      sendReturn();
    }
    catch (InterruptedException ie) { System.out.println(ie); }
    catch (DownloadException de) {
      System.out.println();
      System.out.println("Line " + n + ":");
      System.out.println("  " + de.getMessage());
    }
    catch (IOException ioe) { System.out.println(ioe); }

    // Regardless of what happened, try to clean up.
    try {
      mPortListener.stop();
      mFileIn.close();
      mOut.close();
      mPort.close();
    }
    catch (IOException ioe) {}
    System.exit(0);
  }

  protected void sendReturn() throws IOException, InterruptedException {
    mOut.write('\r');
    mOut.flush();
    Thread.sleep(kCharSleep);
    // Wait for response, or time out.
    long savedTime = System.currentTimeMillis();
    boolean trucking = true;
    while (trucking) {
      if (mPortListener.isComplete()) trucking = false;
      long currentTime = System.currentTimeMillis();
      if (currentTime - savedTime > kTimeOut) trucking = false;
      Thread.sleep(20);
    }
  }

  public class PortListener
      implements Runnable {
    private Thread mThread;
    private BufferedReader mIn;
    private boolean mComplete = false;
    private boolean mError = false;
    private String mLastLine;

    public PortListener(Reader in) {
      mIn = new BufferedReader(in);
      mThread = new Thread(this);
      mThread.start();
    }

    public void run() {
      String line;
      try {
        while((line = mIn.readLine()) != null) {
```

```
              line = line.trim();
              mLastLine = line;
              if (line.indexOf("ok") != -1) mComplete = true;
              if (line.indexOf("redefine") != -1) mComplete = true;
              if (line.indexOf("undefined") != -1) mComplete = mError = true;
              if (line.length() == 0) mComplete = true;
          }
        }
      catch (IOException ioe) {
        System.out.println("PortListener: ioe " + ioe);
      }
    }

  public void stop() throws IOException {
    mThread.interrupt();
  }

  public void reset() { mComplete = false; mError = false; }
  public boolean isComplete() { return mComplete; }
  public boolean isError() { return mError; }
  public String getLastLine() { return mLastLine; }
}

public class DownloadException
    extends IOException {
  public DownloadException(String message) { super(message); }
}
}
```

C

Future Directions

This appendix mentions several interesting technologies related to LEGO robots that didn't make it into the rest of the book. These are things either that weren't quite fully complete as the book went to press or that aren't entirely relevant to a general book on LEGO robots.

RIS 1.5

The first thing to look for, of course, is RIS 1.5. As of this writing (August 1999), there's been only a whisper of it, an off-hand mention in the discussion forums at the official LEGO MINDSTORMS web site. It's supposed to be released in the Fall of 1999, but what actually comprises RIS 1.5 is anybody's guess. One person at LEGO technical support did say it is a software-only upgrade, not a change to the RCX. At this point, though, it's all rumors and speculation; keep your eyes peeled for real announcements.

Java for the RCX

You can program your RCX in C, C++, Smalltalk, Tcl, and Visual Basic; why not Java? The RCXJVM project aims to build a small Java Virtual Machine (JVM) and supporting classes for the RCX. It's based on a JVM developed for a different 8-bit microcontroller, the Motorola 68HC11. (That JVM reportedly was only 6K, which would certainly fit fine in the RCX's 32K of RAM.)

LEGO Robots as JINI Devices

JINI™ is a Java™-based standard from Sun Microsystems™. The basic premise of JINI is that devices should be able to connect and disconnect from networks seamlessly. You should, for example, be able to plug your laptop computer into a hotel network jack somewhere and be able to use the printer, without going through a lot of network configuration gobbledygook. The network vision extends beyond these traditional devices, however, to things like mobile telephones, pagers, Personal Digital Assistants, and, of course, LEGO robots. A detailed article on this demonstration (including source code) is here:

> *http://developer.javasoft.com/developer/technicalArticles/ConsumerProducts/*
> *JavaTanks/Javatanks.html*

At one of the keynote speeches for the 1999 JavaOne conference, in fact, a demonstration of JINI included LEGO robots as JINI devices. Unfortunately, JINI doesn't actually run on the RCX. A proxy system is used instead, such that a JINI proxy runs on a PC, which, in turn, communicates with the robot over the IR link. However, it still makes for an interesting technology blend.

Independent of the JavaOne demonstration, Jan Newmarch has written a JINI tutorial that includes examples with LEGO robots. You can read it for yourself here:

> *http://pandonia.canberra.edu.au/java/jini/tutorial/Jini.xml*

LEGO Network Protocol

LEGO Network Protocol (LNP) would allow two or more RCXs to communicate via their IR ports without prior configuration. While it is possible to exchange messages between multiple RCXs by reserving blocks of message numbers for specific RCX-to-RCX conduits, it's not a generalized solution. LNP is a more general approach, but it's still a work in progress. For more information, see the discussion lists at LUGNET. Here's a discussion from mid-1999:

> *http://www.lugnet.com/robotics/rcx/legos/?n=180&t=i&v=c*

Index

About the Author

"Java" **Jonathan B. Knudsen** is a staff writer for O'Reilly & Associates. He is the author of *Java™ 2D Graphics* and *Java™ Cryptography*, and has contributed to *Java™ Swing*, *Java™ AWT Reference*, and the second and third editions of *Exploring Java™*. He also writes a monthly online column called "Bite-Size Java."

This book represents one of Jonathan's lifelong goals: getting paid to play with LEGO® bricks. He hopes this is the start of something big.

Jonathan works at home with his wife, Kristen, and their children, Daphne, Luke, and Andrew.

Colophon

Our look is the result of reader comments, our own experimentation, and feedback from distribution channels. Distinctive covers complement our distinctive approach to technical topics, breathing personality and life into potentially dry subjects.

The image on the cover of *The Unofficial Guide to LEGO® MINDSTORMS™ Robots* is a mechanical toy rabbit or *automaton*, an automated machine. Biological automata, or androids, are imitations of living beings, animal or human, and have captured the imagination, fears, and hopes of inventors and spectators for many centuries. Especially notable in the long history of automata are the Chinese and Greek cultures. During the Renaissance, European automata and their mechanics or creators were viewed as mystical and magical—conjuring lifelike beings through suspect means. Machinery progressed from water-operated to weight-operated to clockwork structures, incorporating such well-known specimens as dolls who can say "Mama" and "Papa" (c. 1823) and the bejeweled, enameled eggs created by Russian Court Jeweler Carl Fabergé

Mechanical toys have affected the progress of industry and been intertwined with myth, magic, and literature, from Prometheus to Asimov, in the process raising philosophical questions about the nature of life and humanity and the many implications of creating lifelike toys.

Nicole Arigo was the production editor and proofreader for *The Unofficial Guide to LEGO® MINDSTORMS™ Robots*. Melanie Wang and Jane Ellin provided quality control reviews. Nancy Crumpton wrote the index.

Edie Freedman designed the cover of this book, using a 19th-century engraving from the Dover Pictorial Archive. Kathleen Wilson produced the cover layout with

QuarkXPress 3.3 using Adobe's ITC Garamond font. Alicia Cech designed the interior layout based on a series design by Nancy Priest. Whenever possible, our books use RepKover™, a durable and flexible lay-flat binding. If the pagecount exceeds RepKover's limit, perfect binding is used.

The book was implemented in FrameMaker by Mike Sierra. The text and heading fonts are ITC Garamond Light and Garamond Book. The illustrations that appear in the book were produced by Robert Romano using Macromedia FreeHand 8 and Adobe Photoshop 5. All photos were taken by Jonathan and Kristen Knudsen. This colophon was written by Nancy Kotary.

More Titles from O'Reilly

Graphics and Multimedia

Lingo in a Nutshell

By Bruce A. Epstein
1st Edition November 1998
634 pages, ISBN 1-56592-493-2

This companion book to *Director in a Nutshell* covers all aspects of Lingo, Director's powerful scripting language, and is the book for which both Director users and power Lingo programmers have been yearning. Detailed chapters describe messages, events, scripts, handlers, variables, lists, file I/O, Behaviors, child objects, Xtras, and more.

Web Authoring and Design

HTML: The Definitive Guide, 3rd Edition

By Chuck Musciano & Bill Kennedy
3rd Edition August 1998
576 pages, ISBN 1-56592-492-4

This complete guide is chock full of examples, sample code, and practical hands-on advice to help you create truly effective Web pages and master advanced features. Learn how to insert images, create useful links and searchable documents, use Netscape extensions, design great forms, and lots more. The third edition covers HTML 4.0, Netscape 4.5, and Internet Explorer 4.0, plus all the common extensions.

Designing Web Audio

By Josh Beggs & Dylan Thede
1st Edition June 2000 (est.)
250 pages (est.), Includes CD-ROM
ISBN 1-56592-353-7

Designing Web Audio is the most complete Internet audio guide on the market, loaded with informative real-world case studies, interviews with some of the world's leading audio and Web producers, and step-by-step instructions on how to use the most popular Web audio formats.

Web Authoring and Design

Designing with JavaScript

By Nick Heinle
1st Edition September 1997
256 pages, Includes CD-ROM
ISBN 1-56592-300-6

Written by the author of the "JavaScript Tip of the Week" Web site, this book focuses on the most useful and applicable scripts for making truly interactive, engaging Web sites. You'll not only have quick access to the scripts you need, you'll finally understand why the scripts work, how to alter the scripts to get the effects you want, and, ultimately, how to write your own groundbreaking scripts from scratch.

Photoshop for the Web, 2nd Edition

By Mikkel Aaland
2nd Edition November 1999 (est.)
256 pages (est.)
Including multipage color insert
ISBN 1-56592-641-2

In this second edition, author Mikkel Aaland updates *Photoshop for the Web* to include important new techniques and workarounds for the latest Photoshop release – version 5.5. In addition, the new edition covers the latest version of Adobe's ImageReady 2.0 Web graphics production software.

Web Navigation: Designing the User Experience

By Jennifer Fleming
1st Edition September 1998
288 pages, Includes CD-ROM
ISBN 1-56592-351-0

This book takes the first in-depth look at designing Web site navigation through design strategies to help you uncover solutions that work for your site and audience. It focuses on designing by purpose, with chapters on entertainment, shopping, identity, learning, information, and community sites. Comes with a CD-ROM containing software demos and a "netography" of related Web resources.

Web Authoring and Design

Information Architecture for the World Wide Web

By Louis Rosenfeld & Peter Morville
1st Edition February 1998
224 pages, ISBN 1-56592-282-4

Learn how to merge aesthetics and mechanics to design Web sites that "work." This book shows how to apply principles of architecture and library science to design cohesive Web sites and intranets that are easy to use, manage, and expand. Covers building complex sites, hierarchy design and organization, and techniques to make your site easier to search. For Webmasters, designers, and administrators.

PNG: The Definitive Guide

By Greg Roelofs
1st Edition June 1999
344 pages, ISBN 1-56592-542-4

Targeted at graphic designers and programmers, *PNG: The Definitive Guide* is the first book devoted exclusively to teaching and documenting this important new and free image format. It is an indispensable compendium for Web content developers and programmers and is chock full of examples, sample code, and practical hands-on advice.

Other Titles

REALbasic: The Definitive Guide

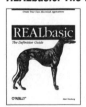

By Matt Neuburg
1st Edition October 1999
686 pages, ISBN 1-56592-657-9

REALbasic allows users to design astonishingly fast, full-fledged applications. Simply put, it is Visual Basic on the Mac. This book documents essential concepts and takes the reader from zero knowledge of programming to the ability to program every aspect of REALbasic. It's a vital reference for the expanding legion of developers who are are discovering the power and flexibility of this program.

Other Titles

User Friendly

By Illiad
1st Edition September 1999
132 pages, ISBN 1-56592-673-0

One of the funniest, most off-beat, and original comic strips to come along in years, *User Friendly* tells the story of Columbia Internet, "the friendliest, hardest-working, and most neurotic little Internet Service Provider in the world." *User Friendly* reads like Dilbert for the open-source community. It provides outsiders a lighthearted look at the world of the hard-core geek and allows those who make their living dwelling in this world a chance to laugh at themselves.

Optimizing Windows for Games, Graphics and Multimedia

By David L. Farquhar
1st Edition December 1999 (est.)
250 pages (est.), ISBN 1-56592-677-3

Every Windows user has spent many frustrating hours trying to figure out ways to optimize system performance. *Optimizing Windows for Games, Graphics and Multimedia* gives you tips and tricks you won't find in any Windows documentation to make your system run faster than ever before. It will answer your questions and save you wasted hours of searching and experimenting to find the practical solutions you're looking for.

O'REILLY®

TO ORDER: **800-998-9938** • **order@oreilly.com** • **http://www.oreilly.com/**

OUR PRODUCTS ARE AVAILABLE AT A BOOKSTORE OR SOFTWARE STORE NEAR YOU.

FOR INFORMATION: **800-998-9938** • **707-829-0515** • **info@oreilly.com**

How to stay in touch with O'Reilly

1. Visit Our Award-Winning Web Site

http://www.oreilly.com/

★ "Top 100 Sites on the Web" —*PC Magazine*
★ "Top 5% Web sites" —*Point Communications*
★ "3-Star site" —*The McKinley Group*

Our web site contains a library of comprehensive product information (including book excerpts and tables of contents), downloadable software, background articles, interviews with technology leaders, links to relevant sites, book cover art, and more. File us in your Bookmarks or Hotlist!

2. Join Our Email Mailing Lists

New Product Releases
To receive automatic email with brief descriptions of all new O'Reilly products as they are released, send email to:
listproc@online.oreilly.com
Put the following information in the first line of your message (*not* in the Subject field):
subscribe oreilly-news

O'Reilly Events
If you'd also like us to send information about trade show events, special promotions, and other O'Reilly events, send email to:
listproc@online.oreilly.com
Put the following information in the first line of your message (*not* in the Subject field):
subscribe oreilly-events

3. Get Examples from Our Books via FTP

There are two ways to access an archive of example files from our books:

Regular FTP
- ftp to:
  ftp.oreilly.com
  (login: anonymous
  password: your email address)
- Point your web browser to:
  ftp://ftp.oreilly.com/

FTPMAIL
- Send an email message to:
  ftpmail@online.oreilly.com
  (Write "help" in the message body)

4. Contact Us via Email

order@oreilly.com
To place a book or software order online. Good for North American and international customers.

subscriptions@oreilly.com
To place an order for any of our newsletters or periodicals.

books@oreilly.com
General questions about any of our books.

software@oreilly.com
For general questions and product information about our software. Check out O'Reilly Software Online at **http://software.oreilly.com/** for software and technical support information. Registered O'Reilly software users send your questions to: **website-support@oreilly.com**

cs@oreilly.com
For answers to problems regarding your order or our products.

booktech@oreilly.com
For book content technical questions or corrections.

proposals@oreilly.com
To submit new book or software proposals to our editors and product managers.

international@oreilly.com
For information about our international distributors or translation queries. For a list of our distributors outside of North America check out:
http://www.oreilly.com/www/order/country.html

O'Reilly & Associates, Inc.
101 Morris Street, Sebastopol, CA 95472 USA
TEL   707-829-0515 or 800-998-9938
       (6am to 5pm PST)
FAX   707-829-0104

Titles from O'Reilly

WEB

Advanced Perl Programming
Apache: The Definitive Guide,
    2nd Edition
ASP in a Nutshell
Building Your Own Web Conferences
Building Your Own Website™
CGI Programming with Perl
Designing with JavaScript
Dynamic HTML:
    The Definitive Reference
Frontier: The Definitive Guide
HTML: The Definitive Guide,
    3rd Edition
Information Architecture
    for the World Wide Web
JavaScript Pocket Reference
JavaScript: The Definitive Guide,
    3rd Edition
Learning VB Script
Photoshop for the Web
WebMaster in a Nutshell
WebMaster in a Nutshell,
    Deluxe Edition
Web Design in a Nutshell
Web Navigation:
    Designing the User Experience
Web Performance Tuning
Web Security & Commerce
Writing Apache Modules

PERL

Learning Perl, 2nd Edition
Learning Perl for Win32 Systems
Learning Perl/TK
Mastering Algorithms with Perl
Mastering Regular Expressions
Perl5 Pocket Reference, 2nd Edition
Perl Cookbook
Perl in a Nutshell
Perl Resource Kit—UNIX Edition
Perl Resource Kit—Win32 Edition
Perl/TK Pocket Reference
Programming Perl, 2nd Edition
Web Client Programming with Perl

GRAPHICS & MULTIMEDIA

Director in a Nutshell
Encyclopedia of Graphics
    File Formats, 2nd Edition
Lingo in a Nutshell
Photoshop in a Nutshell
QuarkXPress in a Nutshell

USING THE INTERNET

AOL in a Nutshell
Internet in a Nutshell
Smileys
The Whole Internet for Windows95
The Whole Internet:
    The Next Generation
The Whole Internet
    User's Guide & Catalog

JAVA SERIES

Database Programming with
    JDBC and Java
Developing Java Beans
Exploring Java, 2nd Edition
Java AWT Reference
Java Cryptography
Java Distributed Computing
Java Examples in a Nutshell
Java Foundation Classes in a Nutshell
Java Fundamental Classes Reference
Java in a Nutshell, 2nd Edition
Java in a Nutshell, Deluxe Edition
Java I/O
Java Language Reference, 2nd Edition
Java Media Players
Java Native Methods
Java Network Programming
Java Security
Java Servlet Programming
Java Swing
Java Threads
Java Virtual Machine

UNIX

Exploring Expect
GNU Emacs Pocket Reference
Learning GNU Emacs, 2nd Edition
Learning the bash Shell, 2nd Edition
Learning the Korn Shell
Learning the UNIX Operating System,
    4th Edition
Learning the vi Editor, 6th Edition
Linux in a Nutshell
Linux Multimedia Guide
Running Linux, 2nd Edition
SCO UNIX in a Nutshell
sed & awk, 2nd Edition
Tcl/Tk in a Nutshell
Tcl/Tk Pocket Reference
Tcl/Tk Tools
The UNIX CD Bookshelf
UNIX in a Nutshell, System V Edition
UNIX Power Tools, 2nd Edition
Using csh & tsch
Using Samba
vi Editor Pocket Reference
What You Need To Know:
    When You Can't Find Your
    UNIX System Administrator
Writing GNU Emacs Extensions

SONGLINE GUIDES

NetLaw   NetResearch
NetLearning   NetSuccess
NetLessons   NetTravel

SOFTWARE

Building Your Own WebSite™
Building Your Own Web Conference
WebBoard™ 3.0
WebSite Professional™ 2.0
PolyForm™

SYSTEM ADMINISTRATION

Building Internet Firewalls
Computer Security Basics
Cracking DES
DNS and BIND, 3rd Edition
DNS on WindowsNT
Essential System Administration
Essential WindowsNT
    System Administration
Getting Connected:
    The Internet at 56K and Up
Linux Network Administrator's Guide
Managing IP Networks with
    Cisco Routers
Managing Mailing Lists
Managing NFS and NIS
Managing the WindowsNT Registry
Managing Usenet
MCSE: The Core Exams in a Nutshell
MCSE: The Electives in a Nutshell
Networking Personal Computers
    with TCP/IP
Oracle Performance Tuning,
    2nd Edition
Practical UNIX & Internet Security,
    2nd Edition
PGP: Pretty Good Privacy
Protecting Networks with SATAN
sendmail, 2nd Edition
sendmail Desktop Reference
System Performance Tuning
TCP/IP Network Administration,
    2nd Edition
termcap & terminfo
The Networking CD Bookshelf
Using & Managing PPP
Virtual Private Networks
WindowsNT Backup & Restore
WindowsNT Desktop Reference
WindowsNT Event Logging
WindowsNT in a Nutshell
WindowsNT Server 4.0 for
    Netware Administrators
WindowsNT SNMP
WindowsNT TCP/IP Administration
WindowsNT User Administration
Zero Administration for Windows

X WINDOW

Vol. 1: Xlib Programming Manual
Vol. 2: Xlib Reference Manual
Vol. 3M: X Window System
    User's Guide, Motif Edition
Vol. 4M: X Toolkit Intrinsics
    Programming Manual,
    Motif Edition
Vol. 5: X Toolkit Intrinsics
    Reference Manual
Vol. 6A: Motif Programming Manual
Vol. 6B: Motif Reference Manual
Vol. 8 : X Window System
    Administrator's Guide

PROGRAMMING

Access Database Design and
    Programming
Advanced Oracle PL/SQL
    Programming with Packages
Applying RCS and SCCS
BE Developer's Guide
BE Advanced Topics
C++: The Core Language
Checking C Programs with lint
Developing Windows Error Messages
Developing Visual Basic Add-ins
Guide to Writing DCE Applications
High Performance Computing,
    2nd Edition
Inside the Windows 95 File System
Inside the Windows 95 Registry
lex & yacc, 2nd Edition
Linux Device Drivers
Managing Projects with make
Oracle8 Design Tips
Oracle Built-in Packages
Oracle Design
Oracle PL/SQL Programming,
    2nd Edition
Oracle Scripts
Oracle Security
Palm Programming:
    The Developer's Guide
Porting UNIX Software
POSIX Programmer's Guide
POSIX.4: Programming
    for the Real World
Power Programming with RPC
Practical C Programming, 3rd Edition
Practical C++ Programming
Programming Python
Programming with curses
Programming with GNU Software
Pthreads Programming
Python Pocket Reference
Software Portability with imake,
    2nd Edition
UML in a Nutshell
Understanding DCE
UNIX Systems Programming for SVR4
VB/VBA in a Nutshell: The Languages
Win32 Multithreaded Programming
Windows NT File System Internals
Year 2000 in a Nutshell

USING WINDOWS

Excel97 Annoyances
Office97 Annoyances
Outlook Annoyances
Windows Annoyances
Windows98 Annoyances
Windows95 in a Nutshell
Windows98 in a Nutshell
Word97 Annoyances

OTHER TITLES

PalmPilot: The Ultimate Guide
Palm Programming:
    The Developer's Guide

O'REILLY®

TO ORDER: **800-998-9938** • **order@oreilly.com** • **http://www.oreilly.com/**
OUR PRODUCTS ARE AVAILABLE AT A BOOKSTORE OR SOFTWARE STORE NEAR YOU.
FOR INFORMATION: **800-998-9938** • **707-829-0515** • **info@oreilly.com**

International Distributors

UK, EUROPE, MIDDLE EAST AND AFRICA (EXCEPT FRANCE, GERMANY, AUSTRIA, SWITZERLAND, LUXEMBOURG, LIECHTENSTEIN, AND EASTERN EUROPE)

INQUIRIES

O'Reilly UK Limited
4 Castle Street
Farnham
Surrey, GU9 7HS
United Kingdom
Telephone: 44-1252-711776
Fax: 44-1252-734211
Email: josette@oreilly.com

ORDERS

Wiley Distribution Services Ltd.
1 Oldlands Way
Bognor Regis
West Sussex PO22 9SA
United Kingdom
Telephone: 44-1243-779777
Fax: 44-1243-820250
Email: cs-books@wiley.co.uk

FRANCE

ORDERS

GEODIF
61, Bd Saint-Germain
75240 Paris Cedex 05, France
Tel: 33-1-44-41-46-16 (French books)
Tel: 33-1-44-41-11-87 (English books)
Fax: 33-1-44-41-11-44
Email: distribution@eyrolles.com

INQUIRIES

Éditions O'Reilly
18 rue Séguier
75006 Paris, France
Tel: 33-1-40-51-52-30
Fax: 33-1-40-51-52-31
Email: france@editions-oreilly.fr

GERMANY, SWITZERLAND, AUSTRIA, EASTERN EUROPE, LUXEMBOURG, AND LIECHTENSTEIN

INQUIRIES & ORDERS

O'Reilly Verlag
Balthasarstr. 81
D-50670 Köln
Germany
Telephone: 49-221-973160-91
Fax: 49-221-973160-8
Email: anfragen@oreilly.de (inquiries)
Email: order@oreilly.de (orders)

CANADA (FRENCH LANGUAGE BOOKS)

Les Éditions Flammarion ltée
375, Avenue Laurier Ouest
Montréal (Québec) H2V 2K3
Tel: 00-1-514-277-8807
Fax: 00-1-514-278-2085
Email: info@flammarion.qc.ca

HONG KONG

City Discount Subscription Service, Ltd.
Unit D, 3rd Floor, Yan's Tower
27 Wong Chuk Hang Road
Aberdeen, Hong Kong
Tel: 852-2580-3539
Fax: 852-2580-6463
Email: citydis@ppn.com.hk

KOREA

Hanbit Media, Inc.
Sonyoung Bldg. 202
Yeksam-dong 736-36
Kangnam-ku
Seoul, Korea
Tel: 822-554-9610
Fax: 822-556-0363
Email: hant93@chollian.dacom.co.kr

PHILIPPINES

Mutual Books, Inc.
429-D Shaw Boulevard
Mandaluyong City, Metro
Manila, Philippines
Tel: 632-725-7538
Fax: 632-721-3056
Email: mbikikog@mnl.sequel.net

TAIWAN

O'Reilly Taiwan
No. 3, Lane 131
Hang-Chow South Road
Section 1, Taipei, Taiwan
Tel: 886-2-23968990
Fax: 886-2-23968916
Email: taiwan@oreilly.com

CHINA

O'Reilly Beijing
Room 2410
160, FuXingMenNeiDaJie
XiCheng District
Beijing, China PR 100031
Tel: 86-10-86631006
Fax: 86-10-86631007
Email: beijing@oreilly.com

INDIA

Computer Bookshop (India) Pvt. Ltd.
190 Dr. D.N. Road, Fort
Bombay 400 001 India
Tel: 91-22-207-0989
Fax: 91-22-262-3551
Email: cbsbom@giasbm01.vsnl.net.in

JAPAN

O'Reilly Japan, Inc.
Kiyoshige Building 2F
12-Bancho, Sanei-cho
Shinjuku-ku
Tokyo 160-0008 Japan
Tel: 81-3-3356-5227
Fax: 81-3-3356-5261
Email: japan@oreilly.com

ALL OTHER ASIAN COUNTRIES

O'Reilly & Associates, Inc.
101 Morris Street
Sebastopol, CA 95472 USA
Tel: 707-829-0515
Fax: 707-829-0104
Email: order@oreilly.com

AUSTRALIA

WoodsLane Pty., Ltd.
7/5 Vuko Place
Warriewood NSW 2102
Australia
Tel: 61-2-9970-5111
Fax: 61-2-9970-5002
Email: info@woodslane.com.au

NEW ZEALAND

Woodslane New Zealand, Ltd.
21 Cooks Street (P.O. Box 575)
Waganui, New Zealand
Tel: 64-6-347-6543
Fax: 64-6-345-4840
Email: info@woodslane.com.au

LATIN AMERICA

McGraw-Hill Interamericana
Editores, S.A. de C.V.
Cedro No. 512
Col. Atlampa
06450, Mexico, D.F.
Tel: 52-5-547-6777
Fax: 52-5-547-3336
Email: mcgraw-hill@infosel.net.mx

O'REILLY®

TO ORDER: **800-998-9938** • **order@oreilly.com** • **http://www.oreilly.com/**

OUR PRODUCTS ARE AVAILABLE AT A BOOKSTORE OR SOFTWARE STORE NEAR YOU.

FOR INFORMATION: **800-998-9938** • **707-829-0515** • **info@oreilly.com**